CURRENT THEMES IN TOURISM
Series Editors: Chris Cooper (*University of Queensland, Australia*),
C. Michael Hall (*University of Otago, New Zealand*)

The Politics of World Heritage
Negotiating Tourism and Conservation

Edited by
David Harrison and Michael Hitchcock

CHANNEL VIEW PUBLICATIONS
Clevedon • Buffalo • Toronto

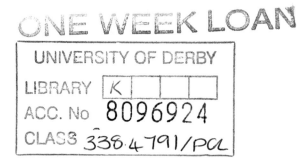
Library of Congress Cataloging in Publication Data
The Politics of World Heritage: Negotiating Tourism and Conservation/Edited by David
Harrison and Michael Hitchcock. 1st ed.
Current Themes in Tourism
Includes bibliographical references.
1. World Heritage areas. 2. Heritage tourism. I. Harrison, David. II. Hitchcock, Michael.
III. Current Issues in Tourism. IV. Series.
G140.5.P65 2004
363.6'9–dc22   2004021452

British Library Cataloguing in Publication Data
A catalogue entry for this book is available from the British Library.

ISBN 1-84541-009-2 (hbk)

Channel View Publications
An imprint of Multilingual Matters Ltd

UK: Frankfurt Lodge, Clevedon Hall, Victoria Road, Clevedon BS21 7HH.
USA: 2250 Military Road, Tonawanda, NY 14150, USA.
Canada: 5201 Dufferin Street, North York, Ontario, Canada M3H 5T8.

Copyright © 2005 D. Harrison and M. Hitchcock and the authors of individual chapters.

The contents of this book also appear in the journal *Current Issues in Tourism*, Vol.7, Nos.4&5.

Printed and bound in Great Britain by the Cromwell Press.

Contents

Foreword

Francesco Bandarin
Director, World Heritage Centre, UNESCO

The major theme running through this collection of papers concerns the complex and sometimes fraught relationship of World Heritage Sites and tourism. While applications for World Heritage status are made on the basis of conservation, tourism is an attendant phenomenon. Inscription to the World Heritage list not only confers recognition in terms of conservation, but also raises a site's profile and stimulates tourist demand. In internationally well known sites, such as the Tower of London, World Heritage status may have little impact on visitor numbers, but in less established destinations inscription is usually accompanied by an upsurge in tourism.

Tourism is, however, a double-edged sword, which on one hand confers economic benefits through the sale of tickets and visitor spending on hotels, restaurants and other tourism-related services, but on the other, places stress on the fabric of destinations and the communities who live in them. Venice, my home city, is a case in point since it benefits financially from its buoyant tourism industry, but struggles to cope with the attendant conservation problems associated with such a large annual influx of tourists. Visitors have long sought peace, tranquillity and inspiration in Venice, but today the city is so popular that it attracts 13-15 million visitors a year, almost 40 for every one of its inhabitants. Such are the problems associated with tourism, ranging from littering to over-crowding, that Armando Peres, the man responsible for tourism in Venice, believes that tourism is on the verge of destroying the city. Tourism officials are experimenting with a 10-point code of conduct to try to make life more bearable there, which ranges from always keeping to the right when walking around the city to how to file a complaint. The rules will be conveyed to visitors via cards and posters, which will also carry information and useful phone numbers.

Venice is, however, in the relatively fortunate position of being able to explore ways of managing visitors on its own terms because it is so well established as a destination that it is assured repeat visitation. Problems arise, however, with relatively new World Heritage Sites, particularly those in lesser developed economies that are anxious to acquire the developmental benefits of tourism. For such countries the fact that tourism can be an environmental or cultural threat is far outweighed by its perceived advantages. Even though there are positive impacts from tourism, it is not invariably the people who live in World Heritage Sites who benefit. Some sites, for example, charge as much as US$20 for entrance, which is a great deal of money in a developing country, but there may be little transparency about how this money is used. High entrance fees may also deter local visitors who risk being excluded from learning about their own heritage in favour of foreign tourists.

Tourism is now widely regarded as one of the largest industrial sectors along-side financial services and manufacturing, and careful attention needs be paid to the global repercussions of this many-sided phenomenon. The impact of tourism is such that progressive strategies are vital to ensure that tourism is managed in a culturally and environmentally sustainable manner. It is UNESCO's mission to help the 190 Member States in preparing their policies while reconsidering the relationship of tourism and cultural and environmental integrity, tourism and intercultural dialogue, and tourism and development. UNESCO aims to contribute to the struggle against poverty, and the protection of the environment and mutual appreciation of cultures, but it has no 'one size fits all' management blueprint for how this may be achieved. World Heritage Sites are simply too varied for UNESCO to be able to include a standard set of recommendations for each newly inscribed site. Instead, it prefers to use its coveted World Heritage Site programme as a means of spreading best practice in sustainable management, but to do this it needs the scientific and cultural insights of practitioners and researchers. UNESCO itself lacks the resources to undertake its own research, but it is able to act as a broker and a forum for the exchange of ideas.

The papers in this collection are to be welcomed because they provide invaluable insights into how tourism and conservation are negotiated in a wide variety of different contexts. The kind of empirical research that is represented by these papers is essential if UNESCO's World Heritage Centre is to fulfil its mission of promoting a discerning type of tourism that is developmentally beneficial on one hand, but is culturally and environmentally sustainable on the other. Negotiation is by definition a political act, hence the title of this volume, but it is a necessary step in the development and exchange of management strategies that will bridge the institutional gap between what is desirable and what actually happens.

Correspondence

Any correspondence should be directed to Francesco Bandarin, Director, World Heritage Centre, UNESCO, 7 Place de Fontenoy 75352, Paris 07SP, France.

Introduction
Contested Narratives in the Domain of World Heritage

David Harrison
International Institute for Culture, Tourism and Development, London Metropolitan University

The focus of this special issue is on the various relationships of world 'heritage' and tourism, and the purpose of this introduction is to raise issues that are germane to the topic, and in the process briefly relate them to the papers that follow.

The scene can be set with an anecdote. Many years ago, one of my neighbours was a Scotsman. He was stereotypically dour, in appearance and manner. A man of few words at the best of times, who struggled to respond to a greeting, he was never one to approach for a cup of sugar. However, once in a while he was transformed. On St Andrew's day, which is of great significance to Scotsmen, he would appear resplendent, immaculate, in kilt, sporran, and all the bright and shiny accessories that accompanied what, to this somewhat ignorant Sassenach, appeared to be a quite royal outfit. On one such day, I congratulated him on his appearance and casually (and undiplomatically) suggested, in passing, that the kilt and the tartan were actually English inventions the Scots had been persuaded to adopt, to the great profit of English tailors and the English cloth trade.

As anyone familiar with the work of Trevor-Roper (1983) would realise, the comment was not original. Nevertheless, it seems to have been unappreciated. I say it seems so, because although we remained neighbours for several more years, it was the last conversation we held. From that time on, my greetings in the street were utterly ignored.

Clearly, heritage is no joking matter. Wearing national costume is a mark or statement of at least two kinds of identity: one that is national or collective, and the other that is individual. And for Scots living outside Scotland, assertions about identity may be more important than for those in Scotland. For those far from 'home', the exile, the refugee or the expatriate, it may be imperative to preserve links with another 'place'. More collectively, in immigrant communities, the things of 'home' take on an additional poignancy, a bittersweet remembrance of things past, which are present, and yet are not. Faced with foreignness, with alienation, the appeal to a collective and individual 'heritage' takes on an added momentum.

Conflicting Inter-subjectivities

Landscapes, too, are often incorporated into individual and collective 'heritage'. The work of poets may reinforce feelings of association, as when Wordsworth writes of the daffodils of the English Lake District or R.S. Thomas describes the bleak Welsh hills, and removal from the 'place' of home may result

1

in alienation and restlessness. Dutch travel writer Cees Nooteboon (1993) recounts the story of an old sailor, recently retired, who was persuaded by his wife to take a holiday in Switzerland. They arrived at night, and in the morning he climbed out of bed and drew the curtains to look outside. Seeing the mountains, he disappointedly turned to his wife, and said 'I want to go home'. 'Why?' she asked, 'we have only just arrived.' 'I can't see the view', he said.

There is nothing 'natural' in our appreciation of landscape. We learn to appreciate it through our backgrounds and socialisation, but the socialisation of the expert may differ from that of the layman, and thus interpretations of what is natural will vary. Another example can illustrate this point. Near Brighton, on the south coast of England, there is a *camera obscura*, a darkened room, situated on a tower, with a lens on the roof through which is projected an image of the surrounding countryside. Through this, with the aid of a commentary provided by an interpreter, can be viewed the South Downs – an Area of Outstanding Natural Beauty. During one presentation, it was explained that South Downs rangers must ensure that the Downs remain pristine, and as part of this task must root out any gorse bushes (spiny yellow shrubs) they see growing, as they are not appropriate. Gorse bushes, it seems, are 'wrong' bits of nature, more like 'weeds', and have no place in an area of outstanding natural beauty.

What precisely is 'natural' about the South Downs can be disputed. A few hundred years ago it was heavily wooded, until the combined needs of the English navy for wood and farmers requiring grazing for their sheep conspired to leave them in their current 'natural' state. However, conflicts over the definition and exploitation of other 'natural' sites and resources are commonplace (Brandon & Wells, 1992), and examples involving tourists and residents can be cited from Newfoundland (Overton, 1980), Australia (Brown, 1999), Canada (Ritchie, 1998), the English Lake District (Clark *et al.*, 1994), South Pacific islands (Baines, 1987), and Kenya (Sindiga, 1999) What is frequently found is that the residents of such areas want to build houses, develop their businesses, harvest the forest or the wildlife, and generally put their surroundings to work. By contrast, town dwellers or tourism promoters, who may exert considerable influence with the politicians, prefer the wilderness untouched, to be visited on vacations, at week-ends, for fishing or photography, perhaps, or to enable outsiders to commune with nature.

Although positions over the use of natural and built environments may seem entrenched, they do change. When tourists first arrived at a Catalan seaside resort in Spain, for example, many local residents regarded them as interlopers, who interfered with the fishing industry. Later, when tourism became established, it was the fishermen who were considered the outsiders (Pi-Sunyer, 1989: 196–7).

There are, then, conflicts over what is natural and what is not, and how 'natural' sites are to be used. Something similar occurs over the built environment, particularly when buildings imbued with special meaning and significance are competed over by different groups, be they ethnic, religious or national. Nevertheless, a territory does not have to be considered sacred for violent conflicts to occur. Indeed, it is perhaps worth considering how many of these conflicts over territory, religious or not, are actually between groups of people who are in most ways very similar. Jews and Moslems, Protestants and Catholics, Turkish

Cypriots and Greek Cypriots: is it because they *are* so similar that the conflicts are so bitter, so violent, so destructive?

Faking it: Heritage, Performance, Commoditisation and Authenticity

Much of what we consider 'heritage' is a form of performance, and there are frequent debates about what is 'authentic' and what is 'fake' (Harrison, 1992: 20–2; MacCannell, 1976: 91–107; Olsen, 2002; Shepherd, 2002). In this context, however, it might be argued that we – and the term is used advisedly – 'perform' heritage for the benefit of people who are not 'us'. Some time ago, for example, in a study of tourism in Brittany, it was reported that there was a renewed emphasis on rural Brittany as a centre of tradition, where the Breton 'heritage', its language, customs, and cuisine, were very much alive. Eco-villages were started, villagers dressed in 'traditional' costume, and old buildings were restored. Middle-class tourists from Paris, seeking a world they thought lost, spent holidays with traditional Breton families, learning their language as they carried on their daily duties, and returned to modern Paris refreshed in the knowledge that Breton tradition was alive and well. For their part, at the end of the tourist season these rustic Bretons breathed a huge sigh of relief, put away the uncomfortable old furniture, and returned to speaking French again. The performance was over (Macdonald, 1987: 131–2).

In MacCannell's terms, the Bretons were putting on a performance of 'staged authenticity' (1976: 98). Was the experience 'fake'? One assumes the hapless visitors were unaware of the deception and, if so, it might be described as a 'genuine fake' (Brown, 1996: 32). Does it matter if it was? Does it matter if buildings considered to be part of heritage are also fake? The Pavilion in Brighton, England, for example, once considered a monstrosity and very nearly pulled down by an irate council earlier last century, is now a crucial feature of Brighton's 'heritage', and some years ago was duly restored. Most visitors to Brighton go there, but at least some of what they see is definitely 'fake'. The turrets, for example, are made of fibreglass – not an 18th-century product – because they are lighter and more resilient to the weather. Does it matter?

Clearly, the debate over what is or is not 'authentic' applies as much to historical objects as to buildings and rituals. It is highly unlikely that most visitors to the British Museum – including Greek visitors – could distinguish the genuine Elgin/Parthenon marbles from plaster casts. Nevertheless, there is continuing dispute about where they should be housed. The debate is not simply about whose *culture* is represented – Greek, British or the world's – but about who is entitled to possess the genuine article. In the West, certainly, much store is set on something being 'the real thing'. A fake Rolex may keep time as accurately as one which came directly from the manufacturer, but (if its provenance is known) is valued far less, and not simply because of the difference in monetary price. It is the *sense* of the real, the authentic. It is what it symbolises. Similarly, no one is going to be that impressed by a fine photograph of the Mona Lisa, and stories about discovered or rediscovered masterpieces are common.

Ultimately, perhaps, what matters are the meanings that people project onto these inanimate objects, these 'things men have made' – to quote D.H. Lawrence.

Such meanings are the result of a complex and continuous process of socialisation, symbolic interaction and negotiation, where we learn the value of x, y or z. Even under conditions of capitalism, these meanings continue to be defined and redefined.

That social scientists may underestimate the ability of members of cultures to adapt and change can be illustrated by reference to Fuentarrabia, in Spain. As reported by Greenwood in the 1970s, the town's annual festival of the *Alarde* celebrated a historic victory over the French, but when it was shortened for the benefit of tourists, and then performed twice rather than once, he considered it had 'lost meaning'. This was symptomatic of a commercialised yet devalued culture, bought and sold in the tourism industry as 'culture by the pound'. In fact, re-visiting Spain several years later, he found that despite tourism, the festival was thriving. However, he *also* discovered its meaning to the participants had changed, and was now perceived by them to be a celebration of Basque nationalism. It was an honest reassessment, an admission that what he had previously written 'was an expression of both anger and concern' (Greenwood, 1989: 181), but one that is rarely mentioned by many tourism commentators, who find his initial analysis more politically correct and convenient.

Tourism may indeed introduce or exacerbate major social change, but it is easy to forget the hardships of work in agriculture in less developed countries, which is often depicted as rustic and idyllic, when life might more accurately be described as nasty, brutish and short. A similar process occurred in 19th century England, when the invisibility of the rural poor 'helped perpetuate and uphold the myth of arcadian beauty which could be seized upon and utilised in selective imagery for a great variety of purposes' (Short, 1992: 2). And Short continues:

> Thus to be truly English by the beginning of the twentieth century was to be rural. But 'rural' did not really mean rural *people*, and especially not *poor* rural people, who might not even fit stereotypes of poverty by living in picturesque cottages. The countryside was made by working people, but the rural idyll of pastoral [life] from the eighteenth to the twentieth century, itself an urban product, has largely banished them from the scene. (Short, 1992: 2–3)

While tourism development is likely to promote or exacerbate the process of commoditisation, this is not necessarily a new phenomenon. The museums and art galleries so beloved of cultural tourists include much that was traded, even in small-scale societies, and it was the market (albeit sometimes a restricted one) that prompted their production and encouraged the use of skills that might otherwise have fallen into disuse. Furthermore, while indigenous arts and crafts have sometimes been undermined by tourism (Graburn, 1984), the literature is replete with examples of where tourism has prompted a creative reaction in local people and has been instrumental in reviving arts and crafts that would otherwise have disappeared (Cohen, 1993; Daniel, 1996; Popelka & Littrell, 1991; Silverman, 2000).

To the Victor the Spoils

According to Hewison, though, it is the promoters of tourism who sanitise the past. In re-presenting it as entertainment, the 'heritage industry' mocks the dark, grim reality of what actually happened. Mines are cleansed of their dirt and their danger, nuclear test sites become 'heritage centres', and museums compete to 'exploit the opportunities for the sale of souvenirs, refreshments and so forth' (Hewison, 1989: 19). He continues:

> History is gradually being bent into something called Heritage, whose commodity values run from tea towels to the country house. My criticism is not simply that it is largely focused on an idealised past whose social values are those of an earlier age of privilege and exploitation that it serves to preserve and bring forward into the present. My objection is that Heritage is gradually effacing History, by substituting an image of the past for its reality. Our actual knowledge and understanding of history is weakening at all levels, from the universities to the primary schools. (Hewison, 1989: 21)

This is a powerful argument, but it does rather assume that someone, some-where, has privileged access to *real* knowledge, to a proper understanding, of what history and heritage are *really* about. By contrast, though, whatever elements of the past are presented as heritage – arts and crafts, events, rituals or buildings – they have already passed through a complex filtering process whereby someone, or some group, has *selected* them. Nothing – but nothing – is automatic heritage material. As Weber put it, 'all knowledge of cultural reality is always knowledge from particular points of view' (1949: 81).

In the United Kingdom in 1983 it may have seemed sensible enough for the Natural Heritage Conference to define 'heritage' 'as that which a past generation has preserved and handed on to the present and which a significant group of the population wishes to hand on to the future' (Hewison, 1989: 16). The definition begs several questions. Why was something considered worth 'handing on'? Who or what is the *'significant group'*? Who does the selecting? As the case studies discussed in this volume show, and as Lowenthal has discussed at length (1985, 1997), when such questions are posed it is apparent that what is presented from the past, and how it is portrayed and interpreted, is a crucial ingredient in the continuous formation and re-formation of perceptions of the present (Uzzell, 1989a, 1989b). It is a process in which numerous groups and agencies jockey for influence and power, and where dealers in 'authenticities' range from casual excursionists to 'objective' ethnographers and museum curators (Cohen, 1988).

If this view is accepted, it becomes much easier to explain the key feature of the process whereby sites are selected for special treatment as 'heritage' sites of some kind or another. It can be crudely summarised as 'to the victor the spoils'. The achievements of vanquished peoples are rarely accorded the luxury of heritage status, and Robben Island, for instance, would never have been nominated for World Heritage Listing by a white government in South Africa.

However, the cultural contributions of the defeated and the subordinate are not necessarily lost. They can be absorbed and/or reinterpreted. The 'Turkish' belly dance, for instance, was an import from Turkey's Arab possessions. Tikka Masala, a dish served in Indian restaurants in the United Kingdom and said by Robin Cook, a prominent British politician, to be an essential component of a 'tra-ditional' Saturday night out in Britain, is a 'South Asian' dish invented specifi-cally for the English palate! At other times, a dominated group may take on at least the semblance of the coloniser's culture. We thus find that Methodism is accorded a key place in 'traditional' indigenous Fijian culture, to the extent that some Fijian nationalists want Fiji (with 45% of its population of Asian origin, and primarily Hindu) to be formally declared 'a Christian country'. By contrast, the cannibalism once practised by indigenous Fijians is little remembered, and when it *is* recalled, it is with a degree of embarrassment.

Let us Forget

In fact, where heritage is involved, collective amnesia is common. What is remembered, as tradition or heritage, is selected from a vast range of built, natural and cultural environments, to celebrate the past and bolster the present. Shameful episodes are rarely given prominence. At least initially, the memorial in Jerusalem to the massacred Jews, *Yad Vashem*, was only possible in Israel – and deals but little with non-Jews who shared the same fate. And as a memorial, like so many other memorials, it serves a dual purpose, enabling visitors to remember the fallen and simultaneously symbolising Israeli nationalism (Bowman, 1992: 129). By contrast, the death camps of Auschwitz-Birkenau in Poland evoke much ambivalence among residents who live in their shadow, and are virtually ignored in some tourist promotional material (Lennon & Foley, 2000: 63–4). Noticeably, while there are many examples of thanatourism, or dark tourism, this complex is rare among World Heritage Sites in that it is a memorial to infamy and shame rather than a celebration of past glories.

Class, status, power and nationalism: all are involved in the presentation and re-presentation of 'heritage', and as groups and classes rise and fall, so, too, do the claims for attention of different sites. In Cambodia, the Khmer Rouge did their best to destroy what they saw as the intellectual element of the society and its achievements and the current regime has to decide how far this resurgent nation should go in publicising what happened in the 'killing fields'. The sites of torture, death and burial are clearly part of the nation's heritage, and in Phnom Penh the former high school now known as *Tuol Sleng*, where the Pol Pot regime tortured its victims, and the nearby Killing Fields, are graphic and gruesome reminders of what happened. Both are much visited by tourists, but there are still many in Cambodia who would prefer to forget – or have others forget – this period of torture, massacre and ignominy.

By contrast, Angkor Wat, the significance of which is debated by Tim Winter in this volume, is a different matter, and there seems to be less of a problem in celebrating this magnificent complex (against Thai assertions) as the achievement of the Khmer nation.

Similar issues arise when one considers how periods of colonialism are portrayed. In this volume, examples are given of the dilemmas faced by governments and tourism promotion agencies in depicting the colonial 'experience' in, for example, Singapore and Fiji. If colonialism was as damaging to the development of the colonised as is usually claimed, why should its buildings and anything else associated with it be celebrated at all, far less glorified as a form of achievement? Are the quaint old buildings in the centre of very modern cities – as in the case of Kuala Lumpur or Singapore – simply there as tourist attractions? If this is so, it might be argued that designating them as 'heritage' is little other than a ploy to attract tourists.

Ambiguities also surround the role of sites related to African slavery in the UK, USA, Caribbean and West Africa. Initially, their existence seems to confirm what Dann and Seaton (2001: 19) describe as a 'domination critique', which 'suggests that the determination of slavery heritage was mainly by powerful business institutions, their commercial agenda and the mainly white audiences they targeted'. If so, this would be a further exploitation of black slaves for white profit. However, as the authors recognise, the available facts are inconsistent with such a hypothesis. Not all sites are financed by private capital or geared to profit, and some are geared to black as well as white consumption. There was also a perception that some black people opposed slavery heritage sites on the grounds that they accentuated and perpetuated social disadvantage. Those who promoted them were in a no-win situation: 'If slavery heritage is not memorialised, it can be read as suppression; if it is commemorated, such heritage may be construed as unethical or compromised truth' (Dann & Seaton: 20).

Narratives of heritage, and the domain that heritage covers, are contested because there is nothing intrinsically sacrosanct about any building, any part of nature, or any cultural practice. As social relations ebb and flow, as one class or pressure group takes ascendancy over another, new perceptions, new views on the past and what was of *value* in the past, also take over. Previous accounts are challenged. Old statues are removed and new ones installed; Marx and Engels are replaced by new icons.

Putting it more phenomenologically, what is considered 'heritage' is continually subject to interpretation and reinterpretation, claim and counter claim, and negotiation. Whether we are dealing with formal categorisations of heritage – on the World Heritage List, or in any national hierarchies – the outcomes will depend on the balance of status and power at any one time and on who among the numerous stakeholders (if, indeed, all can be delineated) has the loudest voice. Who *are* the stakeholders? And how much are those who have the least power *really* involved in decisions about who or what constitutes heritage, or how it should be managed? Studies in this volume of heritage sites in The Netherlands, the USA and Mexico, in Kyrgyzstan, Cambodia, Vietnam and India, and Fiji strongly suggest that their participation is often minimal. The meanings such sites hold for them may be quite different from those propounded by national tourism marketing agencies and UNESCO. Similarly, taking a more historical view of heritage, where can the voices of the previously dispossessed be heard?

Who Decides?

It has been suggested that heritage is about individual and collective identity, that conflict occurs because we are socialised into cultures which predispose us to favour one set of indicators that include us in a specific group or category – hence excluding others from members of our group and ourselves from membership of theirs. Culture includes and excludes. It has been suggested that heritage may be about performance, 'fake' or 'genuine', and that this is linked to notions and judgements about the role of the *market*. Most of all, what is defined as heritage is linked to *power*: the power to impose a view of the world, especially of the past, on others. Perceptions of the past are closely linked to present hierarchies, and the voices of those at the top are often the most likely to prevail. By contrast, the voices of the most lowly stakeholders – whose houses were built of wood or thatch rather than stone – are muted or silent, and those whose lives were blighted by massacre, torture and discrimination are also less remembered. The unknowns of the past lie in unmarked tombs, where no flame burns.

It would be comforting if museum curators and archaeologists could define once and for all what is of world importance, of universal value. Unfortunately, despite occasional claims to the contrary, this is not possible. Like 'lay' members of society, they too are social products of their time, of their cultures, and they too are in the business of articulating *stories*, from their own perspective.

This also applies to guides, whose performance invariably has political ramifications, which may sometimes be quite explicit. Moshe Dayan, an Israeli General, reportedly said he would prefer to contend with an Arab bomber pilot than a Palestinian guide (Bowman, 1992: 131). Even if the comment were apocryphal, it contains the germ of accuracy, as the tourist guide – along with the guidebook – is often the visitors' main source of information about a destination area. Many states have recognised this, and Israel is not alone in ensuring that, as far as possible, international visitors 'see' the sights from the perspective of a guide who has been trained and licensed by the state. By contrast, as Gemma McGrath indicates later in this volume when referring to Peru, there is much to be said for exposing tourists to local guides, and their distinct narratives.

It would be tempting, perhaps, to view the World Heritage Committee as a ruling body, the cultural equivalent of FIFA in association football, that could stipulate what is and what is not 'world heritage'. However, despite its title, it cannot determine which sites should be included on the World Heritage List. The Committee itself does not make nominations. Instead, as indicated in the following pages, these come from nation-states, and an application for World Heritage Listing is far from the end of a complex political process. Even when tentative lists are submitted, and preliminary conditions met by the submitting state party, it is difficult for the Committee to decide which sites are of universal value.

In any case, applications for World Heritage Status are neither made nor received in a global vacuum and, as indicated later in this volume, Europe and Judaeo-Christian monuments and sites continue to dominate the List. Such an international imbalance has been recognised by the World Heritage Committee, and there is now a *political* imperative to go out to other parts of the world and find more sites! Understandable though the desire to widen representation on the List might be, however, such a quest may sit uneasily with the establishment of criteria that clearly establish sites to be of universal significance.

Thirdly, many UNESCO employees are part of an international elite, which others are anxious to join. Academics, archaeologists, surveyors and restorers, for example, have their own interests in working for UNESCO, and inevitably (and quite properly) they develop links with others of like mind in specific nation-states. One consequence of this international network is that UNESCO officials may deliberately or unwittingly seek to influence which built, natural or cultural sites are selected for possible inclusion on the World Heritage List. Indeed, if they can persuade countries or regions with little representation on the World Heritage List to submit other sites for consideration, they might do so at considerable benefit to their careers.

Finally, in UNESCO-organised activities, 'supervision' by experts can sometimes come to mean domination by experts. UNESCO support is valued, prestigious and important, and in many respects UNESCO sets the agenda. Where, even if mistakenly, it is felt inclusion on the World Heritage List might bring more tourists, and would thus increase economic prosperity and status, it might be considered politic to do what the experts suggest.

While it would again be comforting if these dilemmas could be resolved, this is unlikely to occur. The idealistic quest for universals in heritage will always be conducted within the inter-subjective and highly political process in which World Heritage Listing takes place. As Tomke Lask and Stefan Herold suggest, in this volume, there would be clear benefits in setting up what they term 'tourism observation' stations in tourist destination areas, where all stakeholders could come together in a continuous exchange of information and concerns, and where inter-cultural interaction and exchange become genuine possibilities. However, the difficulties in such a project should not be underestimated. Debates and conflicts over 'heritage' take place in an ever-shifting scenario, where the 'achievements' of one class, one ethnic group, one nation-state, one era, are always negotiated and reassessed by the next. History will be doctored, presented and re-presented to suit the demands and the imperatives of the present. The barbarians are always at the gate, but today's barbarians are tomorrow's establishment. And much as we should like it to be otherwise, there is no objective referee 'out there', in Paris, or in any UNESCO office, who can decide for us.

Correspondence

Any correspondence should be directed to David Harrison, International Institute for Culture, Tourism and Development, London Metropolitan University, North Campus, 277–281, Holloway Road, London N7 8HN (d.harrison@londonmet.ac.uk).

References

Baines, G.B.K. (1987) Manipulators of islands and men: Sand-cay tourism in the South Pacific. In S. Britton and W.C. Clarke (eds) *Ambiguous Alternative: Tourism in Small Developing Countries* (pp. 16–24). Suva: University of the South Pacific.

Bowman, G. (1992) The politics of tour guiding: Israeli and Palestinian guides in Israel and the Occupied Territories. In D. Harrison (ed.) *Tourism and the Less Developed Countries* (pp. 120–34). London: Belhaven.

Brandon, K.E. and Wells, M. (1992) Planning for people and parks: Design dilemmas. *World Development* 20 (4), 557–70.

Brown, D. (1996) Genuine fakes. In T. Selwyn (ed.) *The Tourist Image: Myths and Myth Making in Tourism* (pp. 33–47). Chichester: Wiley.

Brown, T. (1999) Antecedents of culturally significant tourist behaviour. *Annals of Tourism Research* 26 (3), 676–700.

Clark, G., Darrall, J., Grove-White, R., Macnaghten, P. and Urry, J. (1994) *Leisure Landscapes: Leisure, Culture and the English Countryside: Challenges and Conflicts*. London: Council for the Protection of Rural England.

Cohen, E. (1988) Authenticity and Commoditization in Tourism. *Annals of Tourism Research* 15 (3), 371–86.

Cohen, E. (ed.) (1993) Tourist arts. *Annals of Tourism Research* 20 (1).

Daniel, Y. (1996) Tourism dance performances: Authenticity and creativity. *Annals of Tourism Research* 23 (4), 780–97.

Dann, G. and Seaton, A. (2001) Slavery, contested heritage and thanatourism. In G. Dann and A. Seaton (eds) *Slavery, Contested Heritage and Thanatourism* (pp. 1–29). New York and London: Haworth.

Graburn, N. (1984) The evolution of tourist arts. *Annals of Tourism Research* 11 (3), 393–419.

Greenwood, D. (1989) Culture by the pound: An anthropological perspective on tourism as cultural commoditization. In V. Smith (ed.) *Hosts and Guests: The Anthropology of Tourism* (2nd edn) (pp. 171–85). Philadelphia: University of Pennsylvania Press.

Harrison, D. (1992) Tourism to less developed countries: The social consequences. In D. Harrison (ed.) *Tourism and the Less Developed Countries* (pp. 19–34). London: Belhaven.

Hewison, R. (1989) Heritage: An interpretation. In D. Uzzell (ed.) *Heritage Interpretation: Volume 1. The Natural and Built Environment* (pp. 15–23). London and New York: Belhaven.

Lennon, J. and Foley, M. (2000) *Dark Tourism: The Attractions of Death and Disaster*. London and New York: Continuum.

Lowenthal, D. (1985) *The Past is a Foreign Country*. Cambridge: Cambridge University Press.

Lowenthal, D. (1997) *The Heritage Crusade and the Spoils of History*. Cambridge: Cambridge University Press.

MacCannell, D. (1976) *The Tourist: A New Theory of the Leisure Class*. London and Basingstoke: Macmillan.

McDonald, M. (1987) Tourism: Chasing culture and tradition in Brittany. In M. Bouquet and M. Winter (eds) *Who From Their Labours Rest?* (pp. 120–34). Aldershot: Avebury.

Nooteboon, C. (1993) The art of travel. Radio 4, British Broadcasting Corporation.

Olsen, K. (2002) Authenticity as a concept in tourism research: The social organization of the experience of authenticity. *Tourist Studies* 2 (2), 159–82.

Overton, J. (1980) Tourism development, conservation and conflict: Game laws for Caribou protection in Newfoundland. *Canadian Geographer* 24 (1), 40–49.

Pi-Sunyer, O. (1989) Changing perceptions of tourism and tourisms in a Catalan resort town. In V. Smith (ed.) *Hosts and Guests: The Anthropology of Tourism* (2nd edn) (pp. 188–99). Philadelphia: University of Pennsylvania Press.

Popelka, C.A. and Littrell, M.A. (1991) Influence of tourism on handicraft evolution. *Annals of Tourism Research* 18 (3), 392–413.

Ritchie, J.R.B. (1998) Managing the human presence in ecologically sensitive tourism destinations: Insights from the Banff-Bow valley study. *Journal of Sustainable Tourism* 6 (4), 293–313.

Selwyn, T. (1996) Introduction. In T. Selwyn (ed.) *The Tourist Image: Myths and Myth Making in Tourism* (pp. 1–32). Chichester: Wiley.

Shepherd, R. (2002) Commodification, culture and tourism. *Tourist Studies* 2 (2), 183–201.

Short, B. (ed.) (1992) *The English Rural Community: Image and Analysis*. Cambridge: Cambridge University Press.

Silverman, E.K. (2000) Tourism in the Sepik River of Papua New Guinea: Favoring the local over the global. *Pacific Tourism Review* 4 (2–3), 105–20.

Sindiga, I. (1999) Alternative tourism and sustainable development in Kenya. *Journal of Sustainable Tourism* 7 (2), 108–27.

Trevor-Roper, H. (1983) The invention of tradition: The Highland tradition of Scotland. In E. Hobsbawm and T. Ranger (eds) *The Invention of Tradition* (pp. 15–41). Cambridge: Cambridge University Press.

Uzzell, D. (1989a) *Heritage Interpretation, Volume 1: The Natural and Built Environment*. London and New York: Belhaven.

Uzzell, D. (1989b) *Heritage Interpretation, Volume 2: The Visitor Experience*. London and New York: Belhaven.

Weber, M. (1949) *The Methodology of the Social Sciences* (trans and edited by E.A. Shils and H.A. Finch). New York: Free Press.

World Heritage as NIMBY? The Case of the Dutch Part of the Wadden Sea

Bart J.M. van der Aa, Peter D. Groote and Paulus P.P. Huigen
Faculty of Spatial Sciences, University of Groningen, P.O. Box 800, 9700 AV,
Groningen, The Netherlands

Acquiring the world heritage label, a reward for establishing and preserving an outstanding environment, is often assumed to be an honour for the local population and a useful leverage for the tourist and environmental organisations. However, the case of the Wadden Sea, a trilateral nomination by Denmark, Germany and The Netherlands, makes clear that this is not always true, and public consultation in The Netherlands has revealed that these local stakeholders do not support such a nomination. It seems they epitomise a 'Not in my back yard' (NIMBY) approach to World Heritage listing. This discussion paper examines the factors that complicate the nomination process. Contrary to common expectation, why do critical stakeholders, like the tourism industry, local inhabitants and environmental organisations become opponents? What are the interests at stake that subvert the balance of benefits and costs of the world heritage status to the extent that nomination is suspended? Is this phenomenon an exception, or an indication that obtaining the accolade is increasingly assessed from a rational rather than an emotional viewpoint, and that 30 years after the convention which created it the world heritage stamp has lost its uniqueness?

Keywords: world heritage nomination process, local opposition

Introduction

The Wadden Sea Conservation Area is the coastal area from Den Helder in The Netherlands to Esbjerg in Denmark (Figure 1). This wetland of 8000 km² is a breeding place for many species of fish and birds. With its tidal system, it is a natural area of exceptional value (Abrahamse & Van der Wal, 1989). Furthermore, the widely recognised archaeological value of the area, the sustained interaction of the population with nature that can be traced in the landscape, the considerable impact of urban culture, the element of tradition, and the awareness of the natural heritage, make the Wadden Sea a cultural area of 'national and international importance' (Vollmer *et al.*, 2001: 12–13).

In the light of these qualities, the World Heritage nomination of the Wadden Sea by Germany, Denmark and The Netherlands seemed to be a straightforward case for the United Nations Educational, Scientific and Cultural Organisation (UNESCO) and its subsidiary organisations. A feasibility study, documented in the Burbridge Report, underlined this. The Wadden Sea qualifies for listing because it fulfils the three most important criteria of outstanding universal value, integrity and the existence of management plans:

> The Wadden Sea Conservation Area is worthy of inscription as a world heritage site as it meets all the UNESCO criteria as a 'natural property' representing one of the world's greatest wetland ecosystems . . . the integrity of a world heritage site could be maintained [and listing] is feasible under the current conservation and management arrangements. (Burbridge, 2000: 1)

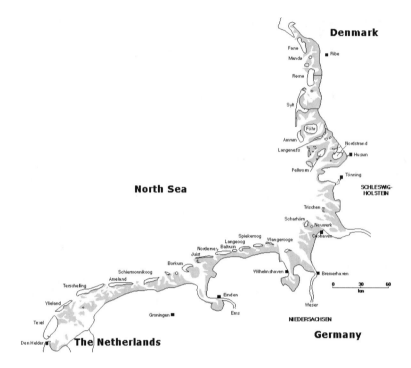

Figure 1 Wadden Sea Area of Denmark, Germany and The Netherlands
Source: Wadsis (2002)

However, despite the accredited qualities and fulfilment of the criteria, the path to listing appeared to be less smooth than expected. Not only is nomination of the Wadden Sea dogged by conflicting opinions on the intrinsic qualities of the wetland and objections from economic players in the area, but also support even from the local (Wadden) population and the environmental and tourism organisations is often absent. It is the lack of support among those who might be considered beneficiaries that makes this case exceptional, which raises the question of how far local objections will become commonplace.

The lack of support is surprising, as it is generally expected that World Heritage listing brings benefits to the local stakeholders. The local population of a proposed site is often in favour of listing, as it is considered a commendation for successful preservation efforts and an honour to live in an internationally recognised area. For example, the population of *droogmakerij* (reclaimed land) of the Beemster in The Netherlands, is proud of the international recognition of their area despite their reservations about the listing (interview with De Jong, Rijksdienst voor Monumentenzorg [State Service for the Conservation of Monuments and Historic Buildings and Sites] (2001).

World Heritage designation can lead to more protection. Indeed, the necessity for international cooperation in the Wadden Sea to ensure that conservation is more coordinated has long been acknowledged (Abrahamse *et al.*, 1976), and the World Heritage emblem of UNESCO could be the natural extension of the trilateral responsibility that started with the *Joint Declaration on the Protec-*

tion of the Wadden Sea put forward by Denmark, Germany and The Netherlands in 1982. And while more protection is not a consequence of World Heritage listing, it could buttress environmental organisations in their protracted appeals for more legal protection for this unique wetland. Many environmentally threatening activities in this region, ranging from oil drilling to the location of windmills, from military activities to the cockle industry, could possibly be halted.

Additionally, World Heritage status can be seen as a 'unique selling point' (Kotler & Armstrong, 1996) and used to attract more tourists and new residents. The Wadden Sea Area would benefit from such recognition, which would enhance its attractiveness and counter the continued reduction in population and relatively high unemployment rate that have afflicted some parts of the region (Provincie Friesland, 1992).

This paper focuses on why presumed beneficiaries did not support nomination to the World Heritage List during the consultation process, queries how far the lack of support is a consequence of a perceived imbalance of costs over the apparent advantages of listing, and discusses the extent to which it is appropriate that the future of a potential World Heritage site is in the hands of the local population. It concludes by raising the possibility that, far from being atypical, the lack of local support for the case of the Wadden Sea may be representative of a more general trend.

Methodology

The process of nominating the Wadden Sea for inclusion on the World Heritage List is interesting because of the resistance it prompted, raising questions both about who opposed it, and for what reasons. Answers to such queries are found, at least in part, in reports drawn up by the *Ministerie van Landbouw, Natuur en Visserij* (LNV – Ministry of Agriculture, Nature and Fisheries) during public consultations. These reports contained an overview of arguments for and against World Heritage nomination, which were later analysed by the authors of this paper. This enabled the presentation and juxtaposition of the arguments, as indicated in Figures 2 and 3.

Public consultations by LNV took place during the summer of 2001. In all, nine groups of stakeholders were consulted. These were the populations of four Wadden islands (Vlieland, Terschelling, Ameland and Shiermonnikoog); the people of Delfzijl (a municipality on the mainland); the municipalities on the mainland in the North Netherlands (Wadden mun. in Figure 2); the platform for agriculture in the North Netherlands (*Noordelijke Land-en Tuinbouw Organisatie*); numerous participants in the tourism industry from all over The Netherlands; the fisheries sector, which was represented by three national organisations. The number of people present at consultations, which were designed to gauge participants' feelings rather than record formal votes, was between 10 and 40, and every group was consulted at least once, sometimes twice, and most of the meetings, especially on the islands, were open to everyone who was interested.

It should be noted that three other groups of stakeholders were not consulted by LNV. These were the local population of Texel (the fifth Dutch Wadden

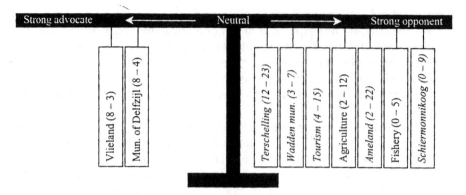

Figure 2 Stakeholder advocates and opponents of World Heritage listing

island), the energy sector, and environmental organisations. As far as Texel is concerned, it is difficult to say what the outcome of consultation might have been, as other Wadden islands were divided in their response, as indicated below. The perspective of the energy sector, represented by the *Nederlandse Aardolie Maatschappij* (personal communication with the Nam, the Dutch Oil Company, April 2002), is neutral, while the views of the national environmental organisations can be deduced from the *Statement of Concern* they wrote, with their Danish and German colleagues, recommending that nomination should be postponed until consultations at community level were completed. Among the signatories were the World Wildlife Fund of The Netherlands, *Natuurmonu- menten* (Natural Monument Association), *Staatsbosbeheer* (State Forestry Service), and the *Waddenvereniging* (Wadden Association).

Results of the Public Consultation

The outcome of the consultation with the nine groups is indicated in Figure 2, and the overall position is clear: more opposed nomination to the World Heritage List than advocated it. Indeed, only people in Vlieland and in the municipality of Delfzijl advocate listing. Stakeholders who unexpectedly failed to support nomination are indicated in italics, the number of arguments for and against within the brackets, and the further a weight is from the pivot, the stronger the actor's viewpoint or the number of arguments. It can thus be seen that the two expected opponents to listing were the fishing sector and agriculture. However, it is the remaining stakeholders to the right of the scale – the three island populations, those who lived on the mainland and the tourism interests – who surprisingly opposed listing, and the rest of this paper will focus on them.

While the scales depicted in Figure 2 indicate the actors' positions, it is more interesting and relevant to know their reasons for supporting or opposing World Heritage listing. In this way, insights can be obtained that might provide clues to how their positions could be changed. In fact, numerous reasons for the stances taken by stakeholders are provided in reports of the consultations, and are indi- cated in Figure 3, which shows the benefits and costs of World Heritage listing, as

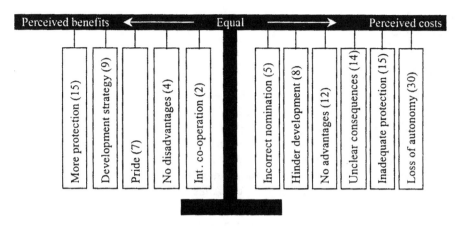

Figure 3 Arguments for and against listing

perceived by the six population groups and tourism organisations. The first, overwhelming reason is concern that listing will simply be another law imposed on the region from outside. Secondly, potential beneficiaries indicate that they believe current protection for the region is inadequate and will not be improved as a result of nomination to the World Heritage List. Thirdly, it is felt that the consequences of addition to the list are unclear.

Interestingly, two explicit arguments balance each other out. First, those who believe the current protection is insufficient for world heritage listing are almost equal to those who believe listing might ensure better protection. Secondly, the number of statements that listing could hinder regional development is expressed just as much as the statements to the contrary, namely that it will encourage development.

In sum, it seems clear that local stakeholders consider world heritage listing would mean more interference from outside the region, would provide no more protection to the Wadden Sea, and that development outcomes would be either non-existent or vague. That said, there may be contradictions in this position. In so far as it is generally accepted that the Wadden Sea must be protected through national legislation, this would seem to entail the loss of some authority at local level. And if it is felt that, at present, the Wadden Sea is inadequately protected, this might suggest that World Heritage listing and internationally recognised status would be an asset to those agitating for more protection. Finally, it would seem that LNV North has done its utmost to dispel stakeholder reservations by distributing folders, clarifying the meaning of listing at every consultation, and emphasising that The Netherlands would withdraw the nomination if UNESCO were to impose more prerequisites. In such circumstances, it is difficult to understand how opponents of listing can argue that they are uncertain about its likely impacts.

General Feelings of Concern

From the expressed views of local stakeholders, two lines of reasoning are apparent. First, they are anxious at the possibility of losing autonomy over 'their' area and, secondly, they are uncertain about the potential impact of World Heritage listing.

Loss of autonomy

The Wadden Sea Area holds only 12% of the Dutch surface area (inclusive water surface) and not more than 2% of the Dutch population (Provincie Friesland, 1992). Nevertheless, the local population perceives that the management of the Wadden Sea is gradually becoming a national issue, and the growing influence of actors from outside at the expense of insiders increasingly fosters frustration and alienation. For example, one in five new members of the Wadden Association have never visited the area (Alles & Beukema-Siebenga, 1991).

Furthermore, the national government and the European Union have stamped their authority on the Wadden Sea by issuing national and international regulations for the area. These include the Planologische KernBeslissing (PKB: Key Decision Planning), the Ramsar convention, the Natuurbeschermingswet (Nature Protection Law) and the Structuurschema Groene Ruimte (Blueprint Environmental Area), to mention but a few. In addition, politicians from The Hague and Brussels have recently flexed their bureaucratic muscles by introducing the Bird and Habitat Directive. The immediate impact of this national law, which is directed from Brussels, is that local governments are allowed to change their planning guidelines only within boundaries that are set at a higher level.

The sense of losing autonomy over the territory may have been strengthened by the way in which the Wadden Sea was short-listed as a prospective natural world heritage site – namely, at the trilateral conference. The affected local communities were informed only after the tentative list, which specified only the cultural parts of the Wadden Sea, was submitted to UNESCO (interview with De Jong, Rijksdienst voor Monumentenzorg, 2001). This might have exacerbated the feeling among the people in the Wadden Sea region that the proposal was not theirs, but just another idea from The Hague, the political centre of The Netherlands. Even worse, they viewed the nomination as something which was pushed forward by ministers who wanted to claim the trilateral conference as a personal achievement.

Not only have there been too many regulations imposed on the area, but also they have also been ineffective. Locals consider that priority has again been given to the national economic sector over the interests of the local population and tourism. For example, the exploitation of resources, whether they be oil, gas, wind or fisheries, is too often seen to be permitted when economic interests prevail over the ecological interests. As expressed in the *Waddenbulletin*, the magazine of the Wadden Association, 'the Wadden Sea may be recognised as an internationally famous nature area, but its protection is compromised as soon as . . . money can be earned' (van der Horn, 1998: 42). A similar view is recorded by Blaak, who notes that exemptions are made for the mussel seed and cockle industry because of the 'large economic interests that are at stake' (1995: 7).

This permissive approach towards major economic players contrasts with the strict approach towards the local population. Revier, manager of the Wadden Association, for instance, expressed local frustration when asking: 'How can you explain to a water sportsman that he is not allowed to sail his boat around

Rottumerplaat, while there are drilling rigs in the same place?' (quoted in Luyendijk, 1997: 21).

In this light, at least, it becomes more understandable that the local population does not want more interference from outside the region.

Lack of clarity

The environmental NGOs of The Netherlands, Germany and Denmark (2001: 4) observed that the negative outcome from consultations result from 'a lack of clarity concerning the consequences of a nomination . . . ' and it is evident that LNV North has been unable to dispel some uncertainties among local stakeholders. For example, it is unclear how far the borders of the natural site, which are the same as the PKB area, will be extended if the cultural qualities are subsumed under the World Heritage site, thereby transforming it into a cultural landscape as well. Despite many attempts to do so, LNV North has been unable to assuage the concern that World Heritage listing will simply be another law imposed on the area. For example, the local population has put much emphasis on a better formulation of the phenomenon 'small-scale historic co-use' to ensure that their children will be able to continue to live in the area and follow the same way of life as their parents.

However, such uncertainties are secondary to the general perception that the repercussions of World Heritage listing are largely unknown. This makes it practically impossible for any executing agency to make much headway. More specifically, during consultations LNV North was restricted to pointing out the possibility of better protection and potential opportunities for development. It is a problem that should be dealt with at the international level, for example, by UNESCO, which should inform local stakeholders of what they might expect to result from World Heritage listing.

Vagueness about the potential outcomes probably also influenced who would attend the consultations. Why should potential advocates attend the consultations if there are hardly any benefits? The necessity to be present seems much greater if one is opposed to a nomination, which may have led to a biased outcome of the consultation sessions.

In short, objections from local stakeholders fell into two main categories. First, they used World Heritage consultations to articulate their general aversion to the policies of the past, which need not be interpreted as an opposition against World Heritage listing *per se*. Secondly, they were unconvinced that listing would lead to significant advantages to themselves. In the light of such explanations, the arguments for and against listing, as indicated in Figure 3, are more finely balanced than initial impressions might suggest.

Discussion: Incident or Trend?

The crucial question here is, of course, whether or not the current lack of support from the local population and the environmental and tourism organisations for World Heritage listing of the Wadden Sea is an exception, or indicative of a more general 'Not in my back yard' (NIMBY) development. Does such resistance threaten the World Heritage Convention 30 years after its inception? Is the

World Heritage label to be commonly regarded as an unwelcome reward, or is the case of the Wadden Sea an isolated one?

It is suggested here that, for three reasons, debates over World Heritage listing are becoming more problematic. First, there is increasingly general opposition to handing over local or national heritage to all mankind, as represented by UNESCO. Secondly, few benefits seem to accrue to local populations and, thirdly, there are many avenues through which local stakeholders can resist attempts to impose World Heritage status upon them. The following sections examine these issues in more depth.

Sharing heritage

Wherever 'heritage' exists, pressure to share it with outsiders, and higher status outsiders at that, is likely to be present. The English site of Stonehenge, for instance, dates back to a period long before such identities as 'English' or 'British' developed, and the monument is visited and valued by people from all over the world. It is a legacy which, at first sight, the English should be prepared to share with others in the Commonwealth, Europe and throughout the world. Nevertheless, although English Heritage (EH), the responsible national agency, was prepared to nominate the site for the World Heritage List, it seems they really wanted to keep it for themselves. As a consequence, rather than indicating that Stonehenge belongs to all mankind and falls under the guardianship of UNESCO in cooperation with English Heritage, the sign at the site reads: 'Stonehenge belongs to the nation and falls under the guardianship of English Heritage'.

Benefits versus costs

The benefits of World Heritage listing are decreasing because listing does not offer more protection. The maximum tourist capacity is often already reached by the time the site is included on the list, and pride is less likely if one's heritage joins the ranks of more than 700 other world heritage sites.

First, despite the guarantee which accompanies World Heritage listing that future protection of the site will be taken on by all humanity, the promise adds nothing to the tangible protection of the site, which has to be arranged at national level before listing is possible. As a consequence, the prospect of more protection is a paper promise without practical value, especially as UNESCO can require that listing is always preceded by a national World Heritage Act. The best example of this system is in Australia (Pearson & Sullivan, 1995), where the World Heritage Properties Act of 1983, later replaced by the Environment Protection and Biodiversity Conservation Act of 1999, has been an effective way of preserving some sites (*World Heritage News*, 2002).

Secondly, the possibility of attracting more tourists as a result of being placed on the list is often less than attractive, as tourist numbers at such sites are often already relatively high. Indeed, Hall and Piggin (2002: 402) query the notion that inclusion on the list will necessarily result in increased visitor numbers. In any case, an increase in tourism to the Wadden Sea is not desirable, as it will strengthen the already existing monoculture of tourism (Gerlings, 2001) and damage the environment.

Thirdly, the reasons for nominating a site for inclusion on the World Heritage List have changed from emotional to rational in nature. Nowadays, the decision whether or not to nominate depends on calculating the actual value such a listing may have, whereas in the past this decision was largely conditioned by the honour accruing to the entire community. With the passing of time, the value of the World Heritage label has depreciated as the number of sites increases.

The example of Cambridge illustrates the first two arguments. This university town in the United Kingdom turned down a World Heritage nomination, proposed by English Heritage. It was felt that listing would bring only additional responsibilities and no additional resources. First, protection of the site is already guaranteed because large parts of the inner city are owned by the university and colleges and 'it is therefore heavily protected by these interests and the subject of sympathetic long-term management'. Secondly, the local tourism authority and the city council felt that publicity from the World Heritage label would be unwelcome, as they were already doing their utmost to deal with the present tourism pressures (correspondence with Brian Human, Head of Policy and Projects, municipality of Cambridge, 15 April 2002).

As returns from listing diminish, the costs for nominating a site are increasing. Proposals are time-consuming in themselves, as they are 'resource-intensive, with input from the property, local and national governments, development agencies' (Leask & Fyall, 2000). A nomination process becomes even more complicated when more than one country is involved, as in the case of the Wadden Sea, as indicated by the fact that the idea of nominating the entire Wadden Sea Area as a World Heritage site was launched in 1991. Even though the intention to nominate the site was included in four subsequent governmental declarations in 1991, 1994, 1997 and 2001, real nomination has been impossible until now. One possible explanation is the difficulty that two national and two regional governments, all with its own political culture, have in agreeing with one another (WAR, 2000).

It is crucial to ask why UNESCO puts so much stress on how nominations should be executed, instead of what is nominated. It already had an opportunity to list the part of the Wadden Sea that belongs to the German Land Niedersachsen (Lower Saxony), which was nominated by the Federal Republic of Germany for natural world heritage status in 1989. However, because this nomination of Wattenmeer, or the Mudflats of Lower Saxony, excluded large parts of the trilateral Wadden Sea Area, the overall integrity of the site was at stake and, as a consequence, the International Union for Conservation and Nature (IUCN) and UNESCO deferred this nomination until the entire area was nominated, including Schleswig-Holstein, Denmark and The Netherlands (UNESCO, 1989).

Of course, stimulating bilateral or multilateral nominations has the immediate advantage that the integrity of a site is strengthened and contact among citizens of the various regions is encouraged, as they are inter-reliant in caring for their shared legacy. However, these two reasons do not counterbalance the possibility of no listing due to unnecessarily complicated nomination processes. The integrity and protection of an internationally recognised site can also be realised through independent national or regional nominations, as demonstrated by the Ramsar list of the most important wetland areas in the world (Ramsar, 2002). All four Wadden Sea regions are included in this list, even though their nominations have been carried out separately at different times between 1984 and 1991. Furthermore, if UNESCO's aim is to facilitate international contact, why then did they allow the separate nomination and listing of the Surdarbans National Park in the border zone of India and Bangladesh, or Iguazu National Park, that straddles the border of Argentina and Brazil? Should the stress on international cooperation not be relieved and replaced by designating more specific parts of an entire site?

Local resistance

The local stakeholders' perception that there are more costs than benefits will often encourage them to object to World Heritage listing. However, objection has not always been possible. For example, in 1993 local communities were almost totally excluded from the nomination process, according to paragraph 14 of the Operational Guidelines published by UNESCO:

> To avoid public embarrassment to those concerned, States Parties should refrain from giving undue publicity to the fact that a property has been nominated for inscription pending the final decision of the committee of the nomination in question. (UNESCO, 1993: 6)

By 1998, the content of the paragraph had been completely changed, and it then stated that 'participation of local population in the nomination process is essential to make them feel a shared responsibility with the State Party in the maintenance of the site' (1998: 4). In fact, the world community has come to depend on local communities, even though the new guideline contrasts sharply with the overall aim of UNESCO to protect the heritage of and by all humanity. One must then ask whether or not the present system of nominating sites, in which such a major role is assigned to local actors, should be sustained, when their resistance could negatively affect all humanity.

In practice, of course, relatively few world citizens would consider the loss of the Wadden Sea as a loss of their heritage. Nevertheless, UNESCO declares that a local or national heritage belongs to all humanity once a nomination by a State Party has been recommended for listing by the IUCN and/or the International Council on Monuments and Sites (ICOMOS). Indeed, even if these NGOs would not recommend the listing of the Wadden Sea, it is worth speculating what UNESCO would have done if local Egyptians or Peruvians had opposed the World Heritage listing of the Pyramids of Gizeh or Machu Picchu.

It is indeed arguable that local permission should be required for issues that concern all humanity. It is especially problematic if local resistance is to World Heritage listing *per se* but more a vote against policies of leading actor(s), which may well occur if locals are frustrated over mistakes they perceive to have been made in their region. In the case of the Wadden Sea, the argument of environmental organisations succinctly expresses the widely held grievance:

> The proposed world heritage nomination can hardly be understood and explained when at the same time the three governments do not react appropriately to continuing or emerging man-made threats to the area. (Environmental NGOs of the Netherlands, Germany and Denmark, 2001: 2)

Aversion to global policies may also be a reason to refute the idea of World Heritage, as indicated elsewhere by the destruction of the Buddhist statues of Bamiyan by Muslim fundamentalists. This occurred not only because of Islamic aversion to the representations of living artefacts (Ashworth & Van der Aa, 2002); it was also designed to demonstrate to the outside world 'frustration at failing to achieve international recognition and the economic sanctions imposed upon the country by the United Nations Security Council' (Gamboni, 2001: 10).

World Heritage Contested

The case of the Wadden Sea demonstrates that the concept of World Heritage is as contested as at any other level. Local populations, the tourism sector, and the environmentalists, all of whom might have been expected to support nomination to the World Heritage List, envisaging an increased sense of pride in the site, more tourists and greater site protection, did not, in fact, support the nomination of the Wadden Sea. Faced with a difficult balance of costs and benefits arising from the nomination, they opted to oppose nomination.

In this case, local resistance stemmed from two reasons: a perceived loss of autonomy and a lack of clarity about the possible impact of nomination. People living at the periphery of The Netherlands have already seen enough mandates from The Hague or Brussels to fear even more layers of protection emanating from UNESCO in Paris, even though there was no evidence that this would occur. In such circumstances, more research on possible impacts of listing, for tourism and for protection, is long overdue.

In fact, inscription as a World Heritage site may no longer be regarded as the highest accolade a site can receive. The costs of inscription are increasingly perceived as outweighing the benefits, especially for those who live and work in cultural landscapes that are being nominated. As local opposition can no longer be ignored, debates over conservation and development are increasingly likely to focus on arguments by those whose response is best summarised as 'Not in my back yard' (NIMBY), a form of opposition that arises from the perception that they might have more to lose than gain through nomination on the list.

It is suggested here that UNESCO should reconsider the role of local opposition to the nomination procedure, and the opportunities it receives, especially as a vote apparently opposing World Heritage listing may, in fact, reflect a different agenda and need not constitute direct opposition to UNESCO. Ideally, the operational guidelines should be far more specific and detailed about which local stakeholders can influence – and to what degree – the outcome of consultation processes.

Correspondence

Any correspondence should be directed to Bart J.M. van der Aa, Faculty of Spatial Sciences, University of Groningen, P.O. Box 800, 9700 AV, Groningen, The Netherlands (b.j.m.van.der.aa@frw.rug.nl).

References

Abrahamse, J., Joenje, W. and van Leeuwen-Seelt, N. (1976) *Waddenzee: Natuurgebied van Nederland, Duitsland en Denemarken*. Harlingen: Landelijke Vereniging tot Behoud van de Waddenzee.
Abrahamse, J. and van der Wal, J. (1989) *Waddenzee: Kustlandschap met Vijftig Eilanden*. Amsterdam: Uniepers.
Alles, J.C.T. and Beukema-Siebenga, H.J. (1991) *De Band met de Achterban: Een Onderzoek*

onder Oude en Nieuwe Leden van de Landelijke Vereniging tot Behoud van de Waddenzee.
Harlingen: Landelijke vereniging tot behoud van de Waddenzee.

Ashworth, G.J. and van der Aa, B.J.M. (2002) Bamyan: Whose heritage was it and what should we do about it? *Current Issues in Tourism* 5 (5), 447–57.

Blaak, R. (1995) De juridische bescherming van de Waddenzee. *Milieu en Recht* (1), 2–8.

Burbridge, P.R. (2000) *The Nomination of the Wadden Sea Conservation Area as a World Heritage Site: A Feasibility Study for the Trilateral Wadden Sea Co-operation / Common Wadden Sea Secretariat.* Newcastle upon Tyne: University of Newcastle upon Tyne.

Environmental NGOs of the Netherlands, Germany and Denmark (2001) *Wadden Sea: Statement of Concern.* Esbjerg.

Gamboni, D. (2001) World Heritage: Shield or target? *Conservation* 16 (2), 5–11.

Gerlings, M. (2001) Toeristen benauwen Texelaars. *Recreatie en Toerisme* 33 (3), 28–9.

Hall, C.M. and Piggin, R. (2002) Tourism business knowledge of World Heritage sites: A New Zealand case study. *International Journal of Tourism Research* 4 (5), 401–11.

Horn, T. van der (1998) Bescherming Waddenzee gebrekkig. *Waddenbulletin* 33 (3), 42.

Kotler, P. and Armstrong, G. (1996) *Principles of Marketing.* Upper Saddle River: Prentice Hall.

Leask, A. and Fyall, A. (2000) World Heritage sites: Current issues and future implications. Paper presented at the conference Tourism 2000 held at Sheffield Hallam University, September.

Luyendijk, J. (1997) In de Waddenzee heersen de oerkrachten. *Intermediair* 33 (17), 21.

Pearson, M. and Sullivan, S. (1995) *Looking after Heritage Places: The Basics of Heritage Planning for Managers, Landowners and Administrators.* Melbourne: Melbourne University Press.

Provincie Friesland (1992) *De Economische Betekenis van de Waddenzee.* Leeuwarden: Drukkerij Provincie Friesland

UNESCO (1989) *Bureau of the World Heritage Committee, Thirteenth Session: Report of the Rapporteur.* Paris.

UNESCO (1993) *Operational Guidelines for the Implementation of the World Heritage Convention.* Paris: UNESCO.

UNESCO (1999) *Operational Guidelines for the Implementation of the World Heritage Convention.* Paris: UNESCO.

Vollmer, M., Guldberg, M., Maluck., Marrewijk, D. and Schlicksbier, G. (2001) *Landscape and Cultural Heritage in the Wadden Sea Region: Project Report.* Wilhelmshaven: Common Wadden Sea Secretariat.

WAR (2000) *Advies met Betrekking tot de Negende Trilaterale Regeringsconferentie over de Waddenzee.* 13 July. Leeuwarden: WaddenAdviesRaad.

World Heritage News (2002) World heritage law acts to halt illegal logging in Wet Tropics of Queensland (Australia). *World Heritage News* 33 (1) (14 February).

Interviews

Jong, R. de (2001) State Service for the Conservation of Monuments and Historic Buildings and Sites, Zeist. 4 December.

Internet sites

Ramsar (2002) http://www.ramsar.org. Accessed 02.05.02.

Wadsis (2002) http://www.waddenseamaps.net/grfx/WWF_wadden.gif. Accessed 07.05.02.

Huddled Masses Yearning to Buy Postcards: The Politics of Producing Heritage at the Statue of Liberty–Ellis Island National Monument

Joanne Maddern
Department of Geography, University of Dundee, Scotland

Located prominently in New York harbour, Ellis Island is part of the Statue of Liberty National Monument, which was inscribed on the World Heritage List in 1984. Formerly an immigration station, Ellis Island is now a powerful commemorative landscape. More than 100 million living Americans can trace their US roots to a man, woman or child who passed through its doors. Because of its popular significance and appeal, hundreds of museum producers endeavoured to create an inclusive, balanced and populist history of the 'peopling of America' within the spaces of the abandoned former immigration station. As part of continuing geographical research this paper draws on in-depth interviews with heritage professionals to explore how complex international immigrant histories have been mobilised by its various producers.

Keywords: Ellis Island, museums, heritage, immigration

Introduction

> 'Throughout history, peoples have exchanged cultural experience, ideas, values and goods through art, trade and migrations', UNESCO suggests in its statement on Intercultural Dialogue. For UNICEF, 'Human history is the tale of such journeys'. (UNESCO, 2004a)

The title of this paper is a play on a line from the famous poem *The New Colossus*, written in 1883 by Emma Lazarus (Vecoli, 1994: 39) and inscribed on the pedestal at the foot of the Statue of Liberty:

> Give me your tired, your poor
> Your huddled masses yearning to breathe free,
> The wretched refuse of your teeming shore.
> Send these, the homeless, tempest tossed to me.
> I lift my lamp beside the golden door.

Named by Emma Lazarus, *The Mother of Exiles* (Vecoli, 1994: 39) the Statue of Liberty stands in New York Harbour, the major port of entry for the 'great waves' of immigration that touched the shores of the US in the 19th and 20th centuries. The Statue of Liberty was one of the first sights seen by the shiploads of immigrants and exiles, as many entered Ellis Island immigration station, often referred to as 'the golden gateway', on their way to new lives in a new land. Between 1892 and 1924 an estimated 12 million migrants entered the US through the station and, as a consequence, millions of Americans have an ancestral connection to Ellis Island.

No longer used by the Immigration and Naturalisation Service (INS) for immigration, detention or deportation, Ellis Island is now owned and administered by the United States Department of the Interior's National Park Service as part of the Statue of Liberty–Ellis Island National Monument complex. Collectively these two heritage sites attract around 5,500,000 visitors per year (National Park Service Accountability Report, 2001). Deemed to be of outstanding universal value, they were inscribed on the World Heritage List in 1984.

Ellis Island Immigration Museum contains three floors of self-guided exhibits (covering 200,000 square feet) and is full of audio/visual displays detailing the history of the immigration processing station between 1892 and 1954. Visitors can tour the Great Hall where immigrant legal and medical inspections took place and are confronted with an array of objects and artefacts on display: baggage, immigrant clothing and costumes, passports, steamer and railroad tickets, ship passenger manifests, etc.

Using a case study of the production of an immigration museum at Ellis Island, this paper explores the dialectical tension that often exists between world heritage as a force which may legitimise inclusive multicultural senses of identity and transnational citizenship, and world heritage as vehicle for nation-building (which often excludes histories and knowledge that lay outside national borders: see for instance Hewison, 1987).

Research was carried out between September 2001 and May 2002 and involved extensive archival analysis of National Park Service documents, and textual analysis of around 40 transcribed interviews with key actors involved in the restoration and running of Ellis Island and the Statue of Liberty from the 1960s to the present day. This contribution traces the contestations between differently positioned sets of social actors involved in inscribing the site with meaning and the paper illustrates the problems of representation and legitimacy often faced by World Heritage Sites in an increasingly interconnected world.

Transnational Migration Histories and World Memory

> The world's memory is composed of more than just kings and heroes, battles and conquests, great cathedrals and monumental undertakings. (UNESCO, 2004b)

Immigrant histories are quintessentially transnational histories that involve the popular mass movements across space of millions of people over time. In this sense, they are histories at the forefront of a new social history that has recently encouraged public historians and heritage professionals to *rewrite* the past at heritage sites (cf. Foner, 1997; Handler & Gable, 1997; National Park Service, 2000). The historic adviser to the Statue of Liberty–Ellis Island project has described the new social history and its impact on museum production at Ellis Island as follows:

> [The new social history] is ... the history of the people – bottom up history if you wish. It is the history of the inarticulate ... It's more the history of the people rather than the politicians. [A] ... history of the people in the pew, rather than the priests in the pulpit. You know it's not popular in the sense

of popularisation, it's not popularising, but it's focused on a different class of people: the inarticulate, the immigrants, the people who work, unskilled labourers, the working class. It's influenced labour history, it's influenced religious history, it's influenced immigration history. (Personal telephone interview with Professor J.P. Dolan, April 2002)

Such an assertion is a rejoinder to cultural institutions which have in the past focused on elite histories to the detriment of more 'popular' versions of the past. Thus, where traditional histories at heritage sites have been 'written from a sedentary point of view' (Deleuze & Guattari, 1987: 23) that stresses 'stability, roots, boundaries and belonging' (Bender, 2001: 5), migration histories necessarily emphasise geographical connectivity and rhizomatic networks that transgress the borders of individual nation-states. Indeed, during the production stage of the museum at Ellis Island, incorporating this level of geographical connectivity into the museum narrative caused difficulties for National Park Service interpretive staff, who were used to dealing strictly with *national* (specifically military or political) histories, as Barry Moreno, Ellis Island's librarian emphasises:

The Park Service was confronted in 1965 by a huge challenge, when President Johnson handed Ellis Island over to the Park Service. The Park Service has run mostly natural sites and biological sites, but they also have been in charge of historic sites – mostly presidential sites or military battlefields connected with the Revolution, the Civil War and the Indian Wars . . . [T]he Park Service knew virtually nothing about immigration. Immigration at Ellis Island is a hugely complicated history and the Park Service was forced to bring in historical experts, historians who know about immigration. Immigration is complicated because it is about the migration from foreign countries of millions of people . . . So suddenly it's not just US history but it's European history . . . *it's world history*. So the Park Service . . . I don't think was capable in the beginning of handling such a complicated museum. (Personal interview, held at Ellis Island Immigration Museum, March 2002)

The suggestion that the museum professionals were dealing with a 'hugely complicated history' at Ellis Island is borne out by the examples presented below, and the many competing narratives of Ellis Island made the production of the museum particularly problematic. The following section provides a short history of the production of the museum, before moving on to particular episodes of the production process and exploring them in greater detail.

Aestheticising the Heritage Landscape: A Short History

From the original proposal for the museum in 1963 nearly 30 years of work went into deciding how best to commemorate a set of social memories that were illustrative of not just an important chapter in American history, but a defining moment in *world history*. The abandoned buildings on Ellis Island had deteriorated rapidly since 1954 and the federal government was anxious to unload what it saw as a surplus piece of property that no longer served any useful purpose. For over 20 years the decaying buildings became objects of disputation among federal, state and local governments, commercial developers and historic preservationists (see Johnson, 1984). Whilst interest in memorialising Ellis Island had been growing steadily in some quarters, the main obstacle to restoration was a lack funds. With federal funding for historic preservation dwindling rapidly under the Reagan Administration, the National Park Service was forced to devise an alternative solution: a major cooperative venture between the private sector and the federal government (Holland, 1993). Though such practices are now commonplace at heritage sites in the United States, Ellis Island was one of the first United States National Park Service historical sites to be underwritten primarily by the private sector.

For many people, this public-private initiative raised serious questions about the role of the private and state sectors in collaborating on a project of such significance. It was feared that the combination of private sector funding and state involvement would not bode well for the staging of a relevant and critical presentation of the past. Johnson, for example, was worried that the lines between 'crass commercial replications of the past' and 'formal historical interpretation' would become thoroughly blurred, and felt that in a worst-case scenario, Ellis Island could become 'a Disney-like "Immigrant land" – with smiling, native-garbed workers selling Coca-Cola to strains of "It's a Small World After All"'(1984: 161).

In 1982, Ronald Reagan appointed Lee Iacocca, (former head of the Chrysler Corporation and an upwardly mobile son of Italian immigrants) as head of the Statue of Liberty–Ellis Island Foundation. With Iacocca lending his corporate celebrity status to the project, this arrangement did nothing to dispel the fears over excessive commercialisation voiced by Johnson. Furthermore, such arrangements fuelled concerns that history museums have often been constructed by members of dominant classes, and have embodied interpretations that supported their privileged positions within the national order (Wallace, 1991, 1996). However, this unease was somewhat tempered by the fact that many others were also involved in the museum, encompassing corporate, voluntary and state organisations. In 1990, after a $150 million dollar restoration, a section of the north side of Ellis Island opened to the public as a new symbol of *America's Immigrant Heritage*.

Visiting Ellis Island Immigration Museum

After a short boat ride today's *recreational migrants* (Kirshenblatt-Gimblett, 1998: **177**) arrive at the 27 acre island by ferries named 'Miss Liberty' and 'Miss New York'. The former immigration centre is an ornate and striking redbrick building with turrets, copper domes and scalloped edges faced in white stone. Upon entering the museum the visitor is immediately faced with a large display of imitation immigrant baggage and high piles of luggage:

> Nearly thirty feet long, cordoned off, accompanied by plaques and vintage photographs it virtually blocks the visitor's progress, along the vast arrival hall. The luggage condenses the experience of immigration to a single visual metaphor and produces a concrete borderline for a national culture, to embody the moment of crossing over to America. (Rogoff, 2000: 41)

The museum utilises the original main building to house photographs, texts, models, oral histories, and such artefacts as immigrant possessions and costumes on three floors of 'self-guided' exhibits. The huge *Great Hall* where immigrants were processed has been left largely empty, except for two large American flags – a flamboyant gesture of banal nationalism (Billig, 1995). Outside the main building can be found The *American Immigrant Wall of Honour*, a series of stainless steel plates attached to a large stone circle. For a 'contribution' of 100 dollars families can 'honour their immigrant ancestors' by having their names inscribed alphabetically. Finally, there is a souvenir shop and fast food hall.

Reactions to the museum have varied. Bodnar, for instance, suggests that the museum negates its responsibility to highlight the injustices faced by immigrants in a new country in favour of a narrative which supposes that immigration was only about progress, both economic and political (1995). In contrast, Ball (1990: 59) argues that the museum was created simply to sustain a heroic image of good immigration, during a time of 'declining global hegemony and increasing ethnic unease'. According to Kirschenblatt-Gimblett, the museum is nothing more than 'a repository of patriotic sentiment' and 'an exemplar of institutional memory under the aegis of corporate sponsorship' (Kirschenblatt-Gimblett, 1998: 177).

The celebratory but selective reading of the American story so readily noted by these authors is certainly evident – nowhere more so, perhaps, than in the promotional material sent to the public by Lee Iacocca, inviting them to inscribe their ancestors' names on the American Immigrant Wall of Honour for posterity:

> Dear Fellow American:
> . . . Parents, Kids and Grandparents alike come to visit [Ellis Island to] learn about the courage of their ancestors, find or register names on the American Immigrant Wall of Honour® and come away with a new appreciation for the freedom and opportunity we enjoy in this country . . . May I count on you to continue your support of a very worthy cause? A cause which unites Americans and makes us proud. A cause which helps educate our children about sacrifice and freedom and our way of life. (Statue of Liberty–Ellis Island Foundation promotional material, 2001)

In this letter, the figure of the immigrant is used in a heroic manner to portray American identity in terms of social mobility, rugged individualism and manifest destiny (Kouwenhoven, 1988). Narratives focus on the professional or industrial achievements of upwardly mobile pursuers of an American Dream. Most notably, this is a reading of migration which downplays conflict between migrant groups and more established first fleet genealogies (Nash, 2003). It also downplays the harsh social, economic and political structures within which migrants often found themselves trapped. Where hardship and injustice *is* mentioned, it is codified as a kind of 'noble suffering' which immigrants tolerated and eventually transcended through heroic personal efforts (Bodnar, 1995).

Another criticism of this reading of immigration is that complex lives of migrants are simplified, abstracted and connected to ideals of patriotic sacrifice and citizenship:

> This [popular] version of the immigration experience [advocated in the museum by President Reagan and Lee Iacocca] simultaneously flattered now comfortable ethnics by lionising their ancestors as rugged and successful individualists, and legitimised the right-wing's dismantling of the New Deal. It also suggested that contemporary immigrants and African Americans should rely on themselves, and implied their depressed situation was a temporary phenomenon. In time, blacks, Asians and Hispanics, too, would move to the suburbs. And if they did not, the record of prior immigrant success would prove their failure to be a matter of insufficient grit and determination. (Wallace, 1996: 57–8)

Wallace has also argued that the Reagan Administration intervened in public memory at Ellis Island, waging a kind of *symbolic war* on the terrain of history, and attempting to legitimise a number of contemporary political projects at Ellis Island. During the restoration, for example, President Reagan was accused of using a version of immigration history to argue for cuts in public relief, saying that African-Americans and other minorities should 'follow the example of the immigrants and work their way out of poverty' (Bodnar, 1995; Wallace, 1991). Wallace argues that Reagan also romanticised the lives of migrants in the past while simultaneously calling for an end to high levels of immigration to the US (Wallace, 1996: 58).

However, patriotic narratives are not the only stories about immigration narrated at Ellis Island. The final section of this paper explores how some museum producers have incorporated insights of the new social history into the museum, invoking the complex nomadologies of mass movements of people back and forth across borders (Deleuze & Guattari, 1987: 23).

Island of Hope or Island of Tears?

Interpretive planners at the National Park Service interpretive headquarters in Harper's Ferry, West Virginia, decided that an important element of the museum would be an orientational film to be shown in the on-site cinema at half-hourly intervals to visitors as they first enter the museum on the ground floor. This film, it was suggested, would provide visitors with a sense of historical context and would be an important element of their overall educational experience at the site. A request for proposals was put out, and Charles Guggenheim, an established American filmmaker and his team, were chosen to produce the film. A black and white montage of historical photographs was to be used, alongside actors' voices and real excerpts from the oral history collection, recounting memories of the 1892–1924 period. The film was to be titled, 'Isle of hope, Isle of tears' alluding to the multiple narratives that have been projected onto the site. However, the making of the film was far from unproblematic. When members of the Historians' Advisory Committee were invited to a screening and asked to submit their written comments of a draft version, their dissatisfaction with the film's stereotypical tone was clear:

> The music with which the film begins is the Godfather theme! It touched off a round of giggles among [the historians' committee]. Bad start! The basic flaw however, is the portrayal of immigrant as victim . . . It is sooo

> heavy-handed, sooo depressing and sooo inaccurate . . . There is a strong
> sentiment among the History Committee members to disassociate our-
> selves from this film and perhaps to go as far as to lodge a public protest
> should it be accepted by the National Park Service in its present form. It
> really is that bad! (NPS archival extract, Private Archive, Charleston Navy
> Yard: Boston National Historical Park, National Park Service)

These critics argued that the film wrongly presented migrants as passive
victims of oppression fleeing persecution and poverty in the Old World. According to them, the emphasis on a benevolent New World and benighted Old World
ignored the fact that many immigrants were, in fact, 'sojourners' or 'birds of
passage' who made repeated trips back and forth to America to earn money.
Their primary loyalty and sense of belonging, however, remained with their
country of origin. Indeed it is estimated that during the 1892–1924 time period in
question, approximately 40% of migrants eventually left the United States to
return to the country of their birth. The academic committee was clearly suspi-
cious of the film's original emphasis on an immigrant population that was unidi-
rectional, and of its focus on immigrant groups who allegedly assimilated
dutifully in the land of 'freedom and opportunity', cutting off all channels of
communication with, and loyalties to, their place of birth in an act of newly found
patriotism towards America.

Another criticism of the film was that it emphasised European migration to
the detriment of other types of migrations. In particular, it is alleged that the film
neglects processes of Asian migration and the forced migration of African slaves.
Although Ellis Island immigrants were primarily Eastern Europeans, Italians
and Jews, many other nationalities emigrated in smaller numbers through this
portal. Historians argued that because of the diverse visitor base that Ellis Island
was likely to attract, the building should be used not only to articulate what
happened at Ellis Island, but also to tell a broader story about the *peopling of
America*. They argued that the museum should include the stories of ethnicities
that have traditionally been marginalised, if not ignored completely, within
predominantly Eurocentric museum narratives, an issue that has also received
wider circulation elsewhere (Hooper-Greenhill, 1997). Such a shift in focus
would involve thinking about American histories that might be completely at
odds with popular histories of migration. Historian Alan Kraut remembers:

> . . . I remember one morning we were discussing all of . . . [the museum
> themes] . . . and someone in the group . . . said 'now you know, lets envision
> a class of New York City public school students coming to Ellis Island,
> including many little African-American kids, what's here for them? What
> are they to make of all of this?' And it was a wonderful question well put,
> because it got us to think about who would be coming to Ellis Island and
> how could we present this in a way that would be inclusive and accurate
> and at the same time engaging, and engaging a very broad public. (Personal
> interview with Alan Kraut, Historians Advisory Committee, October 2001)

From their position as academic experts, the historians were able to create
many exhibits within the museum that contest the patriotic images of American
identity found in the cinematic narrative. Crucially, displays were constructed

which presented *diasporic* histories that were more difficult to appropriate into official versions of national identity. For instance, the section of the museum devoted to immigration history includes displays that attempt to make Ellis Island meaningful to the Native American Indians on the *receiving* end of prejudices from pioneer and settler groups. The displays also provide information about Afro-Americans whose enslaved immigration had less to do with the sentiments espoused by Emma Lazarus in *The New Colossus* (Vecoli, 1994) and more to do with a history of colonial expansionism.

Ellis Island is a world famous tourist site involving a wide range of stakeholders, including numerous and varied social, political and grass-roots institutions, and depicts many diverse ethnic and diasporic populations. As a consequence, it has prompted considerable dispute over the sorts of identities to be represented, including much debate over which stories are deemed *inappropriate* as, for example, arose with temporary exhibits on mass Armenian migration resulting from political turmoil and genocide, and Japanese internment in special 'prison camps' during the enemy alien programme of 1941–1945 (Sengupta, 1997a, 1997b, 1998).

Because of the sheer number of national and ethnic groups claiming Ellis Island as a 'terrain of belonging' (Fortier, 2000: 175) the National Park Service decided not to focus on any one group in particular. They refused such gifts as sculptures and statues for display in the museum offered by ethnic groups which might give this impression. The policy was tested when the Irish American Cultural Institute decided to donate a statue of Annie Moore, the first person to be processed at Ellis Island, to the museum. The offer was rejected on the grounds that accepting it could be perceived as favouritism to Irish-Americans:

> The National Park service seeks to avoid highlighting in a commemorative manner individual nationalities or ethnic groups . . . The restoration strove to achieve an authentic and balanced telling of the Ellis Island story . . . We hope you can understand our policy not to add individual statues to this site that is cherished by visitors of all national and ethnic backgrounds . . . (Private letter from the NPS to the Irish-American Cultural Institute) (National Park Service, 1992)

A later letter expanded upon the reasons for excluding the statue:

> We believe that it is doubtful that a statue of Annie Moore would be perceived as representing all other immigrants. Indeed, park visitors of other than Irish descent would likely view Annie Moore's statue as implying that their ancestors were somehow of lesser importance. Inevitably there would be requests for statues to commemorate the immigrant experiences of Italians, Germans, Poles and other nationalities . . . Her story . . . is not inherently more important than the stories of the millions of other immigrants who braved adversity, danger and the unknown to begin a new life in a new country. (Rust, 1992)

Annie Moore's statue was considered by members of the NPS to be 'too Irish' to be easily assimilated into the national creation mythologies embedded in the museum landscape. Though during her lifetime Annie's migration to the USA signified a desire to become an American, and her successful passage through

Ellis Island meant that she had officially become a US citizen, in the eyes of US officials her enduring Irish-American links and affiliations precluded her statue from being immediately accepted in a national museum almost a century later.

The battle over the inclusion of the statue continued for several months, involving an ever-widening circle of local, national and international stakeholders. John Walsh, the chairman of the Irish-American Cultural Institute, launched a campaign enlisting the support of prominent political figures both in America and Ireland:

> We ran into difficulty with the National Park Service. They did not want to recognise any immigrant group over another immigrant group . . . It was a very difficult time and we had to get former governors, many senators, and many congressmen all to endorse it. It took close to two years to approve it . . . I think the political pressure [eventually changed the mind of the NPS] . . . Every time they said no, I just got somebody else to write another letter. (Telephone interview with John Walsh Chairman of the Irish-American Cultural Institute, March 2002)

Finally, Jeanne Rynhart's bronze statue of the County Cork emigrant was accepted and in 1993 was unveiled by incumbent Irish president Mary Robinson in a dedication ceremony. Today, many Irish-Americans and Irish tourists make pilgrimages to the island to see it, where it can be found on the second floor of Ellis Island Immigration Museum near the Great Hall.

Though the statue was finally included in the museum, the lengthy battle that preceded its acceptance symbolises the complicated relationship that often exists between the diasporic subjectivities of transnational identities and the official histories adopted at 'national' tourist sites. The statue caused concern because it invoked multiple connections and affiliations which stretched well outside the territory and temporality of the nation-state.

Mobilising History: Lessons for World Heritage Sites

> As we cross into the twenty-first century, we . . . have embarked on a journey – whose destination holds out the promise of justice, well-being and a peaceful existence for all. (UNESCO, 2004a)

This case study has provided several insights into different the ways in which history is mobilised at World Heritage Sites. It has been argued that memorials can be:

> Heterotopic spaces . . . that not only order through difference but through competing readings of that difference. It is the very ambivalence and uncertainty of these spaces that allows many voices to be expressed. Heritage landscapes are also contested spaces, spaces with many actors who all wish to project their ideas about society, their utopias, through its space. (Hetherington, 1996: 162)

These 'utopias' are particularly contested at popular World Heritage Sites, where a wide range of stakeholders from a variety of institutional contexts have a legitimate interest in the sorts of knowledge and identities there inscribed. At Ellis Island Immigration Museum, contestation has revolved around such crucial issues as commercialisation and commoditisation, audience relevance, representation and, most crucially perhaps, battles over the types of ethnic, national and international histories narrated at the museum. As the museum librarian remarks:

> You do have to cope with nationalist feeling or ethnic pride or whatever it may be. Groups become angry sometimes at some of our exhibits. . . So we have to deal with some of the ethnic animosity that does come on to Ellis Island brought by these different groups who still have angers or historical grievances against each other and are very sensitive about what is shown at Ellis Island about their history. (Personal interview with Barry Moreno at Ellis Island Immigration Museum, March 2002)

With careful historical interpretation, World Heritage Sites can become arenas for the *working out* of these ethnic differences. However, places designated as relevant to the heritage of all humankind, with the responsibility of acting as receptacles not just of national memory, but of *world memory*, have particular challenges to surmount. Encouragingly, in addressing this problematic, we have seen how some actors at Ellis Island have attempted to construct polysemic versions of history within the museum which challenge exclusionary patriotic versions of history, by stressing instead immigration narratives of the fusion and mixing of different cultural elements over time (Gilroy, 1993; Hall, 1990; Massey, 1993). For instance, the history committee was as much concerned with the lives of the uprooted migrants as their final destination in 'the land of freedom and opportunity' and was instrumental in incorporating more complex stories of migration into the museum displays and orientation film. They initially believed the latter to be excessively nationalistic. Similarly, ethnic organisations such as the Irish-American Cultural Institute were able, through their own campaigning efforts, to become stakeholders in the project and inject new stories and subjectivities. In this regard, immigrant histories are at the forefront of a new social history that highlights most eloquently the spatial interconnections of which we are all a part.

As a former secretary of ICOMOS-UK noted during the 2002 Politics of World Heritage Conference, on which this special issue is based: 'The protection of the world's heritage can reach far beyond technical questions of conservation and site management into the much wider realms of ideology, politics, power and citizenship' (Whitbourne, 2002).

To retain credibility and legitimacy in an age of increasing mobility and spatial interconnectivity, World Heritage Sites must become spaces of *inter-cultural dialogue*, where ethnic animosities can be productively addressed. World Heritage Sites concerned with the narration of the past should aim to promote themselves as transnational rather than national spaces of citizenship, and seek to include rather than *police* ethnically or racially situated 'knowledges' and perspectives within their ideological borders.

Acknowledgements

I should like to thank Luke Desforges and others at the University of Wales for their comments and assistance during the research phase of this project. I would like to register my appreciation to members of the National Park Service, the

History Advisory Committee and the Statue of Liberty–Ellis Island Foundation for taking part in interviews that were drawn on in this paper. I should also like to thank members of the National Park Service for their help in locating and copying archival documents. This project was funded by the Economic and Social Research Council (ESRC) and Institute of Geography and Earth Sciences, University of Wales, Aberystwyth.

Correspondence

Any correspondence should be addressed to Joanne Maddern, Lecturer in Human Geography, Dept. of Geography, University of Dundee, Nethergate, Dundee, Scotland DD1 4HN(j.f.maddern@dundee.ac.uk).

References

Ball, E. (1990) Museum of tears. *Village Voice* 35 (37), 59–87.
Bender, B. (2001) Introduction. In B. Bender and M. Winer (eds) *Contested Landscapes: Movement, Exile and Place*. Oxford: Berg.
Billig, M (1995) *Banal Nationalism*. London and Thousand Oaks, CA: Sage.
Bodnar, J. (1995) Remembering the immigrant experience in American culture. *Journal of American Ethnic History* 15, 3–27.
Deleuze, G. and Guattari, F. (1987) *A Thousand Plateaus: Capitalism and Schizophrenia*. Minneapolis: University of Minnesota Press.
Foner, E. (1997) (ed.) *The New American History* (2nd edn). Temple University: Temple University Press.
Fortier, A. (2000) *Migrant Belongings: Memory, Space, Identity*. London: Berg.
Gilroy, P. (1993) *The Black Atlantic: Modernity and Double Consciousness*. Cambridge, MA: Harvard University Press.
Hall, S. (1990) Cultural identity and diaspora. In J. Rutherford (ed.) *Identity: Community, Culture and Difference*. London: Lawrence and Wishart.
Handler, R. and Gable, E. (1997) *The New History in an Old Museum: Creating the Past at Colonial Williamsburg*. Durham, NC: Duke University Press.
Hetherington, K. (1996) The utopics of social ordering: Stonehenge as a museum without walls. In S. Macdonald and G. Fyfe (eds) *Theorizing Museums: Representing Identity and Diversity in a Changing World* (pp. 153–76). Oxford: Blackwell.
Hewison, R (1987) *The Heritage Industry*. London: Methuen.
Holland, R. (1993) *Idealists, Scoundrels and the Lady: An Insider's View of the Statue of Liberty-Ellis Island Project*. Chicago: University of Illinois Press.
Hooper-Greenhill. E. (ed.) (1997) *Cultural Diversity: Developing Museums Audiences in Britain*. Leicester: Leicester University Press.
Johnson, L. (1984) Ellis Island: Historic Preservation from the Supply Side. *Radical History Review* 28–30, 157–68.
Kirschenblatt-Gimblett, B. (1998) *Destination Culture: Tourism, Museums, and Heritage*. Berkeley, CA: University of California Press.
Kouwenhoven, J. (1988) *The Beer Can by the Highway: Essays on What's 'American' about America*. Baltimore and London: Johns Hopkins University Press.
Massey, D. (1993) Power-geometry and a progressive sense of place. In J. Bird, B. Curtis, T. Putnam, G. Robertson and L. Tickner (eds) *Mapping the Futures: Local Cultures, Global Change* (pp. 59–69). London: Routledge.
Nash, C (2003) Genealogical identities. *Environment and Planning D: Society and Space* 20, 27–52.
National Park Service (1982) *Ellis Island Interpretive Prospectus*. Division of Interpretive Planning, Harpers Ferry Centre.
National Park Service (2000) *History at the National Park Service: Themes and Concepts, The National Park Service's Revised Thematic Framework*. Washington: National Park Service.

National Park Service Accountability Report (2001) *Fiscal Year 2001*. Herndon, VA: Accounting Operations Centre, National Park Service, US Department of the Interior.

National Park Service (1992) Private letter from the NPS to the Irish-American Cultural Institute. Internal documentation, Boston National Park Service Archives, Charleston Navy Yard.

Rogoff, I. (2000) *Terra Infirma: Geography's Visual Culture*. London and New York: Routledge.

Rust, M. (1992) Private letter from Marie Rust, National Park Service Acting Regional Director to Richard A. Moore, American Ambassador, 18 May 1992. Boston National Park Service Archives, Charleston Navy Yard.

Sengupta, S. (1997a) At Ellis Island Museum, dispute on Armenia show: Massacre photographs deemed 'too gory'. *New York Times* (11 September), B3, 5.

Sengupta, S. (1997b) Ellis Island, yielding, permits photos of Armenian massacre. *New York Times* (14 October), B2, 5.

Sengupta, S. (1998) What is a concentration camp? Ellis Island exhibit prompts a debate. *New York Times* (8 March) Section 1, p. 35, col. 2.

UNESCO (2004a) Statement on 'intercultural dialogue'. On WWW at http://www.unesco.org/culture/dialogue/html_eng/index_en.shtml. Accessed 06.07.04.

UNESCO (2004b) Statement on 'regional histories'. On WWW at http://www.unesco.org/culture/history/. Accessed 06.07.04.

Vecoli, R.J. (1994) The lady and the huddled masses: The Statue of Liberty as a symbol of immigration. In W. Dillon and N. Kotler (eds) *The Statue of Liberty Revisited: Making a Universal Symbol* (pp. 39–67).Washington and London: Smithsonian Institution.

Wallace, M. (1987) Hijacking history: Ronald Reagan and the Statue of Liberty. *Radical History Review* 37, 119–30.

Wallace, M. (1991) Exhibition review: Ellis Island. *Journal of American History* 78, 1023–32.

Wallace, M. (1996) *Mickey Mouse History and Other Essays on American Memory*. Philadelphia: Temple University Press.

Whitbourne, P. (2002) The first thirty years. Paper given at the international conference on the Politics of World Heritage, International Institute for Culture, Tourism and Development, London, 2–4 September.

Mundo Maya: From Cancún to City of Culture. World Heritage in Post-colonial Mesoamerica

Graeme Evans
London Metropolitan University, London, UK

Mexico has traded on its world heritage since the first inscriptions in the late 1980s, both to widen its domestic tourism offer of the coastal resorts of Acapulco, Huatalco, Puerto Vallarta, to North American and long-haul European visitors, and to promote a version of Mexicanidad to its own peoples. Since joining the NAFTA, presaging a more 'open' global economy, heritage and tourism have become twin but unequal elements in the country's economic development strategy. The promotion of the Mundo Maya linking heritage sites of pre-Colombian civilisations with the all-inclusive Mayan Riviera resorts of Cancún and Cozumel, has extended tourism development to the south-east and bordering countries. However, residual Mayan communities still inhabit these areas and service the resorts, but less so the heritage sites. The spatial relationship between these sites, city hubs and city resorts, is therefore explored from the perspective of international, national and regional policy towards heritage and tourism, and the fourth world communities whose inheritance is 'on offer'.

Keywords: cultural tourism, Mexico, world heritage, resorts, community

Introduction

> Mesoamerican civilization, like its art, is a complex of forms brought to life through a strange but coherent logic: the logic of correspondence and analogy. The history of these people, whether dealing with politics or war, is expressed, or rather manifested, in rituals and symbols. Like the conch shell, its history is both an object and a symbol, a screaming sculpture. Mesoamerican culture can be seen as an immense and dramatic ritual. The subject of this ritual, repeated incessantly in myriad variations, is none other than the myth of origins: creation/destruction/creation/destruction/creation... the abolishing of linear, sequential time: the myth (history) is repeated again and again, eternal as the days and nights, years and eons, planets and constellations. (O. Paz, cited in Cambiassi, 1997)

The following article considers the evolution and operation of (World) heritage sites in *Mesoamerica*, in particular the constructed *Mundo Maya* in the Yucatan/Quintana Roo region of south-eastern Mexico. This is considered from the perspective of Mexico's regional and national political economy in the post-NAFTA era. It examines the power relations between indigenous and state/dominant groups; and the marketing of Mayan living and monumental heritage as part of a 'hub and spoke' tourism trail, and as iconic symbols used to promote *Mexicanidad* ('Mexicanness') to visitors and to Mexicans. The relationship between city and resort hubs and the heritage sites themselves is assessed in terms of tour operator and hotel provision, and regional promotion and place-making. World Heritage Site (WHS) status and impacts are therefore considered in terms of both the geopolitics of heritage site promotion, and the *fourth world* communities whose collective heritage is used for symbolic economic purposes, but who are marginalised in its interpretation and governance. The research on which this paper is based also draws on a larger group international comparative study of world heritage sites in the context of the political, physical and symbolic economies which drive their touristic and cultural formation, under a theme of *Development and Diversity: Social Exclusion and Economic Development*. This theme is also consonant, at least superficially, with a recent World Bank/UNESCO programme *Culture and Sustainable Development*, which seeks to develop a cultural agenda and criteria for development through heritage and tourism (Evans, 2001; World Bank, 1998a).

The attention now paid to heritage sites, monuments and patrimony has transformed this cultural aspect of late-20th-century society from that of benign, specialist and parochial concern to one of international focus, trade and debate. This arises due to the increased interest in conservation and preservation; the universalist effects of globalisation (Wallerstein, 1992); conflicts and environmental impacts (heritage 'at risk'); issues of identity, community development and social exclusion; and the economic benefits and costs of tourism. As Von Droste once pleaded, 'mass tourism risks loving heritage to death' (Von Droste, 1994, cited in Evans, 2001: 83) with heritage-based tourism a mixed blessing. The designation and institutionalisation of world heritage sites and monuments transforms their role as both economic and symbolic capital 'assets' with 'the complex inter-relationship between conservation and visitation that WHS status implies' (Shackley, 1998: 204). As UNESCO maintained over 25 years ago: 'it would be a mistake to assume that the (WHS) List is simply an ever-expanding tourist's guide to hundreds of wonders in the modern world' (1972). In reality, however, world heritage sites and 'wonders' have become just that – 'must see' symbolic attractions in cultural tours, itineraries, tour operator and tourist board marketing, with World Heritage Site award the equivalent of a Michelin Guide 3-star rating (Molstad, 1993).

This attention has been directed at the built ('cultural') and natural heritage, with the support of conservation through public and private (corporate and philanthropic) organisations. However, little consideration or study has been made by these same institutions of the social and cultural impacts of the twin effects of tourism and heritage development (Getty Conservation Institute, 1999). This is not surprising – dealing with inert physical and natural resources is a relatively uncontroversial activity, notwithstanding resource allocation issues and the pressures for modern development, as well as aesthetic and conservation arguments. Reconciling community and human concerns is, however, more complex, challenging and ultimately political – people answer back, 'heritage' is often contested and not fixed, and consensus may not easily be achievable.

As Shackley (1998: 205) also observes: 'The possession of a WHS and the development of cultural tourism can create a (spurious) image of long-term stability and the basis for establishing a national identity, or may become the focus for a new nationalism'. Heritage can therefore be a tool in political and ethnic assertion. It can be discarded (e.g. Lenin Museum); subjected to terrorist attack (e.g. Borobudur, Indonesia; Bamiyan Valley Buddhas, Afghanistan), appropriated (e.g. Jerusalem's old city 'in danger' status proposed by Jordan, but not Israel); or as in the *Mundo Maya* case discussed here, used as a tool in tourism development and dispersion. Underlying the issue of social impacts are therefore the dialectical aspects of power and identity, which are played out in this case between the 'particular' and the 'universal' (Evans, 2002a; Wallerstein, 1992). These are manifested through local governance and governmentality – notably over land-use access, control, and subsidiarity; local amenities and protected sites coexisting with, or crowded out, by tourist usage and facilities; distributive costs and benefits – i.e. to whom do the benefits of heritage tourism and development flow, and who bears the costs: are they equitable? Finally, the issue of sustainability – *economic,* in a fickle international tourism market; *environmental* in terms of fragile sites, structures and ecology; and *cultural* in terms of identity and diversity and therefore representation and control over the management and access to these heritage sites and sacred places.

Culture and Sustainable Development

The renewed interest now afforded heritage sites and monuments can be gauged by a recent initiative by the World Bank, in collaboration with UNESCO and the World Tourism Organisation (WTO) entitled *Culture and Sustainable Development* (World Bank, 1998b). This programme seeks to develop a cultural agenda as part of the Bank's project development and financing assessment of projects in developing countries and post-conflict areas, particularly where heritage and 'at risk' monuments are located. As an indication of the Bank's involvement (and influence), heritage sites currently receiving finance as part of development programmes include amongst others: Angkor; Bethlehem; Bali; Spanish Town, Jamaica and Old Havana, Cuba (World Bank, 1998b). Intervention in Mexican cultural heritage includes a Bank programme to support sustainable management through the involvement of local communities and the creation of links between communities, government and the private sector. This includes 'expansion of successful community-based models for the conservation management of cultural sites; and the financing of small-scale programmes and activities which preserve and build upon living cultural heritage, indigenous knowledge and artisans products' (World Bank, 1998b: 7). No examples or funding of these initiatives are listed or provided by the Bank. Examples in Mexican locations such as Oaxaca (world heritage 'city'), tend to be limited to urban crafts markets and limited trading outside of heritage sites (e.g. Monte Alban and Mitla, Oaxaca – Evans, 1994b, 1999).

This programme is significant for two reasons. Firstly the Bank had lowered the profile of its involvement with tourism in the 1970s, following the short-lived establishment of a Tourism Project Department in 1967. However, by 1977 $345 million had been committed by the Bank to tourism projects: 40% in Africa, 29% in Latin America and the Caribbean. The financing of tourism had therefore continued but not within a tourism policy framework, with projects arising through Environment, Urban Renewal, Regional and the newly established Cultural Heritage department. Examples include Petra, Jordan; Georgia; and cultural heritage developments in St Petersburg and Butrint, Albania – all World Heritage Sites (Evans, 2001). Secondly, the return to tourism as a mainstream economic development sector in the guise of 'heritage' sought to reconcile the issues of community and economic development within countries undergoing reconstruction. It was also to respond to criticism of the Bank's previous disregard for the cultural/heritage dimension to development impacts, including notions of identity and diversity. From the Bank's position, this cultural development dimension to its lending policy is comparable with the adoption of environmental impact assessment and sustainable development criteria a decade earlier. In practice, however, this promotion of heritage and tourism development is focused on high profile 'cultural capitals' and urban heritage sites, locations where indigenous communities have largely been displaced over a long period of colonisation, and most recently, post-industrial gentrification. In South America and the Caribbean this includes Quito, Ecuador, Havana and other colonial heritage sites which are still intact or at least salvageable (Serageldin, 1999).

The collaboration with UNESCO and the WTO therefore reflects the acceptance that heritage conservation, tourism and economic regeneration are mutually supportive and viable strategies for development. The Bank's aim in developing a cultural component to its development finance programme is thus to:

> Address the economic opportunities and requirements to mainstream investments in cultural heritage and the living arts . . . [giving] attention to questions of equity, social inclusion, the opportunities to redress conditions of poverty. Central to the Bank is the exploration of the crucial importance of a cultural base for national development, as well as for such diverse issues as tourism, investment in cultural activities and the essential role of culture in education. (World Bank, 1998a: 1)

How the Bank's profile and capability – this after all is a bank, staffed predominantly by bankers and experts such as engineers and environmental scientists – could deliver and evaluate such intervention, is not clear. Like World Heritage development, delegation and liaison with national government agencies is a prerequisite. Where these same agencies are part of the social exclusion, land-use conflict and ethnic-cleansing problems, such partnerships are unlikely to be effective. They are more likely to reinforce socio-economic divides and the exclusion of indigenous communities, especially from land access and ownership – key factors in heritage sites and adjoining lands.

Cultural Tourism – the Cultural Component of Globalisation?

In Europe – West and East – cultural, or more accurately 'heritage' tourism is a prime and growing component of international and intra-regional visitor activity (Richards, 1996), as well as domestic tourism. Most visits to heritage sites are in fact undertaken by nationals (Prentice, 1993), until an area, whether city or resort-based, becomes primarily tourist-dependent. Heritage sites that fall within this trap inevitably move from their national/historical status to tourist zone, and crowd out local and citizen access, whether by price, carrying capacity or quality of experience ('authenticity', alternative site interpretations). World Heritage Site applications are often made by governments in order to manage this transition (e.g. Maritime Greenwich – Evans & Smith, 2000), but this is often either too late, or part of a tourism rather than heritage planning process. This trend is accelerated by Europeans and other Westerners taking long-haul trips seeking cultural and heritage experience further afield, and one driver of eclecticism and the 'global village' (MacCannell, 1996). The relationship between 'residents' in historic areas and cultural tourist activity is complex, but an observation is that few (if any) residents inhabit the core historic centres and few of the workers who service the tourist and cultural facilities, who are drawn typically from a peripheral and urban fringe zone. Conservation, property gentrification (including tourist hotels) and corporate investment in architectural heritage has ensured that there are very few living communities in the touristic centres of Venice, Florence, or fashionable museum quarters of London, Paris and Madrid. One effect of this sterilisation of cultural heritage areas is the lack of regular (or authentic) exchange between host and guest, the absence of community amenities and a largely faceless and privatised built environment – the historic and cultural quarter as 'theseum' (Batten, 1993). The tourist generator countries and industry therefore export this phenomenon, with self-interest and having shown little resistance in their own countries outside of the conservation of the heritage fabric and immediate environs.

Compared with Europe, where regional development programmes have long supported heritage and cultural tourism (Evans, 1994b), in developing countries resources are meagre relative to need, with cultural sites neglected and even subject to destruction and looting (e.g. Angkor, Cambodia). Annually about US$3m is made available by UNESCO's World Heritage Fund, mainly to Lesser Developed and Low Income Countries, to finance technical assistance to state organisations requesting help to prepare their nomination proposals, or to develop conservation projects. This averages $2,500 per WHS. At the same time LDCs and emerging and post-conflict nation-states look to tourism as a prime economic source of hard currency and 'invisible' [sic] trade, with low entry costs compared with manufacturing and high-tech industrial investment. It is no surprise therefore that development aid and finance agencies are active in supporting government initiatives in conservation and infrastructure improvement (e.g. roads, hotels) with the heritage tourism economy and multiplier effects the prime rationale and source of payback of loans and access by the West. The extent to which local communities, living heritage and identity are considered in master planning and infrastructure projects, as raised by the recent *Culture and Development* initiatives outlined above, is difficult to determine, but nonetheless by its absence it is hard to defend. An infrastructure-conservation approach to heritage development, which has been the norm since the 1972 World Heritage Convention, seems ill equipped to place social and cultural diversity and impacts into the cost–benefit equations. It is unable to reconcile the very real conflicts and tensions between State intervention and compliance with international agency criteria, and local/regional governance and community concerns.

Tourism in Mexico – from Kan Kun to Ki-huic

The Yucatan coast developed in the late 1800s from the cactus-derived sisal ('green gold') trade, which was a short-lived international export product used as a textile material before industrial production replaced this in Europe. Colonial style haciendas (now converting to speciality hotels) dot the flat, limestone landscape from this period. In 1921 Fernando Barbachano Peon convinced a group of passengers to disembark from their ship and tour the Yucatan with him. He is considered to be the country's travel industry pioneer, paralleling Thomas Cook in Britain, and Fred Harvey in South West USA. Harvey first used native American women to ride the trains as exotica, stopping at craft souvenir stalls en route or even for two to three day 'Indian Detours' (Sweet, 1989). Today the Barbachano family operate hotel lodges (hotel, bungalows, haciendas) under the *Mayaland Resort* company at Uxmal and Chichen-Itza, only a short walk from the entrances to these world heritage sites. Fifty years later, a two-hour drive away to the Caribbean coast, an almost surgical approach to the first wave of resort development had 'created' [sic] Cancún.

> Once virtually uninhabited, the area was computer-selected because of its near-perfect climate, peerless white-sand beaches, proximity to major populations (USA and Canada) and its pre-Colombian archaelogical sites. (Evans, 1994b)

Not just scientific selection – the then Mexican President and international financiers (in)famously flew over potential costal sites which were 'virtually uninhabited' where the previously occupied island of Cozumel, offshore Cancún, had apparently: 'Despite considerable development, managed to retain much of its charm from years gone by' (Mexicana, 1992: 3). Once a sacred place for the Mayans and for their descendants and a pilgrimage location for centuries, there are in fact several archaeological sites on *Kan Kun* island (Mayan for 'nest of vipers'), now home to all-inclusives, 200 hotels and a cruise ship terminal. From the first state-led phase of resort development, Cancún received 100,000 visitors in 1975 (75% nationals, 25% foreign), its first year of operation. Between 1975 and 1984 arrivals grew by 38% per year, representing one-tenth of Mexico's foreign tourists, and by 1989 it had become the single most popular destination, dislodging the Mexico City region, Acapulco and the traditional hispanic tourism centres of Guadalajara and Monterrey (Clancy, 2001).

By 1978 Mexico had become the developing country with the highest number of foreign affiliated hotel rooms, and by 1987 71% of the top two classes of hotels in Mexico were tied to foreign chains (Scheidler, 1988, cited in Clancy, 1998: 13). This did not, however, reflect an ultra-liberal free market position. In a country which had since its independence maintained several nationalised industries (e.g. petroleum, airlines) until the pre-NAFTA 1990s, Mexican state intervention in tourism has been one of strong investment incentives and state financing through FONATUR and supply-led hotel and resort expansion. The choice of this region also met government objectives of minimising a perceived threat from left wing and imported political influence from less stable Central American states. In 1991 Cancún received 1.9m visitors, of which 75% were foreigners, and today it is the biggest resort in Mexico and accounts for 30% of Mexico's foreign exchange from tourism. The growth in cruise visitors, which increased by 80% in the early 1990s, is also set to increase further with the development of a cruise ship terminal adjacent to downtown Cozumel island, offshore Cancún, part-financed by the World Bank. This will attract third and fourth generation ships carrying from 750 to 2,500 passengers. The World Bank's assessment of this development stressed local support because of the jobs that would arise. No social, cultural or heritage factors were cited or considered, despite the wide area on which this major infrastructure project will impact.

The Mayan and Pacific coastal resorts contain over 40% of Mexico's 5-star hotels and receive 46% of foreign tourists and 54% of the country's foreign exchange earnings (*Observer*, 2003). Cancún had its profile raised again in 2003, as 'host' to the fifth Ministerial Summit of the World Trade Organisation (WTO). Occupying 7,500 hotel rooms, 10,000 trade ministers and delegates had almost free reign of the resort, and the opportunity to swim with one of 36 dolphins imported from the Solomon Islands for this occasion.

Despite its reliance on foreign operators, Mexican companies have started to buy-back into hotel ownership and enter into international alliances, as its post-NAFTA status allows access to intra-regional and global markets and finance. However, as a result of its highly concentrated resort-led growth and a differentiated tourist market, by the late 1980s state officials were actively attempting to diversify attractions, promoting colonial cities and the Mayan Route (Clancy, 2001) – areas and cultural assets which had previously been ignored. The first World Heritage Site inscriptions in Mexico were not in fact achieved until 1987. The recent inscription of colonial towns in central Mexico (Hidalgo, Morelia, San Miguel d'Allende) reflect this trend towards more urban heritage tourism (and its European roots[2]), with the economies of scale and access they provide, in contrast to the many Mayan and other pre-Columbian sites that remain unlisted and undervisited.

Heritage tourism in Mexico is now therefore a key element in its tourism strategy, which had become over-reliant on US day visitors (98% of visitors and over 85% of overnight tourists come from North America); and on tourists to all-inclusive resorts (e.g. Cancún, Huatalco, Puerto Vallarta); and in response to the growth in cultural tourists from Europe and other regions. Cultural tourism and crafts-based production for both domestic, inter-regional as well as international markets therefore offer a more sustainable development route than the classic tourist resort lifecycle. Growth in arrivals are in large part accelerated by repeated currency devaluations, both pre- and post-NAFTA membership. In terms of arrivals from the USA and Canada, these increased by an annual average of 8% and 6% respectively during the immediate post-NAFTA years (1994–7) compared with 4% and –6% in the pre-NAFTA period (1987–93) (Smith & Pizam, 1998). The volatile tourism flows therefore reflect the currency crises and over-dependence on North America as both tourist generator, lender (via the World Bank and IMF) and capital investor. Hotel occupancy rates have also remained largely static, although hotel expansion has been achieved with over 10% more bedrooms over this period. Cancún has been the exception, consistently with the highest occupancy rate of 72%. However, the *sun, sea and sand* offer alone has, as elsewhere, begun to wane in Cancún, even with the promotion of sports tourism (e.g. scuba diving), and most tourism packages now include trips to the archaeological zones of the ancient Mayan sites of Chichen Itza, Tulum and Uxmal.

Given its peripheral location, migrant labour has served this expanding resort, mainly Mayan workers from villages and small towns on the peninsula. The pull of the tourism labour market has seen migration firstly to Merida, the capital city, where Indians worked in low-pay hospitality jobs. Through this exposure many learned some Spanish and began to wear Western dress and sometimes English words were added to their vocabulary. With these skills Mayans travelled to Cancún, 'their final destination and the mythic site of a new life' (Hiernaux-Nicolas, 1999: 136). Today, nine miles from this narrow spit of land, where the lagoons, coral reefs and wetlands are no longer, a sprawling settlement has grown to over 300,000 people since the 1970s, 40% living without piped water or sewerage, and earning an average of $10 a day.

World Heritage Sites

> The wedding cake outline of the Mayan ruins contrasts sharply with the humble thatch and adobe dwellings of the present Indians, descendants of the ancient builders. These were people who developed a calendar, a system of numbers utilising the abstraction zero, the first writing system in the Americas, and agriculture based on an accurate knowledge of astronomy and the seasons. (Lane, 1963: 82)

Chichen Itza was the major site of the post-classic Maya period. Settlers appeared as early as 300 BC with evidence of urban planning in AD 750. By AD 900 Chichen was a thriving metropolis of an estimated 50,000 people. The city was inexplicably abandoned in 1250 (theories range from famine, over-farming, disease to invasion), and was later reoccupied by descendants of the original settlers, only to be taken over by a Mexican tribe, probably the Toltecs, who superimposed its own culture and architecture. Prior to the Spanish conquests, sacred stones had been used by locals for building, to be followed by looting for the erection of churches. These sites were 'discovered' by European explorers from England and France (French archaeologists exploded some temples in search of objects and internal routes). The English artist, Catherwood, captured the beauty of the Mayan architecture with exotic and peasant scenes in a series of romanticised lithographs. This brought the image of the Mayan pyramids emerging from the Yucatan jungle, to a *Grand Touring* audience in Britain (early ships between the Yucatan and Europe expanded on the back of the sisal trade and an emerging merchant class). The American archaeologist J. Eric Thompson also put these sites on the map by the late 1800s, with Mexican explorers also extending their knowledge and access to the numerous ruins from the 1930s onwards. In the first sub-aquatic recovery mission in the waterhole (*Cenote*) at Chichen Itza led by Edward Thompson in 1904, the treasure trove included 30,000 pieces. Attempts to bring back major stone carvings to the US were blocked but many items reside in museums outside of Mexico (the British Museum opened its sponsored Mexico gallery in the mid-1990s). State (national and regional) museums proudly display their collections of pre-Columbian art and remnants, not least in the National Museum of Anthropology in Chapultapec Park, Mexico City which opened in 1964. These collections promote the sense of heritage and Mexicanness, which has been state policy since the Revolution. It exhorts artists and intellectuals to make better citizens and strengthen control over the populace, by promoting a new *mexicandidad* both to visitors and residents, but this effectively breaks the physical link and access of Mayans and other Indian communities to their own inheritance. Located in regional cities, they are beyond the reach geographically and financially (all charge entry) and present no opportunity for interpretation or curation by *indigenas*.

Chichen Itza was inscripted by UNESCO in 1988 – the first Mexican sites were inscripted in 1987 such as Palenque and Oaxaca/Monte Alban – whilst Uxmal was not inscripted until 1996. This Puuc site flourished from AD 770 to AD 900 and, unlike Chichen, was never a 'lost' city (reports of its existence are dated as early as 1557, 15 years after the conquest of the Yucatan). The Puuc route links a cluster of Mayan sites a few kilometres apart (Kabah, Sayil, Xlapak and Labna). Other Mayan sites, including the oldest known of Dzibilchaltun, Mayapan, dot the province, but are not World Heritage Sites, an indication of both the arbitrary nature of inscription and limited conservation and site management resources. A heritage plan incorporating the whole historic region would serve as a more comprehensive approach than being left to the tourism marketing of the *Mundo Maya* and artificial Mayan route. The concentration of Mayan and other native Indian communities in the highlands of Chiapas, Yucatan and Oaxaca regions, and in neighbouring Guatemala, reflect the long-standing exodus south, away from encroaching urbanisation and political and land exclusion, as much as any post-colonial notion of *Mayaland*.

Here, as in other cultural (e.g. museums) and heritage sites, entry is charged for and controlled by state bodies who are staffed largely by *Ladinos*. Local Mayans and crafts traders can be found here and in ruins such as Mitla or Monte Alban, Oaxaca and who are tolerated as informal guides, but outside of the museum-system (and payroll) itself. The Mayans, whose descendants still inhabit this region (Davies, 1990), work as hotel staff and waiters, but are completely marginalised in the protection, interpretation and exploitation of the heritage sites and artefacts – the economic benefits from their inherited culture are effectively denied them. Guides are non-local university-educated Hispanics (Cheong & Miller, 2000). Mayan images, superimposed on heritage sites, adorn tour operator brochures to 'Latin America' and government agency logos and communications, and show smiling Indian faces and colourful crafts, but the reality is often the reverse in the heritage sites themselves. For example, in an attempt to exploit the heightened millennium market, Mayaland Resorts (1999) packaged the *Mayan Millennium* in which tourists would 'Receive the Millennium surrounded by the magic and mystic of the renown civilisation, The Mayas!' For a week at both Chichen Itza and Uxmal WHS, with an itinerary starting and finishing at Cancún and Cozumel resorts, the package included experiencing an archaeological excavation. On New Year's Eve a ritual was performed supposedly by a X-meen or Mayan High Priest (in fact an actor), who bid farewell to the old millennium, followed by a gourmet dinner and Light and Sound Show. The Judao-Christian calendar and new millennium had no relevance to the Mayan community, who had developed its own accurate calendar and astrological system long beforehand. The 'Light and Sound' show in fact takes place throughout the year at both sites and is produced by floodlights cemented into the 'protected' structures. Run twice daily, once in Spanish, once in English, it is in effect a laser show beamed over the pyramids (on the summer solstice this event attracts over 80,000 visitors).

Questions of ownership, access and management of heritage sites and collections, although increasingly raised by indigenous groups and their vocal leaders, seldom feature in tourism promotion and planning or in strategies for community and local economic development. In sacred sites around Mexico, their access and exploitation has been institutionalised along Western lines. This is hardly surprising given that both finance and conservation expertise (and financial assistance) is from Europe and North America (EU grant aid, for example under the Lôme Convention, is conditional upon European member state input, i.e. Western experts). As Nasution observes:

> To restore their traditional culture and grand monuments, [the] first local heritage advocates . . . turned to former colonists for advice . . . but who misunderstood the complexities of cities that are not just living, but teeming with life . . . their local counterparts and cultural aficionados sometimes failed to translate the ideas of urban rehabilitation into local realities. (Nasution, 1998: 28)

Resort-city Hub – 'City of Culture'

Merida, the Yucatan provincial capital, is known as the 'white city' and was the former Mayan city of *Itza* prior to the Spanish conquest. The city centre was destined for the Europeans/Creoles, whilst to the west of the city two suburbs were to be occupied by Mayans, and one to the east the Atzcapotzqalco Indians who were brought into the city by the Spanish invaders. Later a northern suburb was created to house the 'negroes and half breeds'. These suburbs, small townships, had their own native authority and representative town council under an Indian chief appointed by the regional governor. As exhibited in *Cuidad Museum*, Merida 1999, the centre in time gave over to the encroachment of these 'suburbs' which grew outwards taking their indigenous residents further from the centre, which as a result lost its geometric street layout and spacious form. Merida was designated the first *Americas City of Culture* in 2000, emulating the *European City of Culture* award first hosted by Athens in 1985. Whose cultures were being celebrated in this designation again was a question that was simply not asked (Evans, 2003), the indigenous communities and the layers of settlement were not communicated, nor celebrated in this festival year.

Merida also serves as the city hub linking the all-inclusive tourist enclaves of Cancún in the neighbouring Quintana Roo region and the intermediary heritage sites. They are largely accessed by visitors as part of day trips from these coastal resorts or from the city, served by fast road links (journey time one to two hours). The heritage sites suffer the day trip phenomenon familiar to many western urban heritage sites, from Athens (Acropolis), London (Tower of London, Westminster Abbey), Edinburgh Castle, to the historic quarters of Bath and Québec city (Evans, 2002a). It is little wonder that Westminster does not use the UNESCO logo in its marketing and introduced dual-priced entry for 'non-worshipping' visitors (Evans, 1998; Foster, 2001). This distinction is not of concern in Mexico – all entry is paid for, not once but twice. On queuing for entry to Chichen Itza for instance, the visitor passes two ticket attendants standing inches from one another. One issues a ticket from the heritage conservation body, the other from the tourist board. This apparent lack of joined up government also belies any trust and accountability (or cross-subsidy) between the tourism and heritage agencies. It is no surprise that museum and heritage agencies are under financial and managerial siege from the state government, unlike the more favoured tourism ministry, which dominates this power struggle.

Community

Finally, the question arises of who is the community with a claim to heritage sites and their environs. The notion of 'community' can be considered in terms of four following uses (Urry, in Richards & Hall, 2000: 3):

(1) The idea of community as belonging to a specific topographical location.
(2) As defining a particular local social system.
(3) In terms of feeling of *communitas* or togetherness.
(4) As an ideology, often hiding the power relations,which inevitably underlie communities.

The living Mayan community met all four of these tests, although *communitas* is the most hidden and fragmented today (if it were otherwise this would be perceived as a threat by the state). As Richards and Hall point out, Lash and Urry (1994) and others (e.g. Sassen, 1991) have argued that the place-based notion of community is re-emerging as a vehicle for:

> rooting individuals and societies in a climate of economic restructuring and growing social, cultural and political uncertainty. As political, social and economic structures based on the nation-state begin to be questioned, so local communities have come to be seen as essential building blocks in the 'new sociations' and political alliances . . . In this view local communities are seen as the essential receivers and transmitters of the forces of globalisation . . . (but also) the seat of resistance against the threatened homogenisation or globalisation. (Richards & Hall, 2000: 2–3)

The assertion of ethnic rights and a global 'voice' can also transcend national control, where:

> An ironically reinforcing bond between local identities and international normative patterns leaves the state on the sideline . . . Thus, ethnic groups have secured, at least theoretically, international support in their jockeying for cultural recognition and political influence. (Jacobsen, 2000: 22)

However, for the residual and marginalised 'fourth world' communities located and displaced in *Mundo Maya*, this opportunity for mediation and Foucaldian resistance appears both hollow and sentimental. Edensor, writing on the exemplar World Heritage Site Taj Mahal, puts it more realistically: 'the processes of blending culture and capital have become increasingly disembedded from localities and become the provenance of an international class, who displace the paternalistic control exercised by local agents' (Edensor, 1998: 11), a view echoed most recently by Eagleton: 'The problem at the moment is that the rich have mobility while the poor have locality. Or rather, the poor have locality until the rich get their hands on it' (Eagleton, 2003: 22).

Conclusion

What this example illustrates is that on the one hand the interpretation and 'ownership' of heritage should not be taken for granted or imposed from the outside, whilst on the other, notions of universalist heritage and 'rights' of (tourist) access to such monuments and sites are problematic, even imperialist.

There is the absence of genuine local community and cultural involvement in heritage site management and in some cases interpretation. The approach of private and public agencies and the tourism development process itself has followed a pattern of commodification. Most seriously, it perpetuates a system in which national authorities and power groups (including heritage intermediaries) effectively collude in international agency and corporate foundation programmes and development aid, using the dualistic heritage tourism and conservation rationale for intervention. A greater impact on patrimony would certainly be achieved by a more equitable distribution to a larger number and range of heritage sites and monuments. This would have the effect of both benefiting more local communities and heritage assets and in time spreading tourism activity over a more diverse area – a more sustainable and *Wise Use of Heritage* than is currently the case (Evans, 1999). Lord Rothschilds, former chairman of the Heritage Lottery Board in the UK, remarked in 1998 that a 'Global Heritage Lottery' might be established to distribute heritage and conservation funds more widely – the present situation highly skewed winners and losers scenario – not so fantastic a proposition when one considers that Lotteries gross over US$100 billion worldwide each year and the Heritage Lottery alone has distributed £1.7 billion to over 7500 projects in the UK (Evans, 2002b).

As Shackley advocates, greater application of heritage and tourism management planning, and the imposition of pricing mechanisms are also needed:

> Large visitor numbers, poor interpretation, little available information, crowds, congestion and pollution affect the quality of that experience, a quality which can unfortunately only be maintained at a high cost. (Shackley, 1998: 205)

Who draws up, implements and enforces such plans and controls (e.g. pricing) is an equally important question. One must start with the inheritors and resident communities who have often stewarded heritage sites, but who are typically losers in the master planning process, and in the land-use and development aid distribution. The World Heritage Convention established a formal obligation for states to adopt a general policy, which aims to give the cultural and natural heritage a function in the life of the community (Article 5a). It is up to each member state, however, to define these 'properties of outstanding universal value' (Article 1). There are few cases of such community planning (and management) in practice and examples of cultural resources within which museums and heritage sites play an important part in the regeneration of communities (see e.g. Newman & Maclean, 1998: 149). The definition and delineation of who the community and constituency of a site are, also fails to reflect the displaced or those to whom heritage attaches but who may no longer be resident, or who may even be excluded from the locality itself. In Mexico a highly displaced community, including economic, political and racial migrants/refugees, also generates a highly mobile diaspora of family, friends, ethnic and tribal groups. They take advantage of low cost road travel by bus and coach, and arterial links such as the Pan-American Highway, which served to bring tourism to central and southern America before the growth of air travel.

Community involvement and cultural democracy may therefore need to extend to the displaced and disempowered and engage fair trading approaches to heritage tourism (Evans, 2000; Evans & Cleverdon, 2000). In contrast to Mexico, for instance, pueblos in New Mexico retain resident control: some are closed to visitors, whilst others employ native tour guides and indige-nous-managed tourist facilities ranging from ski-ing and gaming resorts to game-tours, crafts centres and museums (Evans, 1994a, 2000). It is also clear from the heritage tourism process that greater consideration of heritage education and awareness is needed, in some cases more so than in the conservation and heritage fabric itself. Without community involvement and a sense of ownership and pride in locally based heritage (and all cultural heritage sites have a *locale*), any investment is likely to be wasted and may create resentment of the more subtle but nonetheless destructive practice of heritage development. These magnificent structures, silent tributes to the Maya's vast knowledge of astronomy and the ability of their engineers, force us to meditate on the destruction of the Amerin-dian civilisations, initiated on a large scale by the Spanish Conquistadors and clergy of the great 'civilising' empires of Europe. As Cambiassi (1997: 23) reminds us: 'This destruction continues even today in the form of exploitation and denial of the cultural identity of the descendants of the Maya and other Amerindian civilizations'.

Correspondence

Any correspondence should be directed to Prof Graeme Evans, London Metropolitan University (g.evans@londonmet.ac.uk).

Notes

1. *Ki-huic* (Mayan for 'Market'). The Maya World Tourism Ki-Huic is held bi-annually, serving the Mundo Maya region (Mexico, El Salvador, Guatemala, Honduras, Belize). A travel trade market with a crafts Mayan World Fair attached, it is held in the Convention and Exposition Yucatan Siglo XX1 Center, Merida City (Ki-Huic Turistico, 1999).
2. As Ashworth claimed: 'You cannot sell *your* heritage to tourists: you can only sell *their* heritage back to them in your locality. The unfamiliar is sellable only through the familiar' (1994: 2).

References

Ashworth, G. (1994) *Let's Sell our Heritage to Tourists?* London: London Council for Canadian Studies.
Batten, D.F. (1993) Venice as a 'Theseum' city: The economic management of a complex culture. *Proceedings of the International Arts Management Conference*. Paris: HEC.
Cambiassi, C. (1997) *Guide to the Archaeological Cities of the Maya*. Merida: Puerto Impresos.
Cheong, S.-M. and Miller, M. (2000) Power and tourism: A Foucaldian observation. *Annals of Tourism Research* 27 (2), 371–90.
Clancy, M. (1998) Tourism and development: Evidence from Mexico. *Annals of Tourism Research* 26 (1), 1–20.
Clancy, M. (2001) *Exporting Paradise. Tourism and Development in Mexico*. New York: Pergamon.
Davies, N. (1990) *The Ancient Kingdoms of Mexico*. London: Penguin.
Eagleton, T. (2003) *After Theory*. London: Allen Lane.
Edensor, T. (1998) *Tourists at the Taj: Performance and Meaning at a Symbolic Site*. London: Routledge.
Evans, G.L. (1994a) Tourism in greater Mexico and the Indigena – whose culture is it anyway? In A.V. Seaton, C.L. Jenkins, R.C. Wood, P.U.C. Dieke, M.M. Bennett, L.R. Maclellan and R. Smith (eds) *Tourism: State of the Art* (pp. 836–47). Chichester: Wiley.

Evans, G.L. (1994b) Fair trade: Crafts production and cultural tourism in the Third World. In A.V. Seaton, C.L. Jenkins, R.C. Wood, P.U.C. Dieke, M.M. Bennett, L.R. Maclellan and R. Smith (eds) *Tourism:State of the Art* (pp.783–91). Chichester: Wiley.

Evans, G.L. (1998) In search of the cultural tourist and the post-modern Grand Tour. Paper presented to the International Sociological Association, 14th Congress, Montreal, July.

Evans, G.L. (1999) Heritage tourism: Development and diversity. In *The Wise Use of Heritage*. Proceedings of the 12th World Congress of Conservation and Heritage. Mexico: ICOMOS.

Evans, G.L. (2000) Contemporary crafts as artefacts and functional goods and their role in local economic diversification and cultural development. In M. Hitchcock and K. Teague (eds) *Souvenirs: The Material Culture of Tourism* (pp. 127–46). Aldershot: Ashgate.

Evans, G.L. (2001) The World Bank and World Heritage: Culture and sustainable development? *Tourism Recreation Research* 24 (1), 83–6.

Evans, G.L. (2002a) Living in a World Heritage city: Stakeholders and the dialectic of the universal and particular. *International Journal of Heritage Studies* 8 (2), 117–35.

Evans, G.L. (2002b) The UK Lottery and the arts – the first seven years. *CIRCULAR* 14, 21–7. Paris. On WWW at http://www.culture.gouv.fr/dep/catacollect.htm#circular.

Evans, G.L. (2003) Hard branding the culture city – From Prado to Prada. *International Journal of Urban and Regional Research* 27 (2), 417–40.

Evans, G.L. and Cleverdon, R. (2000) Fair trade in tourism – community development or marketing tool? In G. Richards and D. Hall (eds) *Tourism and Sustainable Community Development* (pp. 137–53). London: Routledge.

Evans, G.L. and Smith, M. (2000) A tale of two heritage cities: Old Quebec and maritime Greenwich. In M. Robinson and P. Long (eds) *Tourism and Heritage Relationships: Global, National and Local Perspectives*. (pp.173–96). Sunderland: Business Education.

Foster, K. (2001) World Heritage sites: Who really cares? *Locum Destination Review*, 41–2.

Getty Conservation Institute (1999) *Values and Heritage Conservation*. Los Angeles.

Hiernaux-Nicolas, D. (1999) Cancún bliss. In D.R. Judd and S.S. Fainstein (eds) *The Tourist City* (pp.124–39). New Haven and London: Yale University Press.

Jacobsen, S. (2000) Indonesia on the threshold: Towards an ethnification of the nation? *International Institute for Asian Studies Newsletter* (22 June), 22.

Ki-Huic Turistico (1999) *Mundo Maya Merida '99*. Merida: Yucatan.

Lane, B.C. (1963) *Mexico* (3rd edn) (1st edn, 1955). California: Sunset.

Lash, S. and Urry, J. (1994) *Economies of Signs and Spaces*. London: Sage.

MacCannell, D. (1996) *Tourist or Traveller?* London: BBC Education.

Mayaland Resorts (1999) *Mayan Millennium*. Merida, Mexico.

Mexicana (1992) *Tourist and Industrial Guide South/Eastern Mexico: Reprivatisation of Mexicana Complete*. Mexicana No. 2 (September). Mexico.

Molstad, A. (1993) The great monuments which belong to all humanity. *European* (31 December), 6.

Nasution, K.S. (1998) The challenge of living heritage. *Urban Age* (p. 28). Washington, DC: World Bank.

Newman, A. and MacLean, F. (1998) Heritage builds communities: The application of heritage resources to the problems of social exclusion. *International Journal of Heritage Studies* 4, 143–53.

Observer (2003) Mexico: On the international agenda, pp. 1–6. On WWW at http://www.images-words.com/mexico2003.

Prentice, R. (1993) *Tourism and Heritage Attractions*. London: Routledge.

Richards, G. (ed.) (1996) *Cultural Tourism in Europe*. Oxford: CAB International.

Richards, G. and Hall, D. (2000) The community: A sustainable concept in tourism development? In G. Richards and D. Hall (eds) *Tourism and Sustainable Community Development* (pp. 1–13). London: Routledge.

Sassen, S. (1991) *Global City: New York, London, Tokyo*. Princeton: Princeton University Press.

Serageldin, M. (1999) Preserving the historic urban fabric in a context of fast-paced change. In *Values and Heritage Conservation* (pp. 51–8) Los Angeles: Getty Conservation Institute.

Shackley, M. (1998) Conclusions. In M. Shackley (ed.) *Visitor Management: Case Studies from World Heritage Sites* (pp. 194–205). Oxford: Butterworth-Heinemann.

Smith, G. and Pizam, A. (1998) NAFTA and tourism development policy in North America. In E. Laws, B. Faulkner and G. Moscardo *Embracing and Managing Change in Tourism* (pp. 17–28). London: Routledge.

Sweet, J.D. (1989) Burlesquing the 'other' in pueblo performance. *Annals of Tourism Research* 16 (1), 62 –75.

UNESCO (1972) *Convention Concerning the Protection of the World Cultural and Natural Heritage*. Paris: UNESCO.

Urry, J. (1995) *Consuming Places*. London: Routledge.

Wallerstein, I. (1992) The national and the universal: Can there be such a thing as world culture? In A. King (ed.) *Culture, Globalization and the World-System* (pp. 91–106). Basingstoke: Macmillan.

World Bank (1998a) *Culture and Development at the Millennium: The Challenge and the Response*. Washington, DC: World Bank.

World Bank (1998b) *Culture and Sustainable Development. Projects in Partnership, Regional Summaries*. Washington, DC: World Bank.

Landscape, Memory and Heritage: New Year Celebrations at Angkor, Cambodia

Tim Winter
Asia Research Institute, Singapore

This paper examines tourism, memory and notions of heritage at the World Heritage Site of Angkor, Cambodia. Rather than viewing heritage and social memory as abstract concepts, the paper explores domestic tourism at Angkor as the context within which Cambodia's recent history is re-articulated and made meaningful for a population recovering from decades of national turmoil. In exploring the various values and meanings associated with the national festival of Khmer New Year, the paper argues that an understanding of Angkor as a form of 'living heritage' remains neglected within a management framework which conceives the site as a form of material culture of the 'ancient' past. It is therefore suggested that exploring the values and meanings associated with Angkor's cultural heritage in this way provides valuable insight into the complex relationships of landscape, memory and identity.

Keywords: Angkor, Cambodia, Heidegger, heritage, identity, memory

Landscapes of Heritage and Memory

> In Angkor – a geographical region, an archaeological site and a cultural concept – lies much of Cambodia's future. (UNESCO, 1996: 165)

In recent years, considerable attention has been given to the fundamental dialectic between time and space within studies of landscape and place. By conceiving each as mutually constitutive, increasingly sophisticated conceptualisations have been offered regarding the often complex role landscapes play within notions of heritage and memory (Boswell & Evans, 1999; Edensor, 2002). Attention has also been given to the role heritage landscapes play in the formation of collective identities articulated in either cultural, religious or national terms (Edensor, 1998; Picard, 1997). In the case of the Acropolis, for example, Yalouri argues that the site not only reflects certain identities, but also serves to communicate and reproduce the values and meanings that underpin those identities. As she states:

> The study of monument is then of necessity also a study of time and of memory . . . the Acropolis [is] a 'vehicle of agency' which informs the way Greeks understand their national identity. (Yalouri, 2001: 17)

Underpinning this literature is an implicit understanding that heritage and landscape are not normative concepts. By contrast to earlier conceptualisations of landscape as abstract, objective and value neutral, recent studies have centred around ideas of spatial multiplicity and the contestation arising from the variegated social actualisation of place (Bender, 1993; Macnaghten & Urry, 1998; Prazniak & Dirlik, 2001). One notable example has been Bender's extensive analysis of Stonehenge. Outlining the presence of multiple interpretations and historical narratives, she illustrates how contestation arises within a socio-political environment characterised by unequal relations (Bender, 1993,

1999). Exploring spatial diversity through a multi-vocal text, she also high-lights the struggle of certain marginalised stakeholder voices in the face of insti-tutionalised and hegemonic value systems (1999). Similarly, Yalouri (2001) argues that, in the case of the Acropolis, the desire to re-present the site for both national and international tourism consumption creates a tension around the selective presentation of memories and their mode of narration. Together with Edensor's analysis of the Taj Mahal (1998), Yalouri identifies the complex polit-ical web arising from a discourse of heritage attempting to encapsulate inter-secting local, national and global memories of place.

Such authors are part of a rich vein of academic enquiry that explores the complex interplay of local, national and global formations of landscape and heri-tage and their intersection with the politics of ethnicity, religion and culture (Leask & Fyall, 2000; Oliver, 2001; Walsh, 1992). This paper attempts to explore these issues further in the context of a festival which holds immense symbolic significance for a Cambodian population still recovering from decades of social turmoil.

By examining tourism as a form of social praxis, it is suggested that rather than viewing Angkor as a monumental landscape of the 'ancient' past, the site needs to be considered as a form of 'living heritage' pivotal in the articulation of contemporary cultural and national identities. Accordingly, it is argued that such understandings remain marginalised within a discourse of cultural tourism which gains its hegemony from a desire to present Angkor as a site appropriate for international touristic consumption. In this respect, the paper illustrates how spatialised formations of power underpinning dominant paradigms of tourism, culture and heritage act to conceal and marginalise alternative values and prac-tices.

This paper draws on recent emphasis on the inter-relationships of identity, place and history in terms of memory (Connerton, 1995; Hue-Tam Ho Tai, 2001; Küchler, 2001). Eschewing the idea that history is situated in the landscape itself, the focus on memory switches attention to the ways places and times are actively constituted and reconstituted in multiple ways on an ongoing basis (Duncan & Duncan, 1988). In this light, landscapes as *lieux de mémoire* (Nora, 1998) also conceptually emerge as the medium through which multiple histories are simul-taneously remembered and forgotten (McCrone, 1998).

In attempting to appreciate how both Cambodia's recent and ancient histories are articulated as social memories through the practice of tourism, Heidegger's concept of *Dasein* is considered instructive here. For Heidegger, 'Being' in the world is fundamentally temporal, where abstractions of a social, public time are derived from an 'existential time' of the self (Heidegger, 1962). By centring the subject around its temporality, Being becomes a practice rather than a fixed state. Effectively, this temporal practice of engaging with the world is captured in his notion of *Dasein*, in which the subject finds 'itself already enmeshed in a series of social and material relationships' (Thomas, 1996: 41).

> World and self are never two separate entities which exist side by side with each other. Rather they are inextricably linked parts of a structure of Being. (Heidegger, 1962: 81)

Heidegger draws attention not only to how the embodied experience of place is given meaning through the imagined presence of subjective pasts and futures, but also to the process that serves to articulate understandings of abstract public times – in this case, recent events in Cambodian history. In effect, it is argued here that the practice of 'playing at being a tourist' (Urry, 1990: 101) actually serves to give meaning to that history in subjective, embodied and reflexive ways. Examining the tourist encounter in this way addresses the intimate and dynamic relationship between Cambodian tourists and their space of consumption. In addition, it clarifies how Angkor is understood as a place where recent histories are simultaneously erased, remembered and re-appropriated as socially practised collective memories.

Monumentalising Angkor

The World Heritage Site of Angkor occupies around 400km^2 of flat plains in northwest Cambodia. The landscape incorporates four main elements: tropical forest, areas of cultivated land, a number of isolated villages, and the architectural legacy of the Angkorean period. Although assigning precise dates to 'The Angkor Period' remains a subject of debate amongst historians, it is generally recognised that the kingdom emerged as a major seat of power early in the 9th century CE. This period lasted until the capital was abandoned in the middle of the 15th century (Tarling, 1992). Indeed, today's architectural remains testify to both the scale and wealth of Southeast Asia's greatest empire, an empire that covered much of today's Thailand, Laos, Vietnam and Cambodia.

As the region absorbed the cultural influences of early Indian traders, a fusion occurred of Hinduism and Buddhism and the already well-established indigenous forms of spirituality and religion (Chandler, 1996a). It was a synthesis which elevated Jayavarman II, who ascended to the throne in 802 and is popularly regarded as the first Angkorean king, into a *'Devaraja'*, or god king. Proclaiming himself the kingdom's first 'universal monarch', Jayavarman II was the first ruler to reign over a centrally governed and largely unified state: one that would later become Cambodia.

Although a number of Angkorean kings built little or nothing, those who enjoyed prolonged periods of prosperity and peace often followed increasingly extensive construction programmes, typically including irrigation work and vast reservoirs, statues of deceased parents or ancestors, and mountain temples dedicated to the ruling king himself (Chandler, 1996a). It was a tradition that would culminate in Jayavarman VII's vastly extravagant 13th-century Angkor Thom city complex. Unsurprisingly, the demands of such an extensive architectural programme are often cited by historians as a major factor in the empire's eventual decline around the mid-15th century (Jacques & Freeman, 1997).

The looting of Angkor by the Thais in the early 1430s heralded the beginning of an undistinguished period in Cambodian history and shifted regional power towards Siam (Tarling, 1992). With temple construction superseded by a more trade-oriented society centred on Phnom Penh, Angkor's abandonment meant that the intense tropical climate and surrounding forest savagely attacked the stone temples and destroyed any wooden structures neglected by the few remaining Buddhist villages in the vicinity.

Although some Spanish, Portuguese and Asian travellers visited the region after Angkor's demise, the late 19th-century travel diaries of Henri Mouhot, a French botanist, were pivotal in awakening interest in Europe to the existence of the site (Dagens, 1995). Encountering a labyrinth of monumental structures entangled with tree roots and lichen, in 1860, Mouhot presented an account of his 'discovery' of Angkor and described it as a 'lost', even dead, civilisation (Norindr, 1996). Despite the presence of numerous local villages, a powerful mythology of loss and rediscovery was reinforced by the very aesthetics of Angkor's seemingly abandoned, wild and ruinous landscape. The mythology endures today.

Notwithstanding the dubious nature of Mouhot's account, themes of redis-covery and restitution played a crucial role in legitimising the subsequent politi-cal and cultural construction of the French administrative territory of *Indochine*. Angkor also became central in the constructions of a national history and identity of an emergent *Cambodge* (Wright, 1991). Primarily through the scholarly work of the École Française d'Éxtrême Orient (EFEO) it was temporally and spatially fashioned as a once glorious, yet lost, cultural, national and ethnic heritage of the 'ancient' past. However, as Edwards notes, while the vision of a Cambodian nation was largely moulded around French colonial agendas, the inscription of Angkor as a national monument also involved a vital fusion of 'native and Euro-pean . . . ideas of culture and politics' (Edwards, 1999: 3). Indeed, as the 20th century progressed, the idea of a noble Khmer, along with a vision of a Cambo-dian cultural heritage and national history all converged on a totemic Angkor and, in particular, on Angkor Wat.

After independence was obtained in 1953, 'an imagining of history and power' (Anderson, 1991: 185) continued to pervade the Khmer psyche and sense of national identity. Throughout subsequent decades, imaginings of a once glori-ous Angkor remained central within Cambodia's political rhetoric. Barnett, for example, argues that during the Sihanouk era (1955–1970), the Prime Minister projected himself as the reincarnation of Jayavarman VII, conflating his own vulnerability with the idea of a Cambodia endangered by its cold war context (Barnett, 1990: 123). Moreover, although Sihanouk maintained a stranglehold over Cambodian politics until his fall in 1970, he was far from alone in seeking political mileage from Angkor. Notwithstanding the ideological variations across individual parties, the political appropriation of an idealised Angkor occurred on a number of levels in the years after independence. First, it repre-sented the opportunity for party leaders to claim guardianship over an invalu-able national heritage. Secondly, Angkor provided the reference points for visions of a national revival and, finally, its regal history supplied the authority for visions of absolutist power (Sorpong Peou, 2000).

Sihanouk's eventual overthrow by military coup in 1970 was also largely legitimised through a particular reading of Angkor's history. Parallels of an Angkorean demise brought about by monarchical decadence were cited by Lon Nol as a way of condemning Sihanouk's style of leadership (Edwards, 1999: 387). Claiming to liberate Cambodia from Sihanouk's indulgent nostalgia for a grandi-ose past, Lon Nol incorporated descriptions of a glorious Khmer culture, Khmer ancestry, Khmer blood and Khmer land into the propaganda of a government Sorpong Peou (2000) has described at length as an authoritarian republic.

In April 1975, paralysed by years of US bombing and civil war, Cambodia witnessed the start of one of the most radical and brutal social experiments ever inflicted on a nation. Promising to free the country from the tyranny of both Vietnamese and American intervention, Saloth Sar, latterly known as Pol Pot, proclaimed the end of 2000 years of history and the return of Cambodia to 'year zero' (Ponchaud, 1978). However, despite rejecting any historical precedents, it will be seen shortly that Pol Pot's extreme socialist ideology was once again partly inspired by the once-glorious agrarian civilisation of Angkor. Tragically, it is now believed that well over one million people, or one in seven of the population, died prior to the eventual liberation of Cambodia's capital Phnom Penh by Vietnamese troops in January 1979.

In recent decades, as well as suffering the short but brutal regime of the Khmer Rouge (Democratic Kampuchea), Cambodians have also endured an extended civil war, the effects of war in Vietnam, and subsequent occupation during the 1980s by the Vietnamese government. As a consequence, Cambodia has only recently begun to make significant progress towards a nationwide cultural, social and economic rejuvenation. However, despite the various political appropriations of Angkor since independence, the site has retained its widespread populist appeal and iconic status as national, ethnic and cultural symbol. Indeed, for a country composed of over 90% Khmers, it is hard to overestimate the deeply symbolic significance of Angkor within Cambodia today, not least because of the suffering endured in recent decades.

The 1990s: Stability and International Tourism

The international isolation of Cambodia under Pol Pot and its subsequent decade-long occupation by a Vietnamese administration meant that Angkor's conservation programme only regained the momentum of previous French efforts during the early 1990s. As Angkor formally came under the umbrella of the World Heritage Committee in December 1992, the International Coordinating Committee for the Safeguarding and Development of Angkor (ICC) was created to oversee efforts to protect the newly listed World Heritage Site.

Incorporating all the major international and domestic organisations involved in Angkor's management, including UNESCO, the ICC met twice a year to review technical and strategic issues relating to monumental conservation and the development of the site for tourism. The ICC was also instrumental in the creation of the Authority for the Protection and Safeguarding of the Angkor Region (APSARA), the Cambodian authority for Angkor which became operational during the mid-1990s. In the virtual absence of a Cambodian tourism industry, and alarmed at the large-scale disrepair of the temples in the early 1990s, both the ICC and APSARA initially set about establishing a body of archaeological and architectural expertise capable of addressing Angkor's need for emergency restoration.

As a consequence, the ICC was overwhelmingly composed of international experts principally concerned with the conservation and restoration of Angkor's temples. The ICC conceived the site as a material heritage of the 'ancient' past – a vision which largely reproduced a construction of Angkor conceived during a period of French colonialism. By focusing on the preservation and restoration of temples in such static and temporally frozen terms, there was little recognition of the monuments, or the site itself, as a living, contemporary landscape. More specifically, anthropological or sociological understandings of the site – in both a historical and contemporary sense – were essentially ignored within a rational, scientific discourse of architectural conservation.

More recently, however, Cambodia's political stability, and the country's position within the heart of a rapidly expanding Southeast Asian tourism industry, has led to increases in international visitors to Angkor of about 30% a year, with some 466,365 visitors in 2000 (Ministry of Tourism, 2000). The pattern is likely to continue for the foreseeable future.

As a response to this new era UNESCO and such transnational bodies as the World Tourism Organisation (WTO) have set about constructing a language of 'cultural tourism' as a key to Angkor's future development. In so doing, they are attempting to reap the optimum social and financial rewards of tourism whilst affording protection to the cultural 'assets' it draws upon. Such a strategy is commonly associated with the promotion of 'quality tourism', as evident in a recent UNESCO publication on Angkor:

> The challenge will be to improve the quality of the experience, while increasing the capacity of the sites to meet the demand and to develop facilities for cultural tourism so as to prevent the onslaught of low quality mass tourism provoking irreversible destruction of Angkor's cultural and natural heritage. (UNESCO, 1996: 157)

The suggestion that 'a policy encouraging high quality / high price tourism . . . is indispensable'(UNESCO, 1996: 159) clearly implies the aim of reaping the maximum benefit from low numbers of tourists while minimising the impact on an infrastructure recovering from decades of social and economic turmoil.

When promoting cultural tourism, it is undoubtedly hard to integrate cultural and economic values in a mutually beneficial relationship. However, such a discursive abstraction of tourism marginalises understandings of the ways in which Angkor is produced as a tourist space by socially contextualised, reflexive and knowing agents. Moreover, although UNESCO recognises the need to improve 'the quality of the [tourist] experience' and safeguard a 'natural heritage', the architectural inclinations of the ICC referred to earlier have forged cultural tourism policies overwhelmingly centred on the protection of Angkor's 'ancient' monumental culture. As a consequence, a particular spatial representation has emerged which firmly regards Angkorean culture as of the past, frozen, even dead. It is a policy that clearly resonates with Bender's concerns regarding the commodification of such landscapes through heritage:

> More often than not, those involved in the conservation, preservation and mummification of landscape create normative landscapes, as though there was only one way of telling or experiencing. They attempt to 'freeze' the landscape as a palimpsest of past activity . . . freezing time allows the landscape or monuments in it to be packaged, presented and turned into museum exhibits. (Bender, 1999: 26)

Such authors as Dahles (2001) and Picard (1997) have pointed out that programmes of cultural tourism have recently emerged as powerful resources for numerous countries attempting to formulate notions of national identity. Within a context of international tourism, the Cambodian government has also taken inspiration from previous colonial readings of Angkor as an architectural masterpiece and glorious, powerful kingdom of the past. Indeed, this reassertion of Angkor as a glorious national and cultural heritage has become the principle asset for a government attempting to profit from the highly lucrative, yet competitive, industry of Southeast Asian tourism.

To conclude, we can see that a discourse of cultural tourism has been offered in an attempt to maintain an appropriate balance between the preservation of a material culture of the past and the presentation of a 'high quality' tourist desti-nation. However, as the following analysis of domestic tourism will demon-strate, a concept of cultural tourism which principally conceives Angkor as an 'ancient' templed landscape fails to incorporate more inclusive understandings of how the site is imagined, practised and valued by Cambodians today.

Khmer New Year

It is argued that an exploration of the values and meanings associated with Angkor's cultural heritage provides valuable insight into the complex relation-ship between landscape, memory and identity. In developing this argument, there is a focus on the Khmer New Year celebrations held in April 2001. The responses presented here are drawn from 29 interviews conducted with individ-uals, couples and families at three different sites within the Angkor park: Angkor Wat, the West Mebon and at Srah Srang. These three sites were selected because lengthy interviews could be undertaken while subjects, who were randomly approached, were picnicking, talking to friends, or simply relaxing by the water. Discussions were semi-structured in nature and centred on a series of themes. Interviewees were asked about their activities at the Angkor complex, their modes of transport and length of stay, why it was important for them to attend the festival, what they knew about Angkor prior to arrival or how they imagined it, as well their attitudes towards conservation and development. Essentially undertaken as 'conversations with a purpose' (Burgess, 1990: 103), these inter-views were conducted in Khmer through a translator, and recorded on mini-disc. They lasted between one and two hours.

Additional material was obtained from interviews conducted with the chief monks of two monasteries located inside the Angkor Thom complex. Under-taken in Khmer with a translator, these focused primarily on the role played by monasteries in the festival and on the reasons they are visited by Cambodians today.

In turning to consider Khmer New Year, the aim is to identify certain values and meanings Cambodians ascribe to a festival which has become an important yet overlooked aspect of Angkor's development as a tourist space. In particular, the analysis presented below examines the New Year festival in relation to the atrocities endured across Cambodia in recent decades. Crucially, however, Heidegger's notion of *Dasein* reminds us that such historical events do not exist only as external realities for Cambodians; instead, it focuses our attention on how such realities are articulated through subjective, embodied experiences at Angkor today. It will be argued that in recent years this annual event has come to symbolise a recovery from the social, political and economic forms of oppression which have characterised Cambodia's recent past. However, before developing this argument, it is necessary to provide a brief outline of the festival itself.

For most Cambodians, the new year serves as a welcome 'liminal, time out' (Turner, 1995) from the agricultural efforts of an increasingly hot dry season. Although not officially promoted or advertised by the government, a decade of relative political stability has enabled increasing numbers of Cambodians to travel to Angkor from around the country for the mid-April celebrations. At the time of writing, statistics on such journeys were not available. While a significant proportion of the tourists interviewed came from provinces across the country, infrastructural constraints meant that a large proportion of domestic visitors to Angkor travelled from areas linked by major highways, most notably Phnom Penh.

Because there is no ticketing system, assessing the scale and scope of the festi- val over recent years is difficult. However, as indicated below, the suffering and destruction endured during the Vietnam war and Pol Pot regime – which essen- tially removed any possibility of large-scale celebrations – means that the number of Cambodians visiting Angkor over the New Year period today remains unprecedented. The lack of accurate data was acknowledged during the ICC technical conference in December 2000, and again recognised at an interna- tional conference on Cultural Tourism held in the same month where estimates of domestic visitors to Angkor over the New Year period ranged from 100,000 to 250,000 (Veng Sereyvuth, 2000).

Staying in local hotels and guesthouses, these tourists typically spend between two and four days visiting Angkor. There are no formally organised events or celebrations, and the festival is characterised by families, couples and individuals moving across a broad range of activities. In addition to visiting the numerous Angkorean temples within the park, regular visits and offerings are made to a number of modern Buddhist monasteries. Typically, hot afternoons are spent swimming at the West Mebon reservoir, driving around the park in open-top vehicles, or relaxing at picnic spots, the most popular of which is the west gate of Angkor Wat. With a strong emphasis placed on socialising and meeting new people, the four-day festival is defined by an interweaving of leisure, tourism and religion as visitors continually move between swimming, picnicking, temple visits and prayer.

As noted earlier, for Cambodians, Angkor represents the material legacy of a once glorious past. In illustrating this, the following interviews also show how the site plays a pivotal role in articulating contemporary formations of cultural, national and religious identities – collective formations that have become greatly reified through the events of recent decades. Indeed, even the ostensibly innocu- ous activities of drinking, praying, swimming and picnicking at Angkor over New Year signify a departure from the 'dark years' of the 1970s, and as such denote a national passage of time. As Meng, a local businessman from Siem Reap, who is in his 30s, states:

> It is good to see a lot of people here, and to see a lot of people employed. If there is no life at the temples then it feels like the time of Pol Pot. So I like to see many people at the temples, both visiting and working. If there is

no-one selling things and no life it is like the dark years of Pol Pot. It is relief from the war to see people going to the temples and visiting them regularly. This really started from 1980 onwards, people started putting incense at the temples, so this needs to carry on today. Before, we were not allowed.

The sense of social liberation expressed in incense burning by Meng here remains a powerful dimension to today's New Year celebrations for a number of reasons. In April 1975, Pol Pot's revolutionary party (*angkar*) swept into Phnom Penh, declaring the end of '2000 years of Cambodian history' (Chandler, 1996a: 214). As Kiernan states, 'history was to be undone, in terms of population as well as territory' (1996: 27) by cleansing Cambodia of its religious, educational, legal and other social infrastructures.

Despite Pol Pot's claims of returning Cambodia to 'year zero', significant elements of his radical ideology drew inspiration from a vision of a once glorious Angkorean period. In particular, Pol Pot's vision of wealth creation through the annual export of a rice surplus was taken from a reading of Angkorean history (Vickery, 1999). It was believed that self-sufficiency could be achieved through the planting of rubber, cotton and coconut crops, a notion that drew considerably on the hydraulic theories of early 20th-century French scholars (Barnett, 1990). In fact, Pol Pot's attempt to massively reproduce Angkor's irrigation technology was to have horrific consequences for the population.

> The Angkorean dream entertained by the Pol Potists, for which tens of thousands of Cambodians died as they slaved building canals, was in large part historical fantasy. (Barnett, 1990: 121)

Based on misguided beliefs that multiple, season-defying harvests could be achieved through complex irrigation systems, grossly unrealistic aims were to lead to progressively worse annual famines. From his examination of party speeches, Chandler indicates that Angkor was cited as an example of the power of mobilised labour and 'national grandeur which could be re-enacted in the 1970s' (1996b: 246). A vision of a glorious Angkorean history thus ensured the site remained protected and was even appropriated as a political resource within the revolutionary ideology of the Khmer Rouge.

Under Pol Pot, however, ordinary Cambodians had no freedom of travel and were thus denied the opportunity to visit and experience Angkor as a landscape of collective heritage.

> The regime had its own form of nationalism, defined in particular by hatred of Vietnam. At the same time, however, it denied its citizens a celebration of their own cultural heritage . . . [and] . . . traditional Cambodian holidays were not observed. (Gottesman, 2003: 13)

Today, after two decades of steady recovery, the modern festivities therefore represent a reclaiming of the site as a collective 'memory', a populist symbol of history enabling Cambodians to better 'understand their national identity' (Yalouri, 2001: 17).

As Meng, a local businessman commented:

> Angkor Wat is a symbol and creation of Khmer culture, a symbol of national culture. That is why it is important for me, and why it is important for me to come here.

His words were echoed by Sovanna, another informant in her 30s from a village 20 kilometres north of Angkor:

> Angkor is the Khmer ancestor heritage and each year we like to see more and more people here at new year. It is a place many people want to come and it is good fortune to come as many people are still unable. After the war many people want to see Angkor, to see their heritage.

Kiernan's reference to the undoing of history in territorial terms raises the importance of spatiality in this reclamation of a Cambodian 'imagined community' (Anderson, 1991). Subsequent to the evacuation of the country's major urban centres in April and May 1975, the country was divided into seven zones (*phumipeak*), comprising 32 administrative areas (Chandler, 1996a: 209–26; Kiernan, 1996: 31–101; Vickery, 1999: 69–201). In an effort to destroy religious traditions, abolish private land ownership, maximise human resources, and to fundamentally reconfigure the country's political demography, major programmes of forced migration across these regions were implemented. With most families dispersed to camps of forced labour, all freedom of movement was abolished. In effect, Pol Pot's revolutionary experiment represented one of the most profound severing of ties between an entire national population and its geographical base.

It was also a four-year period that was straddled by further major political and social turmoil. Indeed, from the American bombing campaigns across eastern provinces during the early 1970s, until the Khmer Rouge's retreat to the provinces adjacent to the Thai border in the late 1990s, Cambodia's physical infrastructure suffered long-term destruction and neglect. Such events, combined and associated with abject poverty, meant that Cambodians were politically, economically and physically inhibited from freely travelling within their own country. In such a historical context, the possibility of travelling to Angkor from different provinces today represents an ongoing rehabilitation from this situation. As Howan, aged 40, a shop owner from the northwest town of Battambang, puts it:

> Yes. I like the crowds over the New Year period. It's a good atmosphere meeting people from other provinces. I like to see that and I like to talk to people from other provinces because we are the same nation. I like to come and see people from different parts of the country. Since I was young, people came to Angkor Wat, up until 1968, before Lon Nol, and then it started again in 1979. But it was more local people then because it was under Vietnamese control . . . Since the late 1980s more and more people can come, which is good for Cambodia.

Similar sentiments were expressed by Li, a woman in her 50s from Kampong Cham, near the Vietnamese border:

> We met when we came here, some of us met in Phnom Penh. But we are all from different provinces now, but we are family, we are all Khmer. We are

staying three days. We have heard about Angkor for a long time, and it is
the first time we are all able to come together after many dark years for
Cambodia. But it is Khmer heritage, built by our ancestors. We wanted to
meet here.

Likewise, for Hong, a 30-year old man from Pailin, an area occupied by the
Khmer Rouge as recently as 1998, New Year clearly represents a new era of
national stability and freedom to travel:

It's good we can now come here over New Year to see the crowds, to
worship in the temples. I used to come for one day on my own since 1994,
but it was not safe to bring my family as we live near the Thai border. I was a
soldier on the Thai border.

Such quotes demonstrate that the festival period represents a metaphoric
rebuilding of the nation through a reclaiming of traditions, territories and material heritage. These personal touristic experiences of Angkor over New Year
enable the events in Cambodia's recent history to be simultaneously remembered and forgotten. In this respect, the festival facilitates the emergence of a
social memory which valuably informs the articulation of a collective identity.

By understanding New Year as a series of sociocultural practices, we are
reminded of Turner's notion of *communitas* (1995). He argues that festivals represent liminal moments occurring in both time and space within which collective
identities can emerge. Meeting people and developing friendships is an experience that depends on the dynamics and symbolic potency of Angkor's landscape. Crouch's account of tourism as practice may also be applied in this
context. He suggests friendship 'is embodied because it . . . makes particular use
of space. People being physically together, sharing activities, the body becomes
aware of a shared body space that is also social space' (Crouch, 1999: 272).
Crucially however, it is only over the time of new year when this social space is
fully constituted through the collective picnicking, praying, swimming and
socialising of thousands of Cambodian visitors. It can thus be suggested that this
festival represents a unique time/space moment of *communitas* within which a
sense of a nation in socioeconomic and cultural recovery is collectively articulated. This is further illustrated in the following responses:

We come every year to see Angkor Wat, to have fun with the family, to see
lots of people. We just drive around. A few families from our village have
come. We've been coming for the past five years and now it's different in
that there are a lot more people here and there has been more restoration.
We don't know much about the history, so we like to picnic here [Angkor
Wat] and the baray [reservoir]. These places have the most people, the other
places are too quiet. We like to see it crowded, both with foreign people and
Cambodian people. No matter how busy we are, we come here over new
year, we feel we have to come to see the people at this time. (Hok and
Huant, husband and wife, both in their 30s, farmers, who travelled from
Kampong Cham Province)

We like to picnic here at the waterwheel, at the Baray or at Angkor Wat. It's
cooler, close to the water, good for picnics and it's a good atmosphere at

those places. Over new year we like to feed the monks at the Bayon, go to Phnom Kulen to see the waterfall and people there and worship the spirits of Khmer mythology at Banteay Srei, Neak Pean, Preah Khan I feel it is very important for my family to see this, to do these things and be here at this time. (Sok, farmer, in his 20s, from Siem Reap Province)

Among those visiting Angkor over the New Year there is also a noticeable optimism that many of the temples from the Angkorean Period will be significantly repaired over the coming years:

Yes. I would like to see the temples restored because the country has suffered four generations of war and so a lot of Cambodian people aren't knowledgeable about the Khmer history. I was born in Siem Reap. I used to come to the temples during the Sihanouk period and I used to come to the temples until Pol Pot, when I had to leave. I had to move 200 kilometres away, but I returned here in July 1979, I came back to Angkor. I am happy to see it being restored, especially the Baphuon temple. Philip Groslier was restoring it up until the war and now they are doing it again, which I am happy to see. People in the country are so poor and for them to see the glories of these temples restored makes them happy to see Cambodia's glory restored once again. Yes it makes people very happy. (Chhin, in her 50s, farmer and mother of six, on a family day trip from a village 15 miles north of Angkor)

Yes. I want to see Angkor as a modern tourist site, but they need to keep the traditional structures. They should restore the outer moat of Angkor Wat for Cambodian people to sit on, and restore these ruined temples for Cambodians to see their heritage. Cambodia is now at peace and to see Angkor restored is good for the country. (Sok in his 20s, a farmer from Kratie Province, who came by truck and is staying at Angkor for four days)

Yes, to see more restoration is good. It would be nice for foreigners and Cambodians to see Angkor Wat and all the other temples restored. Cambodians need to be proud of their heritage and country and for many it is only now that they are able to come here. It is important for them to see Angkor rebuilt. It gives strength to our poor country. (Hong, shop owner in his 30s, from Pailin, staying for three days)

Architecturally, Angkor is symbolically charged not only through its Angkorean temples, but also through the presence of numerous Buddhist pagodas that have been constructed during the last 15 years. Over the new year period, the frequent visits to pagodas centre around prayer, blessings and the personal merit attained from feeding monks and financially supporting the ongoing reconstruction of the buildings, many of which were damaged or destroyed during the 1970s. The following responses given by two head monks of pagodas situated within the Angkor Thom complex vividly illustrate the important role their monasteries play during the festival:

There are many people that come here, they come from town, from villages and they go to many monasteries, not just this one. They want to pray here because the monks are here. They use the old temples in the same way as the pagodas, using incense, praying to the Buddha. Many people like to pray for their relations so they bring food to the monks. They believe food earns them merit as when they give food to the monk he prays for their relative so the food feeds the spirit . . . People have given money to help build the *Vihear* (congregation hall). It brings them good luck and when that happens they believe in that pagoda and keep coming.

Similarly,

People come from Siem Reap town, the province, Battambang, and from the border with Thailand. They especially like to come during the festivals. They like to come to Angkor during the festival time. They like to give money. They believe all the pagodas inside the Angkor area are more significant than pagodas in their local areas, so they like to give donations.

Clearly, the potency of these pagodas is derived not only through the long-standing religious traditions they embody, but also from a series of value regimes very contemporary in nature. More specifically, they are valued because they are active, living sites. Nevertheless, during the first six months of 2002, significant speculation surrounded the future of these pagodas. Local government officials referred to them as 'eyesores', a 'security hazard to the temples' and a 'threat to foreign tourists' (*Cambodia Today*, 2002)

According to reports in the Cambodian media, local authorities intended to evict around 170 Buddhist monks and nuns from pagodas that were deemed 'illegally built'. Despite such strong claims, ascertaining their legal status is far from straightforward, and is beyond the scope of this discussion. However, it can be argued that objections to the presence of these pagodas were directly related to the development of the site's international tourism industry. Local officials drew on the lack of historical authenticity of the pagodas as a justification for their othering within a policy oriented towards the aesthetic presentation of an 'ancient' monumental landscape.

The director of APSARA, Angkor's management authority, subsequently gave an assurance that the monasteries would be safe. But this dispute provides an example of how the practices and values of domestic visitors to Angkor have come to be a frustration for some within the government aspiring to present the site for international cultural tourism. Indeed, these monasteries, considered by Ang Chouléan as 'the most striking manifestation' (1988: 36) of Cambodia's characteristic syncretism between Buddhism and animism, can be regarded as a 'living heritage'. They are potentially under threat from the desire to construct an all-encompassing relationship between the conservation of 'ancient' monuments and the presentation of the site for international tourists.

By contrast, it is suggested here that Angkor is important to a population recovering from a period characterised by US bombing campaigns, a domestic genocidal regime, and the political incursions of neighbouring Vietnam. At Angkor, there is a convergence of past histories, both glorious and tragic, erased, remembered and transposed into optimism about the future. Moreover, Angkor's increasing popularity as a national festival site and the ongoing reconstruction of its architecture are symbolically elevated into an optimistic vision for the country's future. It is a feeling expressed by Suoan, a young businessman in his 20s from Phnom Penh, who was visiting Siem Reap for four days:

> Angkor Wat is for the young generations. It is good to see the crowds coming; it is good for the younger generation to see more and more people coming to the temples. I believe they will restore it one day. Angkor Wat is different from other countries in terms of the architecture. It gives strength to the Khmer people and the nation.

In recalling Heidegger's notion of *Dasein*, we can see that such temporalities of history do not exist as abstract, external realities for such visitors as Suoan. Rather, they are articulated through the personal, embodied experiences of visiting Angkor today. In this respect, Angkor serves as a metaphoric space for a nation in recovery. Not only is it a recovery of the geographical and ethnic presence of a population, but also it is a recovery of their past, present and future.

By contrasting these tourist narratives with the spatial representations of the ICC, we can see that the role of Angkor as a 'living heritage' remains inadequately understood within a framework which conceives and values Angkor as a material culture of the 'ancient' past. The focus on the international tourism market has meant that there has been little or no understanding of Angkor's role as an important landscape in *domestic* tourism. It thus follows that the importance of such festivals as Khmer New Year also remains unrecognised by a management oriented primarily towards presenting Angkor's temples for an international tourism market.

Conclusion

In examining tourism at Angkor as a form of spatial practice, it has been argued that the presence of certain prevailing discourses and framings, in this case cultural tourism, serves to marginalise alternative understandings of heritage and memory. By viewing formations of landscape and heritage as inherently contested, and thus far from normative, the analysis offered here has highlighted some of the tensions underpinning Angkor's recent transformation into commodified tourist space.

The arrival of large-scale international tourism in Cambodia undoubtedly necessitates difficult decisions regarding both the preservation and the presentation of Angkor. While the current strategy of developing cultural tourism succeeds in presenting a 'high quality' landscape of 'ancient' monuments for an international audience, the practices and values of domestic visitors remain inadequately appreciated.

By contrast, this paper has drawn upon the concept of memory to illuminate how the recent traumatic historical events of a nation are simultaneously re-appropriated, remembered and forgotten through the personal experiences of being a tourist at Angkor today. Examining tourism through the Heideggerian lens of *Dasein* has powerfully illustrated the ways in which activities such as picnicking, swimming and driving are symbolically and metaphorically imbued with a sense of national recovery for Cambodians today. We have also seen how the ongoing reconstruction of Angkor's temples and modern pagodas, in the context of an increasingly popular festival, also provides Cambodians with an optimism regarding the country's future.

Addressing the complex interplay between time and space in this way provides valuable insight into the processes through which encounters with heritage landscapes can be translated and abstracted into formations of collective identities. Clearly, new year at Angkor is an example of a tourism practice whereby the 'the activity and its space are enlarged in the imagination' (Crouch, 1999: 271).

As post-conflict Cambodia vividly demonstrates, the material heritage of 'ancient' monumental landscapes does not merely remain part of a nation's past, but can actively serve as a living heritage contributing to the ongoing constitution of national, cultural and ethnic identities. This analysis of domestic tourism at Angkor, as a series of creative sociocultural practices, is thus offered in an attempt to advance the understanding of such vital processes

Acknowledgments

The author would like to thank Mr Khin, Po Thai for his extensive assistance in translating the interviews used for this paper.

Correspondence

Any correspondence should be directed to Dr Tim Winter at tcwinter@ hotmail.com.

References

Ang Chouléan (1988) The place of animism within popular Buddhism in Cambodia: The example of the monastery. *Asian Folklore Studies 47*, 35–41.
Anderson, B. (1991) *Imagined Communities: Reflections on the Origin and Spread of Nationalism.* London: Cornell University.
Barnett, A. (1990) Cambodia will never disappear. *New Left Review 180*, 101–25.
Bender, B. (1993) *Landscape, Politics and Perspectives.* Oxford: Berg.
Bender, B. (1999) *Stonehenge: Making Space.* Oxford: Berg.
Boswell, D. and Evans, J. (eds) (1999) *Representing the Nation: A Reader, Histories, Heritage and Museums.* London: Routledge.
Burgess, R.G. (1990) *In The Field: An Introduction to Field Research.* London.
Cambodia Today (2002) Monks, pagodas near Cambodia's Angkor Wat can stay, official says. Associated Press release, Phnom Penh, distributed by Cambodia Daily, 22 June 2002. On WWW at http://go.to/CambodiaToday. Accessed 01.09.02.
Chandler, D. (1996a) *A History of Cambodia.* Colorado: Westview.
Chandler, D. (1996b) *Facing the Cambodian Past: Selected Essays, 1971–1994.* Chiang Mai: Silkworm.
Connerton, P. (1995) *How Societies Remember.* Cambridge: Cambridge University Press.
Crouch, D. (1999) The intimacy and expansion of space. In D. Crouch (ed.) *Leisure/Tourism Geographies: Practices and Geographical Knowledge.* London: Routledge.
Dagens, B. (1995) *Angkor: Heart of an Asian Empire.* London: Thames and Hudson.
Dahles, H. (2001) *Tourism, Heritage and National Culture in Java: Dilemmas of a Local Community.* Richmond: Curzon.
Duncan, J. and Duncan, N. (1988) (Re)reading the landscape. *Environment and Planning D: Society and Space 6*, 117–26.
Edensor, T. (1998) *Tourists at the Taj: Performance and Meaning at a Symbolic Site.* London: Routledge.
Edensor, T. (2002) *National Identity, Popular Culture and Everyday Life.* Oxford: Berg.

Edwards, P. (1999) Cambodge: The cultivation of a nation 1860–1945. Unpublished PhD Thesis, Monash University.

Gottesman, E. (2003) *Cambodia After the Khmer Rouge: Inside the Politics of Nation Building.* New Haven: Yale University Press.

Heidegger, M. (1962) *Being and Time.* Oxford: Blackwell.

Hue-Tam Ho Tai (2001) Introduction: Situating memory. In: Hue - Tam Ho Tai (ed.) *The Country of Memory: Remaking the Past in late Socialist Vietnam.* Berkeley: University of California Press.

Jacques, C. and Freeman, M. (1997) *Angkor: Cities and Temples.* London: Thames and Hudson.

Kiernan, B. (1996) *The Pol Pot Regime: Race, Power and Genocide in Cambodia under the Khmer Rouge, 1975–79.* New Haven: Yale University Press.

Küchler, S. (2001) The place of memory. In A. Forty and S. Küchler (eds) *The Art of Forgetting* (pp. 53–72). Oxford: Berg.

Leask, A. and Fyall, A. (2000) World Heritage sites: Current issues and future implications. In M. Robinson, N. Evans, P. Long, R. Sharpley and J. Swarbrooke (eds) *Tourism and Heritage Relationships: Global, National and Local Perspectives.* Sunderland: Centre for Travel and Tourism and Business Education.

Macnaghten, P. and Urry, J. (1998) *Contested Natures.* London: Sage.

McCrone, D. (1998) *The Sociology of Nationalism.* London: Routledge.

Ministry of Tourism (2000) *Cambodia Tourism Statistical Report 2000.* Phnom Penh: Ministry of Tourism.

Nora, P. (1998) From lieux de mémoire to realms of memory. In P. Nora and L. Kritzman (eds) *Realms of Memory: The Construction of the French Past* (pp. 15–42). New York, Columbia University Press.

Norindr, P. (1996) *Phantasmatic Indochina: French Colonial Ideology in Architecture, Film, and Literature.* London: Duke University Press.

Oliver, P. (2001) Re-presenting and representing the vernacular: The open air museum. In N. AlSayyad (ed.) *Consuming Tradition, Manufacturing Heritage: Global Norms and Urban Forms in the Age of Tourism.* New York: Routledge.

Picard, M. (1997) Cultural tourism, nation building, and regional culture: The making of a Balinese identity. In M. Picard and R. Wood (eds) *Tourism, Ethnicity and the State in Asian and Pacific Societies* (pp. 181–214). Honolulu: University of Hawai'i Press.

Ponchaud, F. (1978) *Cambodia Year Zero.* London: Allen Lane.

Prazniak, R. and Dirlik, A. (eds) (2001) *Places and Politics in an Age of Globalization.* Oxford: Rowman and Littlefield.

Sorpong Peou (2000) *Intervention and Change in Cambodia,* Chiang Mai: Silkworm.

Tarling, N. (1992) *The Cambridge History of Southeast Asia. Volume 1.* Cambridge: Cambridge University Press.

Thomas, J. (1996) *Time, Culture and Identity.* London: Routledge.

Turner, V. (1995) *The Ritual Process: Structure and Anti-structure.* New York: Aldine de Gruyter.

UNESCO (1996) *Angkor – Past, Present and Future.* Phnom Penh: Authority for the Protection and Safeguarding of the Angkor Region (APSARA).

Urry, J. (1990) *The Tourist Gaze: Leisure and Travel in Contemporary Societies.* London: Sage.

Veng Sereyvuth (2000) Angkor Wat – the pillar of the Cambodian tourism industry. Paper given at International Conference on Cultural Tourism, Siem Reap, Cambodia, 11–13 December.

Vickery, M. (1999) *Cambodia 1975–1982.* Chiang Mai: Silkworm.

Walsh, K. (1992) *The Representation of the Past: Museums and Heritage in the Post-modern World.* London: Routledge.

Wright, G. (1991) *The Politics of Design in French Colonial Urbanism.* London: University of Chicago Press.

Yalouri, E. (2001) *The Acropolis.* Oxford: Berg.

Levuka, Fiji: Contested Heritage?[1]

David Harrison
International Institute for Culture, Tourism and Development, London
Metropolitan University, London, UK

The complex links between heritage and tourism, and the ways in which attitudes towards historical built environments vary over time and place, are demonstrated in a study of Levuka, on the small island of Ovalau, Fiji. The town was founded by traders of European origin, and for a few years was Fiji's first colonial capital. Since the late 1800s, however, it has remained undeveloped, despite periodic efforts by tourism interests, resident expatriates and some government departments, to raise its profile and conserve its buildings and ambience through the development of tourism. Over the past decade, these attempts have crystallised in moves to nominate the municipality for listing as a UNESCO World Heritage site. This paper describes Levuka's origins and its continued association with the colonial past, discusses the impetus within Fiji to nominate it, analyses UNESCO's role in supporting Levuka's case, and indicates the variety of perceptions to 'heritage' in the town, across Ovalau, and more widely in the Fiji Islands.

Keywords: Levuka, Fiji Islands, tourism, heritage, UNESCO

Introduction

The Fiji Islands, situated in the South Pacific almost 3000 km east of Australia and 1800 km north of New Zealand, are the 'gateway' to the Pacific. The current population of some 800,000 is the result of waves of migration that date back thousands of years, the most recent of which (from 1879 until 1916) involved the transport of thousands of indentured labourers from India to work on the country's sugar plantations (Crocombe, 1989: 3–20; Naidu, 1980; Nunn, 1994). By 1970, when Fiji became independent of Britain, it could legitimately be described as 'three Fijis' (Fisk, 1970: 33–48), as it was then (as now) constituted by culturally and economically distinct categories of indigenous Fijians, Europeans and East Indians. Indeed, shortly before independence, the East Indians were in a majority, with 50% of the population, compared with Fijians 44%, and Europeans and part-Europeans nearly 3%. By 1996, the ratios of the two major ethnic groups had been reversed (Government of Fiji, 1998: 29). As has been described elsewhere, Fiji Islands can be defined as a 'plural society' (Harrison, 1998: 130–1), where citizens of different ethnic groups and cultures 'mix but do not combine' (Furnivall, 1948: 304).

Colonial Fiji was largely developed to supply sugar to the metropolitan power, but early in the 20th century Suva became an important stopping-off point for visitors, mostly en route to destinations in North America and the Pacific. In 1923 the Suva Tourist Board was formed, initially to encourage visitors to go to other parts of Fiji and eventually settle in the Fiji group (Scott, 1970: 1). Growth was slow, but tourism became increasingly important in the 1960s, as indicated in Table 1, and the newly independent government of Fiji 'inherited an economy built upon twin pillars of sugar and tourism' (Plange, 1996: 209).

By the end of the 20th century, tourism was Fiji's main source of foreign

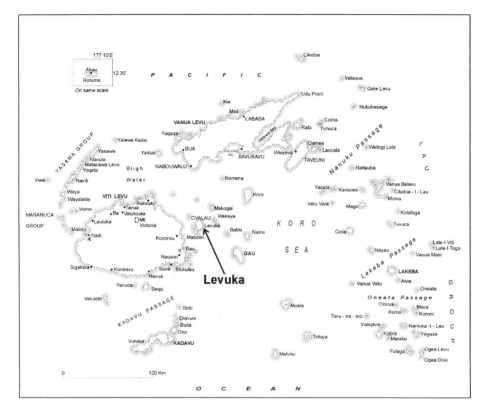

Map 1 Fiji Islands

exchange, with most holidaymakers going to the west/south-west of Viti Levu, or to nearby islands (Ministry of Transport and Tourism *et al.*, 1997: 13–15). Except for periods of insecurity during and after two *coups d'état* in 1987, tourist arrivals grew consistently, and by 1999 exceeded 400,000, with many indications that progress would be sustained. The trend was reversed by another coup, in May 2000, as indicated in Table 1, and while the following years have been characterised by an uneasy political stability, tourist numbers again increased, albeit from the relatively low base of 2000 (Bureau of Statistics, 2003: 4).

The ethnic divisions in Fijian society are reflected in the tourism industry. Fiji's tourism is largely run by people of European descent for visitors from Australia, New Zealand and North America. Indo-Fijians are frequently found 'back stage' of the industry, but the 'front stage' (except for senior management positions) is normally occupied by indigenous Fijians, largely to the exclusion of other ethnic groups (Harrison, 1998). In addition, the advertised sun, sea and sand (the main attractions for most tourists visiting Fiji) are complemented by an emphasis on indigenous Fijian tradition and culture. Put differently, while the sun-seeking hedonist may spend his/her time on the beach, diving or snorkelling, those seeking cultural experiences visit Fijian villages and seek out Fijian customs, traditions, and 'heritage'.

Table 1 International arrivals in Fiji, selected years: 1961–2002

1961	14,722	1990	278,996
1965	40,128	1995	318,495
1970	110,042	1996	339,560
1975	162,177	1997	359,441
1980	189,996	1998	371,342
1985	228,184	1999	409,995
1986	257,824	2000	294,070
1987	189,866	2001	348,014
1988	208,155	2002	397,859

Source: Bureau of Statistics (2001: 4); Bureau of Statistics (2003: 4); Fiji Visitors' Bureau (1999)

In particular, attempts to develop a heritage component in Fiji tourism have focused primarily on the town of Levuka, in Ovalau. Tourism interests have been instrumental in highlighting the town's historical importance as Fiji's first capital, a project in which they have received considerable backing from the United Nations Educational, Scientific and Cultural Organisation (UNESCO). However, as the following pages indicate, recognition of and support for Levuka's contribution to *Fijian* heritage is far from universal. Instead, Levuka's historical importance is contested, and the debate over its significance both illustrates and reiterates the divisions of Fijian society. In order to demonstrate this argument, it is necessary, first, to outline Levuka's history, describe its situation in the early 2000s, and to show how tourism interests and UNESCO combined to prioritise Levuka's case. This leads to a discussion of responses within Fiji, especially Ovalau, to such attempts to position Levuka as a centre of Fijian and, indeed, *world* heritage.

Levuka, 1800–2000: A Brief History

Levuka is on the small island of Ovalau, some 15 miles east of Viti Levu, the biggest island in the Fiji group, and is the administrative and educational centre of Lomaiviti Province. It was founded in the early 19th century by ' beachcombers' (itinerant traders) of European origin, mainly from New South Wales (now part of Australia), New Zealand and North America, who prospered under the protection of *Tui Levuka* – the local chief. In turn, he used them as allies against an inland tribe, the Lovoni, with whom he shared the island and was periodically at war (Derrick, 1953: 50; Ralston, 1978: 1–43).

An important node in the China trade, Levuka was a source of sandalwood, bêche-de-mer (sea cucumber), tortoise shell and pearls and, from the 1830s to the 1850s, the provisioning and repair of whaling boats were important sources of income. In the 1860s, as a result of the American Civil War, there was a brief boom in cotton, and Levuka provided plantations in Fiji with workers, often taken by force from the New Hebrides (now Vanuatu) and Solomon Islands. After cotton, coconut oil became pre-eminent, but by the end of the 19th century copra took over, and remained an important product until the 1950s.

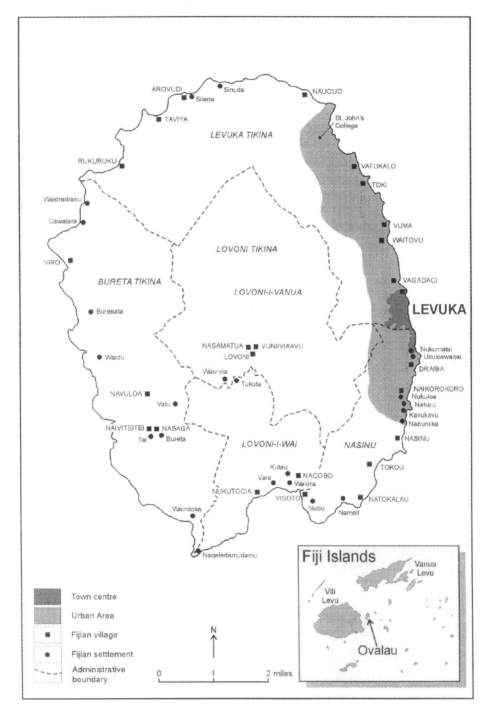

Map 2 Ovalau

The beachcombers, as these early traders basing themselves in Pacific islands came to be known (Ralston, 1978: 20), lived with indigenous Fijian women, fathered their children, and were notorious drunks. They were soon joined by more abstemious Wesleyan Methodist missionaries (Garrett, 1982: 279–88; Ralston, 1978: 23, 124–30), who branded them 'irresponsible adventurers seeking little else than the gratification of their lusts and freedom from the wholesale restraints of civilised society' (Derrick, 1953: 6). However, despite their reputation, beachcombers slowly became settlers, and by the late 1860s Levuka had a population of about 200, 'with a floating population of about 300 more' (Britton, 1870: 40). Within a few years, this population had doubled (Derrick, 1953: 57) and, gradually, the town became established.

Economic prosperity was not initially accompanied by peace and stability. Drunken quarrels frequently occurred 'between half-castes and whites' (Derrick, 1953: 52), and lawlessness predominated (Gravelle, 1979: 115–29). There were also continual hostile encounters between, on the one hand, the *Tui Levuka* and his people and the town's residents, and on the other, the inland Lovoni (Derrick, 1953: 50, 55; Derrick, 1957: 93, 154; Routledge, 1985: 141). The latter held a long-standing grievance that the Tui Levuka and his people, who had originally come to Ovalau from Viti Levu, had taken their land, and subsequently given some to the Europeans to found Levuka municipality.

During this period, the overall insecurity was exploited by the settlers, who jostled for influence and land, often acquired in dubious circumstances. More generally, throughout the 19th century, Fiji was riven by tribal conflict. For a brief period, from 1871, Cakobau, as *Tui Viti*, ruled the 'kingdom' of Fiji, with some settler assistance, but such support was variable (and unmatched by financial contributions) and his claim to kingship was fully accepted neither by Fijians nor Europeans. According to Routledge (1985: 141), even as his government was being inaugurated, for instance, the Lovoni of central Ovalau attacked and killed a chief in Levuka. Another account suggests the specific cause of this conflict was the refusal of the Lovoni to pay tax to Cakobau (Derrick, 1957: 200–201). No doubt longstanding enmities and particular complaints reinforced each other. However, as a consequence, the Lovoni were dispossessed of their land and forced to become plantation labourers, to be only partially reinstated in 1873, an injustice their descendants still bitterly recall (Fisher, 2000: 302–3, 314–15; Gravelle, 1979: 110–14).

Efforts by Cakobau to rule as king of Fiji did not succeed, and eventually he and the warring chiefs approached the British (not for the first time) to take on the responsibility of government. In 1874, Fiji became a British colony, with Levuka as its capital (Routledge, 1985: 186–210).

During the 1860s and 1870s, Levuka prospered. The *Fiji Times* – a newspaper still published – was started there in 1869. Lodge Polynesia, the first Masonic Lodge in the Pacific islands, was consecrated in 1872, moving to a new stone building in 1875, and the Bank of New Zealand opened its first branch in Fiji in Levuka in 1876. In addition, the Levuka Public School in 1879 was a pioneer in the Fijian educational system.

The town's physical layout and appearance were established by the mid-1870s. It then boasted several hotels and wholesale houses, a Wesleyan and Roman Catholic Church, and a Literary Institute (Britton, 1870: 40). The wooden houses, the shops, churches, and the Masonic Lodge, the schools and other public buildings, were clustered along a narrow coastal road bounded on one side by the sea and on the other by steep volcanic rocks, and along a short inland road branching off towards the hills. They were (and remain) European in design and orientation.

The first indentured labourers from India also disembarked at Levuka, where they were placed in a quarantine station. They arrived in 1879, after a catastrophic outbreak of measles in 1874 that wiped out an estimated 25% of Fiji's population, and one-third of that of Ovalau (Gravelle, 1979: 135–9). Introduced by Sir Arthur Gordon, the Governor, the policy had already been implemented in Mauritius and the Eastern Caribbean (Gravelle, 1979: 146–56; Naidu, 1980).[2]

Even after becoming Fiji's first capital, Levuka continued to be associated with Europeans, their form of government, and their offspring (Derrick, 1953: 49, 52). Von Hügel, who stayed in Fiji shortly after it became a British colony, noted the normality of sexual relations across the European/Fijian divide (Roth & Hooper, 1990: 146, 191, 196–7, 222). He concluded: 'It never occurs to me now to expect otherwise than that a man is living with a native woman. I either take it for granted, or if I ask at all it is only as to their numbers, countries or looks' (Roth & Hooper, 1990: 227). Nearly five decades later, another visitor noted 'the half-caste problem' and 'beautiful children, many of them, with sweet and gentle manners [who] are ostracised by the white people, and patronised by others' (Goode, 1922: 35).

Levuka's position as Fiji's capital was short-lived. After colonial status had been gained, efforts were made by the British to improve its infrastructure, including roads and sea walls, but these were temporary measures. Despite having a good harbour, the limitations of its geographical position were apparent (Layard, 1875: 21) and, in 1882, the British moved their capital to Suva, on Viti Levu, and Levuka's development was curtailed.

Levuka in the Early 2000s

Once Suva became Fiji's colonial capital, Levuka became an anachronism, while the rest of Fiji moved on. Except for a fish canning factory, its current appearance is largely unchanged from that of the 1880s. Situated on freehold land, of which there is little more than 8% in all of Fiji (Melrose, 1981: 21), its population (in 1996) was just over 1000. As Table 2 demonstrates, the closer the focus on the old municipality, the higher the proportion of those categorised by the census enumerators as 'Other'.[3] In this respect, the European connection is still at the heart of Levuka.

Since 1963, the fish canning factory has been by far the main employer on Ovalau, at its peak employing more than 600 workers from all over the island (Fisher, 2000: 96–7, 111). Intermittent closures have served to remind the people of Ovalau, especially Levuka traders and residents, that they depend on the factory for their economic survival (McCutchan, 1997; Nadore, 1996a; Rika, 1997). Employment in other sectors is low. From research carried out in Levuka in the late 1990s, Fisher estimates that there were '100 people employed in the education sector, 98 in the local government and utilities sector, and between 600 and 1000 in the canning factory, when it is open' (Fisher, 2000: 111).

Table 2 Population and ethnic distribution in Fiji, Ovalau and Levuka, 1996

	Total population (%)	*Fijian*	*Indian*	*'Other'*
Fiji	775,077 (100)	393,575 (50.8)	338,818 (43.7)	42,684 (5.5)
Ovalau	8,647 (100)	7,275 (84.1)	471 (5.4)	901 (10.4)
Levuka Peri-urban	2,650 (100)	2,046 (77.2)	220 (8.3)	384 (14.5)
Levuka Town	1,096 (100)	627 (57.2)	185 (16.9)	284 (25.9)

Source: Government of Fiji (1998) 1996 Census of Population and Housing, Bureau of Statistics, Suva, Fiji. Parliamentary Paper No. 43.

By contrast, despite the efforts described below, tourism in Levuka is undeveloped. In 2000, there was one hotel (the atmospheric but somewhat run down Royal Hotel, the oldest in Fiji) and three guest houses, offering about 160 beds, many in dormitory accommodation. Although owned by local residents, none was owned by indigenous Fijians and, according to Fisher, in 1997 they employed a total of only 15 people. With 14 more employed in restaurants, three in the travel agency and two in a dive shop (Fisher, 2000: 111), tourism in Levuka could hardly be described as big business. This is reflected in visitor numbers, and it has been estimated that in 1999 there were 7639, of whom 65% were from overseas (Levuka Case Study Team, 2000: 12). After the May 2000 coup, the situation became even more precarious. As the number of international visitors to Fiji plummeted (Table 1), the only travel agent in Levuka (a Canadian) closed his business and left Fiji, and Devokula, a nearby Fijian 'village' constructed especially for tourists, and heavily reliant on the travel agent for guests (Fisher, 2003), also ceased operating.

Levuka as a 'Heritage' Site: Early Initiatives

For much of the 20th century Levuka was ignored by those marketing Fiji as a tourism destination. Even in the mid-1960s, when tourism started to develop, it was barely mentioned, although a new hotel for the town was considered 'particularly desirable' (Harris, Kerr, Forster, 1965: 23). Nearly a decade later, it was reportedly 'the most interesting historic town in Fiji' (Belt, Collins, 1973: 15) and consultants recommended 'moderate' hotel development and the preservation of the town's historic character, under the Fiji National Trust. However, little came of the proposals. Locals were given no financial incentive to preserve decaying infrastructures and, as a later critic noted, few stakeholders had been consulted about the idea (Melrose, 1981: 70).

There were local residents who did want to preserve Levuka's 'heritage'. In 1977, the Ovalau Tourism and Promotion Committee was formed, later to become the Levuka Historical and Cultural Society (LHCS). It subsequently purchased and restored several dilapidated public buildings and, in 1980, started 'Back to Levuka Week' (Baba, 1997; Daya, 1997; Fisher, 2000: 149–51; Melrose, 1981: 42–5). This organisation was developed by an Australian and his North American wife, and supported primarily by people of European and part-European origin, including many not residing in the town (Fisher, 2000: 149–50).

Soon afterwards, the tourism industry started to take an interest. In the mid-1980s, a Task Force of the Pacific Area Travel Association (PATA) visited the town to assess its cultural and heritage significance, recommend how it might be enhanced, how restoration might be financed, and how the town should be marketed (PATA, 1985: 1). The subsequent report, supported by the LHCS (1985: 64–7), noted Levuka's decaying buildings, stagnating economy and few tourist arrivals, praised the 'commitment of Levuka's citizens in establishing the Community Centre' (1985: 9), and found 'civic groups and commercial interests . . . eager to participate in a programme to revitalise the environment, the community and the regional economy' (1985: 2).

Like the Belt-Collins Report, the PATA Task Force saw tourism as the major means of achieving this aim, especially as many 'modern tourists' wanted 'contact with "real" culture and environmental experiences' (1985: 3). It was felt that Levuka – 'the cradle of modern Fiji' – would widen the appeal of Fiji to international visitors, show residents that their town was valued, and had

> the potential to focus the attention of all Fiji's disparate community groups on a common national identity, thus emphasising their shared heritage and providing a potential boost to national awareness and national morale. (1985: 3)

As Fisher remarks, this assumed that indigenous Fijians shared the perceptions of Fijian citizens of European descent about the historical importance of Levuka (Fisher, 2000: 143). Nevertheless, following the Report, in 1987 the Fiji Government accorded some protection to Levuka's historic buildings by designating it a National Heritage Town and Fiji's First Historic Town (Fisher, 2000: 143; Francis, 1998: 136).

Levuka and 'World Heritage' Listing

Crucially, the PATA Task Force recognised that Fiji lacked the financial resources to restore Levuka, and suggested that international assistance should be sought, perhaps from the National Trust of Australia or UNESCO, to start a restoration programme (1985: 5, 47, 49). This moved Levuka's conservation and restoration from a purely local to an international agenda.

The recommendations had some effect, for over the next few years two significant developments took place. First, in 1991, following key initiatives by young graduates (expatriate and from the Fijian Islands) in the Department of the Environment and by the Director and others at the Fiji Museum, the Fiji Government signed the World Heritage Convention (Amato-Ali, 1998: 90). The same people *also* played an important part in the second development: the formation in 1992 of the Levuka Conservation Committee (LCC), which was to bring together technical expertise and political interests to act in the interests of conservation. While the Mayor of Levuka and two Levuka Councillors were included on the Committee, others were from outside the town. The latter were notably the Town and Country Planning Officer, the Director of the Fiji Museum, the General Manager of the Levuka fish cannery, and representatives of the Provincial Office, the District Office and the Ministry of Tourism. The role of the LCC was to act as an intermediary between the Town Council, which forwarded plans for building alterations to them for comment, after which they would be sent on to the Director of Town and Country Planning.

The issue of international assistance was again raised in 1994 in yet another PATA-sponsored document (the Hubbard Report). This repeated several of the conclusions of its 1985 predecessor, of which only one – the PATA-funded appointment of short-term Heritage Advisers – was really taken up. It also recognised, however, apparently for the first time in print, that the nomination of Levuka for World Heritage listing was being actively canvassed in Fiji (HJM Consultants & Hubbard, 1994: 59–60). In this respect, the Hubbard Report counselled caution:

> Under this Convention, the National Government of Fiji must, should it nominate any places in Fiji to the World Heritage List, be able to show that it has legislative measures in place to properly protect any such places . . . At present, Fiji has no such legislation . . . Nomination to the World Heritage List is a time-consuming and expensive exercise and not one to be undertaken without serious thought. Whilst World Heritage Listing can be an advantage in a couple of ways, particularly in providing an additional aspect to sell to visitors and tourists, it also carries with it obligations upon the National Government to manage and conserve the place to the required standard. (HJM Consultants & Hubbard, 1994: 59–61)

Arguably, this advice was already too late. Since 1991, when Fiji signed the World Heritage Convention (Amato-Ali, 1998: 90), the possibility of World Heritage Listing had increasingly been mooted in some government departments, most notably the Environment, Town Planning, and the Fiji Museum.

UNESCO Seeks Greater Pacific Representation

During the early 1990s, then, the conservation activities of several quite different organisations in Fiji were converging. In Levuka, there was the LHCS. Elsewhere, the Department of Town Planning and the Fiji Museum were similarly active and were linking with other organisations, including the National Trust of Fiji. And PATA's intermittent activities, in funding reports and employing short-term Heritage Advisers, were also important.

These moves, often prompted by expatriate advisers and enthusiasts, were increasingly linked to the activities of international institutions, especially UNESCO. The connections were not new. Since the late 1970s, for example, regional museums had been involved in a programme known as PRIMO (Preservation in Museums in Oceania), and the Pacific Islands Museum Association (PIMA) – itself a sub-programme of the International Centre for the Study of the Preservation and the Restoration of Cultural Property (ICCROM) – was started in 1979. By the late 1990s it had an office at the Fiji Museum in Suva.

From the mid-1990s, however, a changed pattern in these relationships seems to have emerged. In essence, the links between UNESCO and Fiji were increasingly promoted not by initiatives from the latter but by imperatives emanating from the former. Indeed, while the 1994 Hubbard Report was advocating caution in Fiji, a very different perspective was emerging from UNESCO and, in particular, the World Heritage Committee. At the 18th Session of UNESCO's World

Heritage Committee, held in Thailand in November 1994, it was noted that Europe, historic towns and religious buildings, especially from Christian traditions, and elitist architecture were all over-represented in the list of World Heritage Sites. However, 'traditional' cultures, 'with their depth, their wealth, their complexity, and their diverse relationships with their environment', were largely absent (UNESCO, 1994: 3).

As a result, it was decided to try to make the World Heritage List more 'representative, balanced and credible', and to take more cognisance of *cultural* property and heritage (UNESCO, 1994: 3). This was to be done by adopting a 'Global Strategy', which would

> identify the major gaps relating to types of property, regions of the world, cultures and periods in the list ... through a small number of thematic studies, carefully targeted and forward-looking, and concentrating on new or little known aspects of the heritage, especially that of under-represented nations such as Africa or the Pacific. (UNESCO, 1994: 4)

Furthermore, there would be a move away from large conferences to a series of regional meetings in under-represented regions, and in advance of which 'States Parties are encouraged to develop tentative lists of properties for inscription as an additional working document' (UNESCO, 1994: 5–6).

The decision to target less-developed regions, hitherto poorly represented on the World Heritage List, and to substantially expand the *criteria* for inclusion on the List, was subsequently confirmed at later UNESCO meetings, including a meeting of 'Heritage Experts' at Amsterdam in March, 1998 (UNESCO, 1998a). An even more specific focus on the Pacific, and especially Pacific Island Nations, was confirmed at the 22nd Session of the World Heritage Committee, held in Kyoto from November to December 1998. This was informed that of 23 Pacific countries, only 14 were member states of UNESCO, and only five were parties to the World Heritage Convention. Furthermore,

> There are a total of only 15 World Heritage properties located in the five Pacific States Parties to the Convention. Thirteen of these ... are located in Australia and two in New Zealand. (UNESCO, 1998b: 30)

The overall message was clear. Any Pacific island nation that had signed the World Heritage Convention and wished to nominate sites for the World Heritage List would receive every encouragement to do so. And this was matched in Fiji by a corresponding willingness to engage in the process. After Fiji signed the World Heritage Convention in 1991, the links of the Fiji Museum with UNESCO increased, especially with its Bangkok office, as indicated below, and the museum seems to have coordinated Fiji's 1994 submission of four tentative sites for World Heritage Listing to the World Heritage Committee. Those chosen as National Heritage Sites (and confirmed in 1997 and 1999) were Sigatoka Sand Dunes (a National Park administered by the National Trust) and the Sovi Basin (both in Viti Levu), the Yadua Taba Crested Iguana Sanctuary (a small island off the coast of Vanua Levu), and Levuka, Ovalau township and island. Perhaps it was a coincidence, but this submission occurred at *exactly* the same time as the 18th Session of the World Heritage Committee was bewailing the lack of Pacific World Heritage sites.

UNESCO's 'Global Strategy' and LEAP

From the mid-1990s, then, UNESCO's policy was to expand representation on the World Heritage List and to raise UNESCO's profile in the region. In Asia-Pacific, this involved two separate initiatives. From Paris, UNESCO implemented the Global Strategy and generally encouraged nations to apply for World Heritage Listing, while its Asia-Pacific office, in Bangkok, initiated its own project (LEAP), which aimed more generally to link heritage conservation, tourism and local development.

Formally entitled 'Integrated community development and cultural heritage site preservation in Asia and the Pacific through local effort', and abbreviated to Local Effort and Presentation (LEAP) (UNESCO, 2001, 2002a), UNESCO's Asia-Pacific initiative dates from 1996, when it first focused on five pilot sites – Luang Prabang (Laos), Hoi An (Viet Nam), Lijiang (China), Vigan (Philippines) and Bhaktapur (Nepal). Its aim was

> to make the local communities themselves the custodians and protectors of their own communities and in doing so to enable them to develop their ancient towns into modern cities with their heritage intact. It is a people-centred development project addressing within and from the perspective of heritage preservation and advancement, such varied issues as: poverty alleviation, environmental conservation, rural degradation, urban renewal and the globalization of culture caused by international tourism. (UNESCO, 2002a: 1)

While it is not possible here to analyse UNESCO's initiatives in detail, it is necessary to outline Fiji's participation in some of their activities. Perhaps the most crucial was the Third World Heritage Global Strategy meeting held in Suva, Fiji in 1997. Funded by UNESCO, and organised by the Fiji Museum and the National Trust, it was also the first Global Strategy meeting for the Pacific Islands and was designed to increase local and regional interest in the World Heritage List. Among papers presented by museum directors from the region, one was by the Director of the Fiji Museum, who introduced the four sites identified by Fiji in 1994 as possible contenders for World Heritage Listing.

For Fiji, the Suva conference of 1997 had several major consequences. Fijian citizens and others interested in conservation were brought into personal contact with UNESCO representatives from Paris and (especially) Bangkok. Equally importantly, a direct result of this interaction was the decision that Levuka should be the first site for which Fiji would apply to the World Heritage Committee for nomination on the World Heritage List.

Once this decision had been made, others followed. Responsibility for World Heritage submissions was moved from the Fiji Museum to the National Trust, and the Ministry of the Environment formed regional committees to submit nominations for heritage status (a brief moved in 1998 to the Ministry of Women and Culture). Also in (April) 1998, and following recommendations from UNESCO's Regional Advisor for Culture in Asia-and the Pacific, a request was made to the World Heritage Committee in Paris for a Preparatory Assistance Grant of US$15,000 to help prepare Levuka's application for nomination to the World Heritage List. This was complemented locally by the establishment in

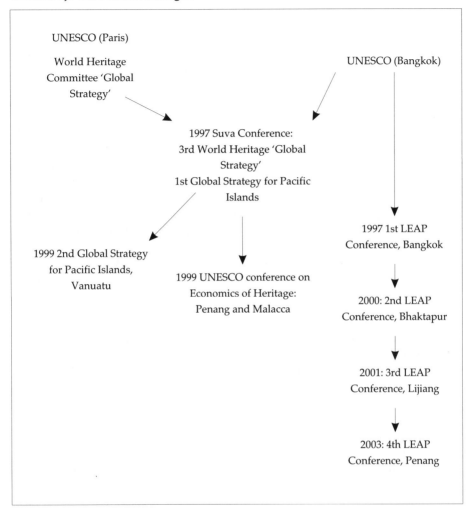

Figure 1 Some results of the 1997 Conference, Suva

1999 of the Levuka Heritage Committee, a government initiative to advise Levuka's residents on how they could assist the process.

Once established, personal links were reinforced through attendance at other UNESCO-sponsored conferences, as indicated in Figure 1. Broadly speaking, these fell into two categories. The first involved the implementation of the Global Strategy in the Pacific, with the overall aims of increasing the number of island signatories to the World Heritage Convention and then generating applications from them for World Heritage status. As a result, a representative of the Fiji Museum attended the Second Global Strategy Conference for the Pacific Islands in Vanuatu in 1999. Delegates were much encouraged by the success of Solomon Islands in nominating East Rennell, part of the largest raised coral atoll in the world, for World Heritage listing.

Secondly, details emerged at the Suva conference of UNESCO's (Bangkok)

LEAP project and (on the invitation of UNESCO's regional representative) the Director of the Fiji Museum subsequently attended its first workshop, on site management, held at Bangkok in November 1997. As a consequence, Levuka was added as the ninth case study area in the project, joining the first five sites, along with recently added Malacca (Malaysia), Hahoe (South Korea) and Kandy (Sri Lanka), ensuring it would thenceforth benefit from UNESCO's expert advice and interest.

Fiji delegates, from the Fiji National Trust and the Fiji Museum, subsequently attended further LEAP workshops. At the second, in Bhaktapur (2000), which was on 'Enhancement of Stakeholder Co-operation in Tourism Development and Heritage Preservation', they presented a case study of Levuka, outlined its history, gave an inventory of its buildings, indicated the extent of its tourism industry and its potential, and detailed its financial needs. The third, at Lijiang in 2001, focused on models of cooperation of stakeholders in tourism and conservation, and was attended by the Acting Director of the National Trust and two Levuka citizens. Finally, the fourth, in Penang in January 2003, was again attended by a representative of the National Trust and a resident of Levuka.

Local Responses to UNESCO Initiatives

From the accounts of numerous participants, and from sources in Levuka, one clear result of the 1997 Suva conference was that Levuka became the favoured site for nomination for World Heritage status in Fiji. Nevertheless, although new institutions were established to facilitate the process, it is unclear how effective these were in promoting grass-roots enthusiasm. Some attempts were undoubtedly made – if, for no other reason, because UNESCO stipulated local consultation. In 1999, for example, the National Trust made a presentation to the Great Council of Chiefs in Fiji (the stronghold of Fijian nationalism) and held four 'Stakeholders World Heritage Workshops'. The first, in Levuka in January, explored the claims of Levuka as a World Heritage site, and aimed to facilitate its nomination. However, a minority of those involved, as participants, presenters of papers, or as members of the Levuka Heritage Committee, were local residents, and it was largely a top-down exercise to agree an agenda for future activities (Fiji National Trust, 1999a). The other workshops, held in November in Labasa (Vanua Levua), Lautoka and Suva, aimed to provide local people (especially chiefs) with general information about World Heritage Listing and explain the advantages and obligations it would involve (Fiji National Trust & Fiji Museum, 1999b). How far these workshops really succeeded in gaining the support of other stakeholders, especially local residents, is doubtful. In any case, the momentum was short-lived, for the May 2000 coup, led by George Speight, and carried out in the name of indigenous Fijian interests (Lal, 2000), resulted in chronic political unrest and a general and pervasive lack of effective government for years rather than months.

The overall effect of the LEAP meetings is also difficult to assess. Attendance at the first, in 1997, was arranged at the last minute and involved no more than the introduction of the four sites officially favoured in Fiji for World Heritage Listing. For the second, at Bhaktapur, a considerable amount of useful data was brought together on Levuka, on its buildings and on local and visitor attitudes.

The 2001 workshop, in Lijiang, did indeed lead to a proposal for a 'flagship' project to restore a wharf (in effect, a small slipway) in the old town. It was a worthy enough aim, but had been mooted more than five years previously (Fisher, 2000: 152; Nadore, 1996b) and by July 2003 insufficient funds had been made available to start the repairs.

Although such a distinction is rarely made in Fiji, the functions of UNESCO's headquarters in Paris must be distinguished from those of its Bangkok office. While the former has an interest in increasing Pacific representation on the World Heritage List, and has been sympathetic to requests for assistance from Levuka, it has also stressed the need to consult and inform stakeholders, as state parties are expected to do as part of the nomination process. In addition, several consultants answerable to UNESCO in Paris, when attending the Vanuatu conference in 1999, reportedly questioned the extent to which Levuka epitomised *Fijian* heritage.

By contrast, UNESCO's Bangkok office has been considerably more proactive. For example, in July 1997, during the Global Strategy Conference in Suva, UNESCO's Regional Adviser for Culture in Asia and the Pacific reportedly visited Levuka. For an audience including two government ministers and representatives of the Pacific Asia Travel Association, he gave 'a presentation on the prospects of Levuka becoming a "World Heritage Site"'. Wittingly or otherwise, the impression was created that nomination was likely, for accompanying the report was a photograph of the town's seafront, with the caption: 'The Levuka Town – chances likely for Levuka to become a World Heritage Site' (Anon, 1997: 2b).[4]

The LEAP programme, which is supported by NORAD, the Norwegian aid programme, is also an initiative of UNESCO's Bangkok office. As indicated earlier, Levuka joined the programme after it had started and, compared with other case studies in the pilot scheme, receives far fewer tourists (in 1999, less than 8000). By contrast, Kandy, Lijiang, Malacca and Hahoe are mass tourism destinations. In addition, and again compared with other sites, Levuka lacks 'attractions' and opportunities for generating funds for restoration and conservation. Such differences have not prevented organisers of LEAP workshops, and some consultants, trying to impose a 'one size fits all' policy and framework on all the participating case studies, irrespective of their socio-economic background. More seriously, perhaps, there may be a tension in the LEAP project in Asia-Pacific between the aims of encouraging 'people-centred projects,' and encouraging local communities to conserve their heritage 'under the supervision of conservation professionals' (UNESCO, 2001: 1). Whereas the former aim assumes autonomy, the latter implies a considerable degree of direction.

The Process Stalls

Despite efforts in Fiji and UNESCO to promote Levuka's cause, by the end of the 1990s the process had stalled. Within Fiji, it has been alleged that the (then) Director of the National Trust was slow in forwarding relevant documents to Paris but, in any case, the coup of May 2000 meant that no further preparation on Levuka's application for listing occurred. The lack of progress in carrying out stakeholder consultation over the nomination can be gauged from the fact that, of the requested US$15,000 for Preparatory Assistance (PA) submitted to UNESCO in 1998 (finally agreed in 1999), only US$5000 was ever disbursed. The remaining sum was earmarked for consultants' fees and report preparation, but was withdrawn by UNESCO early in 2003 because it had not been claimed. Later, in May 2003, another application for PA for stakeholder consultation over World Heritage Listing, with no mention of a specific site, was made. This was accompanied by a second request, this time for consultants to carry out a Comparative Analysis of the claims for Levuka for nomination to the World Heritage List.

Perhaps even more damaging to Levuka's chances of nomination, the municipal elections of October 2002 led to radical changes in the composition of Levuka's Town Council. Before the elections, of the seven councillors, only two were of indigenous Fijian origin, with the remainder of mixed race (three), Indian and European origin. By contrast, the new councillors were primarily indigenous Fijians from the SDL (the United Fiji Party), also, since August 2001, the party of an uneasy and insecure national government. Committed primarily to furthering the interests of indigenous Fijians, since its election it has shown little interest in furthering Levuka's case for nomination to the World Heritage List. Some grounds for optimism might be discerned in the establishment, in September 2003, of a World Heritage Committee to assist the National Trust in nominating Levuka and other sites to UNESCO, but the chances of Levuka being the first choice have been substantially reduced. Instead consultations have started afresh as to which sites in Fiji might be nominated and arguably it is likely that the efforts of those who have supported Levuka's case, both within Fiji and further afield, have been in vain.

Whose Heritage? Whose Participation?

Two basic analytical issues arise from this case study. The first concerns the role of UNESCO and its personnel in encouraging the nomination of Levuka as a World Heritage Site. Indications have already been given that while both support the expansion of World Heritage listing to islands in the South Pacific, the leading role in promoting Levuka's cause has been taken by the Bangkok office.

The second issue is Levuka's status within Fiji. As Fiji's first European capital, and that for only a brief period, it has undoubted charm, as residents assert and many visitors have found. However, the process that led to the preservation of its 19th-century atmosphere has also made it an anachronism. The capital's early association with Europeans, the emergence of a high proportion of mixed-race citizens, and its subsequent lack of development, have together marginalised Levuka within Fiji in much the same way that these 'Others' have also been marginalised within Fiji society. The character of Fiji as a plural society is indeed reflected in the lack of consensus over the town's possible inclusion that has emerged among the town's residents and other stakeholders.

Awareness of divisions within Levuka is not new, for previous commentators have suggested that Levuka's history might not be 'owned' by other Fijian Islanders, whether indigenous Fijian or Indo-Fijian (Melrose, 1981: 70; Takano, 1996: 17) Indeed, while no unambiguous pattern emerges of attitudes of

Levuka's residents to the proposals that it become a World Heritage Site, there is evidence that support for the town's 'heritage' follows 'racial' or ethnic lines, simply because people in different ethnic categories tend to fall into different occupational categories. Informal interviews with residents conducted in June 1996 and January 2001 clearly indicated that those living in colonial-style properties were generally supportive of the idea, *provided* they could obtain financial support for maintaining their properties in the agreed condition. However, as such support had not been forthcoming, the restrictions – which (if enforced) entailed higher maintenance costs – were resented.

Interviews with residents also confirmed Fisher's view that those of European or part-European origin would prefer Levuka to remain much as it is, with some assistance from revenues of tourism. Chinese and Indian shopkeepers appear to tolerate conservation, and even go along with it, provided it brings them some financial benefit (Fisher, 2000: 153–7), but such views are not surprising, given that Chinese and Indians are most likely to be involved in retailing. Most residents of European origin either live in the town (and in colonial-style properties) because of its architectural charms or because they are actively involved in tourism, which depends heavily on Levuka's architectural image (2000: 167–9). That said, even among those committed to tourism development, there have been disagreements, perhaps because of competitive self-interest. Anxious to make their mark in a short time, for example, Heritage Advisers have frequently clashed with residents, who value the slow pace of life in the town. Similarly, the entrepreneurial activities of the Canadian inbound tour operator gave rise to considerable local resentment – from taxi drivers, whose prices he tried to undercut, and from 'elite' families of 'European' origin, whom he antagonised in his search for business.

By contrast, indigenous Fijians, most of whom live near but not in the town, are largely dismissive of the need to conserve Levuka's built environment (Fisher, 2000: 159–61). In part, as Fisher suggests, this may be because they have a different attitude to history, considering that its essence is retained in the location, the place, rather than the buildings. While agreeing that tourists came to Levuka because of its past, for instance, one of his informants nevertheless advocated that old buildings in Levuka should be pulled down. After all, she added, 'the history is still here' (Fisher, 2000: 160).

Developing this theme, Fisher suggests that, in Levuka, indigenous Fijians and people of European origin have two quite different ways of perceiving and referring to 'heritage':

> The first is that of the indigenous Fijians, for whom buildings and artefacts are of little consequence compared with the land – mere adjectives in a flowery piece of prose. The second is the language of the Europeans, both local and visitors, for whom buildings are the substance and structure of the writing, without which the meaning becomes obscured (Fisher, 2000: 135).

Importantly, he also notes that indigenous Fijians have no sense of ownership of the municipality:

> Levuka Town (as opposed to Levuka Vakaviti) [the village of indigenous
> Fijians next to the municipality] was created by Europeans and is still seen
> as a European town. It is not Fijian. As was noted earlier, arguments put
> forward for the preservation of the town included the belief that the town is
> the birthplace of the nation . . . One respondent said this is not of much
> concern to most Fijians. They see their origins in the legends of their ances-
> tors' arrival in Fiji and, more importantly, in the area in which their *yavusa*
> [broadly, their clan] originated. These stories are still told on Ovalau. The
> people of Lovoni trace themselves back to the first arrival on the island who
> swam there to escape persecution on Viti Levu. (Fisher, 2000: 161)

More succinctly, as one informant remarked to the author, there is a view
among indigenous Fijians that Levuka's history is 'half-caste history', while
another, of mixed race, commented that Fijians 'are not like us Europeans and
part Europeans. They can be very violent'.

An apparently unrelated issue, too, is the right of the Levuka municipality to
the freehold land on which it is situated. While only 8.2% of the total area of Fiji
Islands is denoted as freehold, even this is resented by some indigenous Fijian
nationalists, who demanded its return to Fijian ownership during the Speight
coup in 2000 (Lal, 2000: 185). That this is a source of conflict from which Levuka is
not immune was graphically illustrated during the 2000 coup when, on the
morning of 10 July, a large group of Lovoni came into the town, apparently intent
on causing trouble. After rampaging through the town, and trying and failing to
capture the Tui Levuka, they converged on the Masonic Lodge. Singing hymns
and prayers, they set it on fire, allegedly looking for tunnels to the Town Hall and
the Royal Hotel, leaving the building gutted and the Mayor of Levuka in tears.

One of the author's informants, with relatives in the group, said their hostility
had been fanned by a local Methodist minister, who had consistently preached
against the Lodge. However, she had also been told 'it was time they got their
land back'. The prevalence of this view was confirmed by the District Officer
(personal communication, 19 January 2001), who had been in Levuka for nine
months. Professing ignorance of 'heritage issues', he was nevertheless aware of
the Lovoni claim that Levuka land had been taken from them, and that they felt
their position was supported by the (indigenous Fijian) interim government of
the time. He added that there was a general feeling among Fijians that while
tourism was desirable, Levuka should not be developed to the detriment of the
rest of Ovalau.

A similar perspective was expressed by the *Roko Tui* (administrative head) of
Lomaiviti Province (personal communication, 19 January 2001). While not
formally opposed to World Heritage Listing for Levuka, he argued that any
application should include the prehistoric sites of Ovalau, to be identified by
indigenous Fijians in the villages, and that the process should then be agreed by
them through traditional and formal channels. He also observed that while the
hospital in Levuka had been modernised, people could not understand why the
old buildings had been retained, and felt that preservation had taken precedence
over the need for a completely new hospital.

From the Lovoni attack on the Lodge, the reasons given for it, and the
comments of prominent Fijian administrators after the event, several issues of

direct concern in this paper emerge. Once again, the historical hostility of the inland Lovoni to the municipality of Levuka (and to the *Tui Levuka*) emerges, along with the claim that the town was at least partly built on *Lovoni* land, which – despite its freehold title – was morally and spiritually theirs. Secondly, by destroying the Masonic Lodge, one of oldest and most valued of the few stone buildings in Levuka, a direct attack was *also* mounted on European and mixed-race heritage in Levuka. The Lodge was a solid yet mysterious symbol of the colonial past, set on land allegedly taken from the Lovoni. It was a source of much pride to European and part-European residents of the town, whose predecessors had founded it and historically made up the vast majority of its members (Patterson, *c.* 1976). And although the responses of the two senior Fijian administrators for Levuka and the wider province of Lomaiviti did not condone the violence of the attack, they clearly sympathised with the Lovoni cause and felt that Levuka received more favourable treatment than the rest of Ovalau.

Internal disputes over Levuka's 'heritage' (and who is to pay for it), are matched by differing interpretations from outside Ovalau. The Fiji Visitors' Bureau, the marketing arm of the Ministry of Tourism, has always adopted a low profile concerning Levuka's claim to World Heritage status. Its officials assert that local residents always bicker among themselves, whereas residents complain at the town's minimal presence in Fiji's tourist brochures, which are designed to appeal to a larger-scale market. For a considerable time, too, there was ill-feeling between the National Trust (which has to coordinate the application to the World Heritage Committee) and members of the Levuka Town Council. It had its roots in the contested responsibility for running the former Morris Hedstrom retail store (one of the earliest retail outlets in Levuka), now the community centre (Daya, 1997). However, Levuka people also feel the Trust has been slow to process the application for World Heritage listing and has not kept them informed of its progress. For his part, the former Director of the Trust argued that he needed the boundaries of the site to be agreed before further work could be done on the application.[5]

Those promoting Levuka's case are aware of such problems. During their first LEAP workshops, the Fiji delegates noted:

> With regards to heritage, support is rather muted. The villagers [i.e. indigenous Fijians in the *village* of Levuka, on the town's eastern boundary] are quite supportive of it but they have been spared the cost of maintaining these buildings since their houses are not heritage homes. However, heritage house owners do support the concept of heritage conservation but feel that the government should assist them in maintaining their homes in cash or in kind. (Levuka Case Study Team, 2000: 72)

A year later, at the Lijiang workshops, the Acting Director of the Fiji National Trust referred to

> . . . the lack of awareness by the [Levuka] community of heritage conservation. Because of its history, it has always been associated with negativity. For the residents, it was seen as restricting development for the town, an extra set of rules when townsfolk want to develop their property etc. The

lack of information dispersal by the council has not helped the situation. (Amato-Ali, 2001: 2)

Conclusion

If Levuka is to be successfully nominated for inclusion on UNESCO's World Heritage List, supporters of its nomination *must* obtain widespread support within Fiji. It has a small population, a weak economy and, compared with other case studies in the LEAP programme, few international tourists. Even if the Town Council was fully committed to World Heritage nomination, it could neither fund nor maintain a restoration programme. As it is, the main impetus for World Heritage Listing has come from outside Levuka: at various times, PATA, the Fiji Museum (which is no longer actively involved), the National Trust, the Department of the Environment, the former Ministry of Culture and, currently, the Department of Culture and Heritage. Furthermore, most individual participants in this process, although committed to the overall project, live in Viti Levu, and few are indigenous Fijians.

Despite this external support from some (but by no means all) government officials and departments, much still remains to be done. According to UNESCO, inclusion on the World Heritage List

> implies that legislative and administrative measures have been taken to ensure the protection of the group of buildings and its environment. Informed awareness on the part of the population concerned, without whose active participation any conservation scheme would be impractical, is also essential. (UNESCO, 2002b: 7)

Neither government officials nor local residents have reached any such level of 'informed awareness'. The lack of consensus among the latter has already been noted, and few of the former understand the obligations entailed by nomination to the World Heritage List. On being asked about these, one prominent politician, directly involved in promoting Levuka's case for nomination, admitted ignorance of the process and said they would wait for UNESCO to tell them what to do.

In Weaver's terms, Ovalau is a 'periphery of a periphery' (1998), and Levuka itself is even more marginal. Although it is the administrative centre of Lomaiviti Province and the Lau Islands, its future is tied, ironically, to perceptions of its past. Once replaced by Suva as Fiji's capital, it remained a colonial 'intrusion' (Harrison, 1997: 182). It was marginalised by the removal of the European administration, lacking an informal sector and a skilled work force, and without a tax base even to maintain its current infrastructure, far less fund conservation and future growth (Lea, 1996: 129).

Since the mid-1960s, tourism consultants and other interested parties (including this writer) have visited the town and admired what, to many, is a charming, evocative, and slowly decaying reminder of Fiji's colonial past. In searching for solutions, they have co-operated with European and part-European residents, temporary and permanent, and with government officials, who believe that nomination on the World Heritage List will bring tourists, economic growth and conservation to the town. A few – a very few – of these officials also consider that listing as a World Heritage Site would help indigenous Fijians appreciate the intercultural aspects of their past, and thus encourage a greater tolerance of their intercultural present. These local initiatives have been supported by several international organisations, primarily UNESCO, whose representatives since 1994 have tried to implement the Global Strategy and nominate sites in the South Pacific, a task in which they are soon to receive increasing support from the Australian government.[6]

Discussions about Levuka's 'heritage' occur primarily on the mainland, where officials in government departments and parastatals discuss 'action plans' for Levuka with overseas experts, and complain about the sluggish response of Levuka's residents. They, in turn, wonder what is going on. They do not distinguish UNESCO in Bangkok, or UNESCO in Samoa, from UNESCO in Paris. Rather, like residents at other pilot study sites, they simply hope that association with UNESCO will bring funding to make them more attractive to tourists who, in turn, will bring prosperity to their ailing town.

In fact, even Levuka's residents are divided on the benefits World Heritage status would bring, and on Ovalau there is little consensus on the town's historical importance. Most indigenous Fijians consider it, at best, an irrelevance to modern Fiji, while some resent the attention it periodically receives from government and the international community. In general, throughout the Fiji Islands there is little vocal support for Levuka's case or, indeed, for the nomination of any site! Still reeling from the 2000 coup, and apprehensive of further political unrest, most citizens are more concerned about present stability than the niceties of 19th-century history.

As Lowenthal has demonstrated, portrayals of the past are important in the formation and reformation of the present (1985 and 1997), and even presenting the past necessarily involves its interpretation (Uzzell, 1989a, 1989b). What is considered 'heritage' is continually invented and reinvented (Hobsbawm & Ranger, 1983). Such weighty issues are discussed at length elsewhere in this volume, but they are implicit in debates over Levuka's role in present-day Fiji. Clearly, Levuka has no *intrinsic* significance in Fiji. Rather, its role in history and the present is contested, and viewed through lenses which owe much to ethnic group affiliation and material and political interest.

These socially constructed meanings are the result of a continuous process of interaction and negotiation, and are not static over time. If, as Hewison suggests, even the definition of 'heritage' is 'the product of conflicting interests' (Hweison, 1989: 17), they will be reflected in and conditioned by the political process. In the Fijian context, especially, where a multiracial government has been overthrown and replaced by one dedicated to advancing indigenous Fijian interests, Levuka's historical significance – and the financial resources devoted to its conservation – will inevitably be renegotiated.

Finally, as Lowenthal notes, 'heritage is not an inquiry into the past but a celebration of it, not an effort to know what actually happened but a profession of faith in a past tailored to present-day purposes' (Lowenthal, 1997: x). If this is so, it is unclear whose purposes would be served by according pride of place to Levuka as Fiji's first World Heritage Site. This is not to suggest that claims on its behalf should necessarily be rejected, or that efforts to link conservation with increased economic growth through tourism are misguided. It *is* to suggest, though, that such attempts should be accompanied by open reflection and discussion about whose 'heritage' Levuka represents, and that the nomination process must be supported by all stakeholders, especially those who live in Levuka and, more widely, in Ovalau. Unless these conditions are met, the process will simply confirm that these arguments about 'heritage' simply reflect (but do not transcend) the notion that Fiji is indeed a plural society in which different ethnic groups continue to 'mix but do not combine'.

Correspondence

Any correspondence should be directed to David Harrison, International Institute for Culture, Tourism and Development, London Metropolitan University, London, UK (d.harrison@londonmet.ac.uk).

Notes

1. A different and earlier version of this paper appears in *Journal of Pacific Studies*, 2002/3. Many people have assisted in the development of the paper. Elizabeth Erasito is owed a *very* special debt, and thanks are warmly extended to Viane Amato-Ali, David Fisher, Justin Francis, David Kirton, Jotika Singh, Sarah Titchen and Kate Vusoni-wailala, and to George Gibson and many other Levuka and Fiji residents. The author alone is responsible for the conclusions expressed. Data for the paper were obtained over a period of several years. The author first visited Levuka 15–17 June 1996, as a member of a PATA-sponsored team, when he was Coordinator of Tourism Studies at the University of the South Pacific, Fiji (an appointment that was from March 1996 until December 1998). Informal interviews with key actors were held during that visit and continued irregularly during the remainder of the period in Fiji, and formal presentations on Levuka by PATA personnel were also attended. After leaving Fiji, the author received funds from the Centre for Leisure and Tourism Studies, now part of the International Institute for Culture, Tourism and Development, to attend UNESCO's second LEAP conference in Bhaktapur, Nepal, 8–16 April, 2000, where Fiji delegates first presented Levuka as a case study. The Centre also funded a further research visit to Fiji, especially Levuka, in January 2001, and informal interviews were continued during this visit. Finally, in July 2003, the Institute funded a visit to UNESCO in Paris to obtain further information about Levuka's inclusion on the Tentative List of World Heritage sites. As the paper indicates, these interviews were considerably supplemented by data obtained from secondary historical materials.
2. In particular, by decreeing that land was to remain under Fijian control, and denying Indians the right to purchase it, Gordon effectively sowed the seeds of bitter ethnic conflict for many generations to come. His policy in Fiji was in stark contrast to the one he had previously implemented in Trinidad, where Crown Land was opened up for sale to all sectors of the population, including Indians (Wood, 1968: 270–80), and is probably the result of the Social Darwinian view he held of Fijians' place in the human hierarchy (Routledge, 1985: 218).
3. In this case, 'Other' refers to everyone who is neither indigenous Fijian nor Indian, and would thus include Europeans, Chinese and members of other ethnic groups. More generally in Fiji, 'Other' refers to people of mixed race. In fact, the percentage of permanent residents of Levuka in this category is probably much greater than indicated. The municipality of Levuka is the educational and administrative centre for Lomaiviti Province, and within the boundaries of its three enumerating districts there are three secondary schools, with teaching staff and a high proportion of boarders, two squatter settlements of indigenous Fijians, and a hospital. In addition, many Fijian administrators for the Province also live within the old town's boundaries.
4. Indeed, in a recent publication, it is suggested that Levuka has already become a World Heritage Site (Connell & Lea, 2002: 21).
5. In fact, the boundaries of the site remain a matter of some confusion. As indicated

earlier, the reference to Levuka on the Tentative List sent to UNESCO in Paris was to 'Levuka, Ovalau (township and island)', whereas in most discussions the site to be nominated has been considered coterminous with the municipal boundaries – a preference confirmed in May 2002 by a UNESCO consultant on a fact-finding mission to Levuka.

6. The Australian Government is the most recent addition to the grouping of international interests. In May 2002, through its Ministry for the Environment and Heritage, it signed a Memorandum of Understanding with UNESCO to help promote UNESCO's Global Strategy in the Asia-Pacific Region. Designed to operate through the newly formed Asia-Pacific Focal Point for World Heritage Managers, the assistance envisaged includes promoting best practice in heritage management, facilitating requests for international assistance, identifying and securing funds for World Heritage activities, and sharing information and experience on heritage management issues (Asia-Pacific Focal Point for World Heritage Managers, 2003).

References

Amato-Ali, V. (1998) Strategic planning for sustainable heritage tourism: A case study of Levuka, Fiji's old capital. Unpublished MSc in Tourism, Management and Planning, Bournemouth University.

Amato-Ali, V. (2001) *Report on UNESCO's Conference on Heritage Management and Tourism*. Suva: National Trust of Fiji.

Anon (1907) *Cyclopedia of Fiji* (reprinted 1984 and 1988). Suva: Fiji Museum.

Anon (1997) Ministers to be briefed on heritage project. *Fiji Times* (16 July), 2b.

Asia-Pacific Focal Point for World Heritage Managers (2003) On WWW at http://www.heritage.gov.au/apfp. Accessed 14.07.03.

Baba, P. (1997) Carells lead repair work in Levuka. *Fiji Times* (2 September), 15.

Belt, Collins and Associates (1973) *Tourism Development Programme for Fiji*. Suva: United Nations Development Programme, International Bank for Reconstruction and Development, and Government of Fiji.

Britton, H. (1870) *Fiji in 1870: The Letters of the Argus Special Correspondent*. Melbourne: Samuel Mullen.

Bureau of Statistics (2001) Visitor arrivals, 2000. *Statistical News* 3. Suva.

Bureau of Statistics (2003) Visitor arrivals 2002. *Statistical News* 7. Suva.

Connell, J. and Lea, J. (2002) *Urbanisation in the Island Pacific: Towards Sustainable Development*. London and New York: Routledge.

Crocombe, R. (1989) *The South Pacific: An Introduction* (5th edn). Suva: University of the South Pacific.

Daya, M. (1997) National Trust. Letter. *Fiji Times* (19 February), 6.

Derrick, R.A. (1953) The early days of Levuka (first published 1941). *Transactions and Proceedings of the Fiji Society of Science and Industry* 2 (2), 49–58.

Derrick, R.A. (1957) *A History of Fiji: Volume One* (3rd edn). Suva: Government Press.

Fiji National Trust and Fiji Museum (1999a) *Stakeholder Workshop: Levuka World Heritage Site*. Suva: Fiji National Trust.

Fiji National Trust and Fiji Museum (1999b) *Fiji Islands Stakeholders World Heritage Workshops*. Suva: Fiji National Trust.

Fiji Visitors' Bureau (FVB) (1999) In-house statistics. Suva: FVB.

Fisher, D. (2000) The socio-economic consequences of tourism in Levuka, Fiji. PhD Thesis, Lincoln University, Christchurch.

Fisher, D. (2003) Tourism and change in local economic behaviour. In D. Harrison (ed.) *Pacific Island Tourism* (pp. 58–69). New York: Cognizant.

Fisk, E.K. (1970) *The Political Economy of Independent Fiji*. Canberra: Austalian National University Press.

Francis, J. (1998) Tourism development in Fiji: Diversification through ecotourism. Unpublished MA Thesis. Suva: School of Social and Economic Development, University of the South Pacific.

Furnivall, J.S. (1948) *Colonial Policy and Practice*. London: Cambridge University Press.

Garrett, J. (1982) *To Live Among the Stars: Christian Origins in Oceania*. Suva: World Council of Churches/Institute of Pacific Studies, University of the South Pacific.

Goode, A.K. (1922) Fiji of today. A series of articles written by Mrs Agnes K. Goode, JP, of Adelaide, South Australia, after a visit to the Fiji Islands, and published in the Adelaide Register. Read before the Fijian Society at meetings held on 20 September 1921 and subsequent dates. *Transactions of the Fijian Society*, 25–44.

Government of Fiji (1998) *Census of Population and Housing*. Parliamentary Paper No. 43. Suva: Bureau of Statistics.

Gravelle, K. (1979) *Fiji's Times: A History of Fiji*. Suva: Fiji Times.

Harris, Kerr, Forster and Company (1965) *Report on a Study of the Travel and Tourist Industry of Fiji*. Legislative Council of Fiji, Council Paper No. 32. Suva: Government Printer.

Harrison, D. (1997) Globalization and tourism: Some themes from Fiji. In M. Oppermann (ed.) *Pacific Rim Tourism* (pp. 167–83). Wallingford: CAB International.

Harrison, D. (1998) The world comes to Fiji: Who communicates what, and to whom? *Tourism, Culture and Communication* 1 (2), 129–38.

Hewison, R. (1989) Heritage: An interpretation. In D. Uzzell (ed.) *Heritage Interpretation, Volume 1: The Natural and Built Environment* (pp. 15–23). London and New York: Belhaven.

HJM Consultants and Hubbard, T. (1994) *Levuka: Heritage Conservation Study*. Canberra, Hobart and Melbourne: Department of Town and Country Planning and the Pacific Area Travel Association (Fiji Chapter) through the PATA Foundation.

Hobsbawm, E. and Ranger, T. (eds) (1983) *The Invention of Tradition*. Cambridge: Cambridge University Press.

Lal, B.V. (2000) Madness in May: George Speight and the unmaking of modern Fiji. In B.V. Lal (ed.) *Before the Storm: Elections and Politics of Development* (pp. 175–194).Canberra: Asia-Pacific Press at the Australian National University.

Layard, E.L. (1875) Memorandum, for His Excellency Sir A. Gordon, on the most fitting site for the seat of government, further correspondence respecting the colony of Fiji, in continuation of C.1337 of 1875, Levuka. 27 June, 20–23.

Lea, J.P. (1996) Tourism, realpolitik and development in the South Pacific. In A. Pizam and Y. Mansfield (eds) *Tourism, Crime and International Security Issues* (pp. 123–42). Chichester: Wiley.

Levuka Case Study Team (2000) *A Case Study on Levuka, Fiji Islands*. Second LEAP Workshop, Culture Heritage Management and Tourism: Models for Co-operation among Stakeholders, Bhaktapur, 8–16 April.

Lowenthal, D. (1985) *The Past is a Foreign Country*. Cambridge: Cambridge University Press.

Lowenthal, D. (1997) *The Heritage Crusade and the Spoils of History*. Cambridge: Cambridge University Press.

McCutchan, A. (1997) PAFCO closing is big loss. *Fiji Times* (weekend) (21 June), 2.

Melrose, J. (1981) *Town Planning and the Preservation Process: Levuka, Fiji*. Honolulu: Urban and Regional Planning Program, University of Hawai'i.

Ministry of Transport and Tourism, Tourism Council of the South Pacific, and Deloitte and Touche (1997) *Fiji Tourism Development Plan, 1998–2005*. Suva: Ministry of Transport and Tourism.

Nadore, I. (1996a) Levuka hopeful of cannery reopening. *Fiji Times* (5 October), 3.

Nadore, I (1996b) Father's wharf to be rebuilt. *Fiji Times* (9 March), 12.

Naidu, V. (1980) The violence of indenture in Fiji. *Fiji Monograph Series* 3, Suva: School of Social and Economic Development, University of the South Pacific.

Narayan, E. (2004) Special status hinders old capital's growth. *Sunday Times* (8 February), 17.

Nunn, P. (1994) *Environmental Change and the Early Settlement of Pacific Islands*. Honolulu: East-West Center.

Pacific Area Travel Association (PATA) (1985) *Levuka and Ovalau: Tourism Development through Community Restoration*. Sydney: PATA.

Patterson, R.T. (c. 1976) *The History of Lodge Polynesia, No. 562. C: Levuka, Fiji*.

Plange, Nii-k. (1996) Fiji. In C.M. Hall and S.J. Page (eds) *Tourism in the Pacific: Issues and Cases* (pp. 205–18). London: International Thomson Business.

Ralston, C. (1978) *Grass Huts and Warehouses: Pacific Beach Communities in the Nineteenth Century*. Honolulu: University Press of Hawai'i.

Rika, N. (1997) Old capital, new problems. *Fiji Times* (24 May), 7.

Roth, J. and Hooper, S. (eds) (1990) *The Fiji Journals of Baron Anatole Von Hügel, 1875–1877*. Suva: Fiji Museum, Suva, in association with Cambridge University Museum of Archaeology and Anthropology.

Routledge, D. (1985) *Matanitu: The Struggle for Power in Early Fiji*. Suva: University of the South Pacific.

Scott, R.J. (1970) The development of tourism in Fiji since 1923. *Transactions and Proceedings of the Fiji Society* 12, 40–50.

Takano, G.T. (1996) Learning from Levuka, Fiji – preservation in the first colonial capital. *CRM* 3, 15–17.

UNESCO (1994) Convention concerning the protection of the world cultural and natural heritage, World Heritage Committee, eighteenth session, Phuket, Thailand, 12–17 November. On WWW at http://www.unesco.org/whc/archive/global194.htm. Accessed 20.01.02.

UNESCO (1998a) *Report of the World Heritage Global Strategy Natural and Cultural Heritage Expert Meeting. 25–29th March*. Amsterdam: UNESCO World Heritage Centre in Association with the Government of the Netherlands.

UNESCO (1998b) *Convention Concerning the Protection of the World Cultural and Natural Heritage, Twenty-second Session, Kyoto, Japan, 30 November–5 December*.

UNESCO (2001) LEAP online. Office of the UNESCO regional adviser for culture in Asia and the Pacific. On WWW at http://unescobkk.org/leaponline/index/shtml. Accessed 30.03.01.

UNESCO (2002a) LEAP: Integrated community development and cultural heritage site preservation in Asia and the Pacific through local effort. Office of the UNESCO regional adviser for culture in Asia and the Pacific. On WWW at www.unescobkk.org/culture/archive/leap-sum.pdf. Accessed 24.01.02.

UNESCO (2002b) Establishment of the World Heritage list. On WWW at http://www.unesco.org/whc/opgulist.htm. Accessed 27.01.02.

Uzzell, D. (1989a) *Heritage Interpretation, Volume 1: The Natural and Built Environment*. London and New York: Belhaven.

Uzzell, D. (1989b) *Heritage Interpretation, Volume 2: The Visitor Experience*. London and New York: Belhaven.

Weaver, D. (1998) Peripheries of the periphery: Tourism in Tobago and Barbuda. *Annals of Tourism Research* 25 (2), 292–313.

Wood, D. (1968) *Trinidad in Transition: The Years after Slavery*. London: Institute of Race Relations/Oxford University Press.

Post-colonial Politics and Resurgent Heritage: The Development of Kyrgyzstan's Heritage Tourism Product

Karen Thompson
The Scottish Hotel School, University of Strathclyde

In 1991 the Kyrgyz Republic secured its political autonomy from the USSR and set out on the road to cultural and economic independence. Tourism was high on the development agenda, not least because of the country's abundance of natural assets, its experience with health and recreational tourism during the Soviet period and its lack of viable alternatives. During the post-colonial period, tourist activity has been based mainly on the country's mountains and lakes. More recently attempts to develop a heritage tourism product have mirrored the resurgence of ethnic Kyrgyz nationalism and Turkic culture throughout Central Asia. The paper identifies ethnic diversity and nationalist revivalism as potential constraints to the development of heritage tourism in Kyrgyzstan. Moreover, the issue of dissonant interest groups in the protection of the heritage of Kyrgyzstan is addressed. Much of the international interest in Kyrgyz heritage has been directed at the epos of the nomads of the Steppes and it is their protection, rather than that of tangible heritage sites, that has attracted sponsorship from UNESCO and other bodies. Additionally, the tangible heritage sites that have been proposed by the Kyrgyz government for World Heritage status are of domestic and regional, rather than international interest. Implications for the strategic development of Kyrgyzstan's heritage tourism product are discussed, with specific reference to world heritage.

Keywords: tourism, ethnicity, nationalism, heritage, Kyrgyzstan

Introduction

Prior to 1991, Kyrgyzstan, in particular the Ysyk-Köl region, was one of the Union of Soviet Socialist Republics' (USSR) most important recreational resorts. Since the demise of the Soviet Union the principal focus of tourism development in other Central Asian republics has been architectural and archaeological sites, marketed within the framework of the Silk Road (Taksanov, 2003). By contrast, Kyrgyzstan has preferred to concentrate tourism planning and marketing primarily on its natural resources. The combination of remote locations and mountainous topography has led to destination marketing in Kyrgyzstan being focused on adventure, nature and ecotourism. Nonetheless, the country has a wealth of heritage sites, many of which were explored to some extent during the Soviet era, and several of which have been nominated for World Heritage status.

Since independence, a resurgence of Turkic cultural and ethnic consciousness has placed important emphasis on the development of a heritage tourism product. However, Kyrgyzstan's historical and sociopolitical status and ethnic pluralism complicates the strategic development of a heritage tourism product. The population of Kyrgyzstan, as with all Central Asian countries, is made up of a diverse mix of ethnic and religious groups. Ethnic Kyrgyz represent less than 53% of the population and themselves comprise around 40 tribes. The ethnic

Kyrgyz are a Turkic people who are thought to have originated in the Yenesei region of Siberia and whose language belongs to the Ural-Altaic family. Other major ethnic groups in Kyrgyzstan are Russians (18%), Uzbeks (12.9%), Ukrainians (2.5%) and Germans (2.4%), although large numbers of Slavs and Germans migrated back to the Volga region in the wake of independence (CIA, 2002). In light of the ethnic diversity of Kyrgyzstan's population, there is a need to balance the reassertion of ethnic Kyrgyz identity with the desire to develop a fully inclusive civil state. In addition, the culture of the ethnic Kyrgyz majority has been most heavily influenced by their nomadic and tribal past and in particular the epic poems. It is therefore the intangible elements of their heritage with which the Kyrgyz identify most closely. Nonetheless, some tangible heritage sites within Kyrgyzstan's territory have been considered for inclusion on the United Nations Educational, Scientific and Cultural Organisation (UNESCO) list of World Heritage sites. However, the attraction of these sites is currently limited mainly to a domestic and regional visitor market. The paper aims to explore issues of ethnicity and nationalist revivalism that have potentially significant implications for the strategic development of a heritage tourism product within Kyrgyzstan. In addition, the latent conflict of interest between protecting heritage sites of importance to the national and regional population and attracting overseas visitors to Kyrgyzstan will be explored.

Ethnicity, Nationalism and Tourism in a Post-colonial Context

Kellas (1998) suggests that ethnic groups are differentiated from nations on the basis that they are smaller, more clearly based on common ancestry and historically more pervasive. Thus, whilst nations are inclusive, ethnic groups are exclusive. Stalin considered a nation to be created on the basis of a common language, culture, territory, economic life and psychological make-up (Franklin, 1973). In reality, few nations satisfy all of the above criteria. The Central Asian republics, created in the wake of the break-up of the Soviet Union, are multicultural nations, which are home to a variety of ethnic groupings. Since these nations obtained independence in 1991, it is the ethnic groups which have sought to reassert their culture, ideology and ethnicity (see Kamidov, 2002; Megoran, 2000a), whilst the nations have largely practised *cognitive nationalism*, based on a common understanding and acceptance of a shared group identity (Carney & Moran, 2000).

Ten years before the break-up of the Soviet Union, Smith (1981) noted the general occurrence of an 'ethnic revival' (and ensuing ethnic conflict) across the globe. It is by and large inevitable that there should be a resurgence of nationalism and ethnicity within newly independent nations and/or ethnic groups. Indeed the legacy of colonialism is a very important determinant of nationalism in the developing world (Kellas, 1998). In Central Asia itself, Bichel (1997: 3) claims that newly constructed national identities are expressed with a heavy emphasis upon ethnicity and 'have at least as much to do with self-expression and self-assertion as they do with historical evidence, precedent or cultural revival'. Horowitz (1985) contests that one of the common undertakings of ethnic groups after a period of colonisation is to restore the cultural image of the ethnic group, with the aim of fostering inter-group cohesion and increasing the group's external status. Within the context of tourism, it has been suggested that heritage tourism, in particular, can be used as a resource in such endeavours through the marketing and promotion of cultural heritage and an ethnic image to a wider audience (Pitchford, 1995). However, in multiethnic nations, such activities arguably become more sensitive. Whilst Adams (1998) details the Indonesian government's attempts to use cultural tourism as a tool for nation building, she notes that, in some instances, encounters between groups have led to ethnic antagonism. By contrast, Mitchell (2001) and Pretes (2003) argue that a nation's past and the heritage sites representing that past are important factors in constructing a common national identity among a diverse ethnic population.

Trans-national ethnic and religious forces can also be viewed as contributing to nationalism and playing a role in reducing ethnic tension within nations by fostering the idea of a common heritage. Indeed, Gellner (1994) discusses the role of Islam in uniting ethnic groups and differentiating them from outsiders within the context of the demise of the Soviet Union. He further asserts that the mechanisms underlying Muslim fundamentalism reflect those underpinning nationalism. Lewis (1999), on the other hand, draws attention to the difficulties of establishing ethnic identity on the basis of religion in a region such as Central Asia, where much of the population come from mixed ethnic and religious backgrounds. Moreover, Elebaeva (2003) warns that, since ethnic nationalism in Central Asia is closely linked to religious extremism, it has the capability to undermine stability and security in the region. But it is not only a common religious heritage that connects the various ethnic groupings of Central Asia. Since 1991, a pan-Turkic ethnic movement, focusing on common language and culture, has sought to reunite Turkic peoples, with the aim of counteracting extreme nationalism, fundamentalist Islam, and secular westernisation (Badretdin, 2000). Indeed, from a heritage tourism perspective, the tangible and intangible heritage of Central Asia has arguably stronger links to Turkism and Islam than to individual ethnic groups.

Methodology

A combination of desk research and interview-based fieldwork was employed for the research. Newspaper articles, press releases and conference proceedings were the main source of information on post-colonial nationalism and ethnicity in Kyrgyzstan and the Central Asian region. A large element of the paper could therefore be completed using the documentary method, identifying and analysing information that had already been compiled (Jennings, 2001). This desk research included a content analysis of the cultural and heritage tourism marketing literature for Kyrgyzstan. Content analysis is traditionally associated with the breakdown of texts and indeed is often referred to as textual analysis, discourse analysis or rhetoric analysis (Jennings, 2001). However, in tourism research, content analysis has typically been extended to other media.

> Tourism research should involve the examination of texts, not only written texts but also maps, landscapes, paintings, films, townscapes, TV programmes, brochures and so on. (Urry, 1994: 237–8)

Since the heritage tourism sector is very poorly developed in Kyrgyzstan, literature covering this field was extremely basic. The decision was therefore taken to conduct fieldwork in the form of semi-structured interviews using a purposive sample of individuals working within the tourism and heritage sectors in Kyrgyzstan. Although a non-systematic sampling method, purposive sampling is acceptable where the views of particular individuals are sought and where external validity is not required (De Vaus, 1996). Interviews were conducted, through an interpreter, with employees of relevant Kyrgyz government departments and non-governmental organisations, tourism academics and directors of a number of heritage sites throughout Kyrgyzstan. In this way a body of expert opinion and experience was collected on heritage tourism, government strategy and the protection of heritage sites in Kyrgyzstan. The discussion commences with a historical perspective on nationalism and heritage in Soviet Central Asia and, in particular, Kyrgyzstan. It goes on to discuss nationalist revivalism and the resurgence of ethnic heritage within the region as well as the socio-economic situation in Kyrgyzstan, with particular reference to the fledgling tourism industry. The implications of the combination of factors at work in Kyrgyzstan are then explored from the point of view of developing a heritage tourism product, and with particular reference to the role of World Heritage.

Kyrgyz Nationalism and Cultural Heritage under the Russians and Soviets

Prior to the subjugation of Central Asia by tsarist Russia the territory of Kyrgyzstan was occupied by nomadic peoples. Whilst there was a clear sense of nationhood and the population was linked ethnically, economically and linguistically, sociopolitical and administrative structures were centred on family and clan associations (Anderson, 1999; Asankanov, 1995). According to Kyrgyz oral history, they were forced from their ancestral lands on more than one occasion, arriving at their present territory via the Yenesei and Altai regions. The most important legacy the Kyrgyz people possessed were the epic poems telling the history of the struggles of their ancestors. It is significant that the best known of these, the *Manas Epos*, is often referred to as a 'monument' or 'memorial' (*inter alia* Abetekov, 1995; Asankanov & Bekmukhamedova, 1999). However, these epics can be better described as a living heritage in that their influence is discernible in the people's customs, rites and daily activities and, since independence, they have played an important role in encouraging self-expression and raising the level of social consciousness (Asankanov, 1995; Galieva, 1995).

Attitudes and sympathies towards nationalism and national identity in Kyrgyzstan fluctuated throughout the late 19th and 20th centuries in accordance with the balance of power in Saint Petersburg and later Moscow. Whilst tsarist Russia operated a policy of russification throughout the empire in an attempt to strengthen internal cohesion, the Bolsheviks wished to unite the nations of the Russian Empire by granting statehood and self-determination (see Boobbyer, 1998; Duncan, 1990). In the early days of the USSR, the Communist Party heavily promoted a policy of *korenizatsia* which encouraged the use of native languages and ways of life. Indeed it was during the 1920s that the Kyrgyz were encouraged to create a written alphabet. However, in the 1930s under Stalin there was notably less emphasis on native culture; moreover the migration of large Slavic and Germanic populations throughout the Soviet Union in the course of industrialisation precipitated a return to Russian national values (Duncan, 1990).

The period of Stalinist rule saw the gradual introduction of the Russian language into Kyrgyz schools and later throughout the political institutions. Heavy-handed measures were used to intimidate and remove the non-Russian elite on charges of 'bourgeois nationalism'. Between 1920 and 1940 the Union of Militant Atheists demolished scores of religious buildings and cemeteries, destroying literature and persecuting believers. It was not only the influence of Islam on daily life that was curtailed; Kyrgyz culture also came under pressure:

> On the pretext of combating pan-Islamism and pan-Turkism, steps were taken to root out cultural traditions and ideas from the consciousness and memory of several generations. (Bakieva, 1999: 64)

The death of Stalin saw a resurgence of nationalism and the renewal of efforts on the part of the non-Russian elite towards safeguarding aspects of Kyrgyz culture and in particular the epic poems. Such activities, whilst not encouraged by Moscow, were largely tolerated. At the same time, Soviet scholars were increasingly active in excavating and documenting heritage sites throughout the territory of Kyrgyzstan. By the time Kyrgyzstan gained its independence in 1991, a considerable number of important artefacts, clumsily unearthed from sites all over the country, had been removed to Moscow and Saint Petersburg. The formerly nomadic population, meanwhile, had been settled and urbanised; Russian had become the language of academic and political discourse. Islamic practices had been abandoned in public, if not completely in private, particularly in the north of the country.

Economic and Sociocultural Situation in Post-colonial Kyrgyzstan

After the founding of the new Kyrgyz nation on 31 August 1991, the country quickly emerged as the most democratic and liberal of the Central Asian states, a fact that has helped it to attract essential international aid. Nonetheless, several important factors continue to affect economic, social and cultural regeneration. The country's remote location, its lack of natural resources (particularly energy) and poor infrastructure are serious barriers to economic development. Meanwhile, political problems within the region continue to give cause for anxiety. Ethnic disputes in southern Kyrgyzstan, perceived political instability in Central Asia and the recent, high profile military activity in Afghanistan have all contributed to a drop in external investment and have had negative consequences for tourism demand.

Whilst President Akaev has actively attempted to create an open and civil society for all residents of the new republic, in practice democracy has suffered a number of setbacks. Omarov (1999) attributes widespread abuse of power within the Kyrgyz government to the fact that individuals place loyalty to their ethnic group above loyalty to the state. The ethnic divide is further aggravated by the demographic spread between different groups. In some areas of southern Kyrgyzstan Uzbeks outnumber ethnic Kyrgyz, whilst the Russian population is concentrated in the north. Additionally, Islam is strongest in the south of the country, the northern Kyrgyz having been considerably more exposed to Soviet influence during the USSR period. Thus, recent attempts to reconnect the ethnic Kyrgyz with the heritage of their nomadic ancestors have the potential to alienate other resident ethnic groups. Although historical disputes between ethnic groupings have been rare since independence, violence among ethnic Uzbeks, Tajiks and Kyrgyz has recently re-emerged, particularly in the south of Kyrgyzstan (see Kamidov, 2002; Saipjanov, 2003).

Post-colonial Resurgence of National Identity in Multi-ethnic Kyrgyzstan

In the Central Asian republics, the imposed supranational culture and the suppression of ethnic nationalism during the colonial era appear to have unleashed a resurgence of cultural identities linked to pre-communist ethnic heritage. This building of a national self-consciousness is perceived to be a direct response to avoiding being re-conquered. Fairbanks (2001: 52) notes how, 'leaders such as Askar Akaev of Kyrgyzstan have defied long odds to save their countries from dissolution or re-absorption into a new Russian empire'.

In Kyrgyzstan the creation of economic and political relationships within the international community has been accompanied by concerted attempts at reuniting the ethnic Kyrgyz with their pre-colonial heritage and identity. At the same time, the government has tried to create a civil and open society for all residents, regardless of ethnicity. However, some of the measures taken to promote Kyrgyz nationalism in the post-colonial era have not only been controversial, but have ultimately proved counterproductive for both economic and cultural regeneration.

One of the earliest assertions of national identity was the State Language Law of September 1989, which made Kyrgyz the state language of the republic and proposed a rapid switching to the use of the Kyrgyz language in education and administration. However, the consequences of this law were unsatisfactory on two counts. Firstly, the perceived growth in nationalism and the practical difficulties presented by the new legislation led to the exodus of a sizeable Slavic and German contingent, many of whom were professionals whose skills were essential to the new republic. In 1989 there were approximately 100,000 Germans living in Kyrgyzstan but by 1997 only 20,000 remained (Anderson, 1999). Secondly, the intention that Kyrgyz should be the working language for all administrative and educational establishments by 1994 was unrealistic, not least because many ethnic Kyrgyz still feel most comfortable using Russian in the workplace. Thus, in 1996 a change was implemented to the constitution to the effect that Russian could be reinstated as an official state language. Those who support the use of Russian as an official state language have put forward a number of reasons. First, there is the economic value, especially with regard to industrial partnerships with Russia and other CIS countries and the cost of translating documents. Second, there are demographic considerations, particularly with regard to slowing down the migration of Russian speakers. Third, speaking Russian conveys important educational benefits, not least the ability to study in other CIS countries (Anon, 2001). Meanwhile, supporters of the Kyrgyz language link its uncertain future with the disappearance of other visible vestiges of culture from daily life (Bashiri, 1999a).

An important manifestation of the resurgence of national identity is the continuing use of the legendary Kyrgyz warrior-hero *Manas* as a cornerstone of state ideology. The eponymous hero of the *Manas* epos has been identified as an iconic figure, upon which Kyrgyz cultural identity is based and the epic itself has frequently been described as the encyclopaedia of the Kyrgyz nation (*inter alia* Asankanov, 1995; Musayev, 1994). Galieva (1995) notes that the society depicted in the *Manas* epos shows many of the characteristics a fledgling, modern democracy might aspire to. Indeed, President Akaev has repeatedly stressed the need for the Kyrgyz nation to look to the seven precepts of *Manas* in building an ideology for the new state. As has been highlighted by Asankanov (1995), the further role of the *Manas* epos is in consolidating the Kyrgyz tribes into an ethnic community, and in encouraging self-expression and raising the level of social consciousness. It is therefore unsurprising that the epic should be selected as an important means of reuniting the population with their pre-Russian heritage.

Megoran (2000b) argues that this focus on *Manas* suggests an underlying desire for Kyrgyzstan to remain primarily the home of the ethnic Kyrgyz. However, other authors have emphasised the importance of the *Manas* epos to all Turkic peoples and it was this perceived pan-Turkism that primarily led to its suppression by the Soviets.

> Auezov argues *Manas* belongs to all Turkic peoples irrespective of their socio-economic, political or geographical affiliations – as an epic, *Manas* does not recognize any temporal or spatial boundaries. (Bashiri, 1999b)

Nevertheless, whilst the importance of epic poems on a wider level within the region may be argued to further the inclusion of many of the Turkic ethnic minorities resident in Kyrgyzstan after independence, Slavic and Germanic expatriates may scarcely identify with the principles and precepts they promote.

The updating of Islamic codes has also contributed to the renaissance of pre-Soviet cultural activities and traditions in Kyrgyzstan. Bakieva (1999) argues that Central Asians are now looking to Islam as a form of social inclusion and a source of sociocultural memory.

> Islam has . . . for many centuries been intimately interwoven into the life of the region's peoples, and its system of cultural codes is deeply embedded in their minds and their social praxis. (Bakieva, 1999: 69)

The promotion of ethnic identity at both national and regional level and the nurturing of a modern Kyrgyz culture have helped to highlight the potential role of cultural and heritage tourism in the search for viable economic activities. The complex historical, ethno-political and economic factors discussed above have, however, affected regeneration on a more general level, and have also led to a lack of direction and coordination in the development of a heritage product.

Vestiges of Tangible and Intangible Heritage

As a potential tourist destination, Kyrgyzstan's competitive advantage over the other Central Asian republics lies primarily in its natural resources. Large areas of the country are virtually inaccessible and this has helped to conserve a wealth of rare wildlife and alpine plants. Furthermore, the republic was a prime health and nature tourism destination in the USSR. It is therefore not surprising that adventure, nature and ecotourism have been the main focus of international tourism marketing campaigns. However, two factors have stimulated the marketing of heritage for tourism. Firstly the World Tourism Organisation (WTO) Silk Road Project, launched in 1994, focused its efforts for tourism development in Central Asia on the architectural heritage and cultural assets of the Silk Road. Whilst this campaign has been greatly hindered by strict regulations and a lack of cooperation regarding visas, the Silk Road campaign has been important in promoting awareness of Kyrgyzstan outside Central Asia and the former USSR. Secondly, a series of consultancy reports, commissioned and funded by various international organisations as part of the economic regeneration process, highlighted the potential of cultural and heritage products in marketing and promoting tourism to Kyrgyzstan. Whilst these reports identified preserved and emerging culture (in particular handicrafts) as a strength of the tourism product in Kyrgyzstan, they also emphasised the lack of 'significant monuments' in the more accessible north of the country (see BDO Consulting, 1996; Eckford, 1997; Touche Ross/International School of Mountaineering, 1995). The consultancy reports demonstrate a lack of enthusiasm for Kyrgyzstan's tangible heritage, which has been reflected in the dearth of international interest or indeed funding for the protection of sites. This lack of enthusiasm reveals disparities in the interests of the international community and those of the domestic and regional populations with regard to the heritage product. Kyrgyzstan in fact has a wealth of historical sites through which can be traced the various cultures, religions and communities that have occupied the territory throughout its history. Some of the most important relics of the spread of Islam to Central Asia are located on the territory of Kyrgyzstan. These include Safet Bulan, which is an early medieval settlement from where Islam grew and spread throughout the region; it was also an important religious centre in pre-Soviet times. The mausoleum of Shah Fazl at Safet Bulan is now in a dilapidated condition and there have been calls for it to be included in the UNESCO list of World Heritage sites (Begimkulov, 1999).

Other, more ancient sites are connected to some of the religions and spiritual practices that have passed through the territory, such as Christianity, Zoroastrianism, Buddhism and Shamanism. The restored caravanserai on the Silk Road at Tash Rabat is said to have been built by Buddhist monks in the 10th century. The ancient city of Balsaghun, of which only the Burana minaret remains, was one of the three capitals from which the Karakhanids ruled Central Asia in the 11th century and converted its peoples to Islam.

Unfortunately Soviet led excavations and restorations of some heritage sites were clumsy and the pick of the spoils were sequestered in Moscow and Saint Petersburg. Those artefacts which remain in Bishkek are not currently displayed due to the financial constraints. Since Soviet withdrawal and the collapse of the economy, maintenance of heritage sites has been sketchy due to lack of coordination and funding. Whilst the economy remains in a state of development, the preservation of these sites and their interpretation for tourism purposes is low on the government's list of priorities (UNDP, 1999).

Incongruence in the Development of a Heritage Tourism Product

More fundamental determinants, however, may explain the delay in developing a heritage tourism product. Efforts to promote the culture and heritage of the country have tended to reflect the propensity of the Kyrgyz to associate more strongly with their intangible heritage than with historic sites or artefacts. Many of the ancient sites of historic interest within the territory of present-day Kyrgyzstan are relics of peoples with whom the modern Kyrgyz have no ethnic links and who occupied the region prior to the arrival of the Kyrgyz. As regards Soviet heritage, most vestiges of the colonial era were rapidly removed after independence. The nomadic lifestyle practised by the Kyrgyz before collectivisation avoided the construction of permanent buildings. Two exceptions were the mausoleums that were constructed for important personages and the mosques and medressahs that sprang up under Kokhand influence toward the end of the 18th century. Many of these religious buildings were destroyed during the Soviet era. Thus, it has been argued that the elements of heritage with which the Kyrgyz most closely identify are the rights and cultural traditions associated with their nomadic past that have been passed down to them through the epic poems, in particular the encyclopaedic *Manas* epos (*inter alia* Galieva, 1995).

Nonetheless, there is a collection of tangible heritage sites throughout the country that are considered to have religious significance on a regional, if not international level. Furthermore, certain sites associated with the oral tradition, and in particular *Manas*, are visited as sites of pilgrimage by Kyrgyz and other Central Asian peoples. The failure to develop these sites as heritage attractions can be attributed to several factors. Firstly, there is an acute lack of funding for tourism development and resources are channelled primarily towards developing a product for the wealthier outbound markets of Western Europe, America and Japan. Sites associated with *Manas* and Islam are not considered to be of interest to international visitors from outside Central Asia (Akmatova, 2001). Moreover, the demand for domestic tourism within Central Asia is very small, due to the lack of disposable income. Further obstacles include the remoteness of many of the sites and the inadequate internal infrastructure which precludes any clustering or packaging of sites for overseas visitors.

A content analysis of the English language tourism marketing literature reveals those aspects of Kyrgyz heritage which are considered to hold interest for the wider international market. These mainly include sites along the Silk Road restored by the Soviets in the 1970s and 1980s, such as the caravanserai at Tash Rabat, and the minarets at Burana and Uzgen. Of these sites, only Burana benefits from any kind of interpretation, which is entirely in the Russian language. The same applies to museums and galleries, which are largely omitted from the main tourist brochures.[1] The Soviet built National Historical Museum in the capital, Bishkek, demonstrates the separation of Kyrgyz and Soviet heritage whilst displaying an absence of historical artefacts. The history of 20th-century Russia occupies the first floor of the museum, whilst the second and third floors are filled with 20th-century Kyrgyz household objects and musical instruments, many of which are still in regular use in rural areas. The only evidence of important archaeological findings is a catalogue of objects found on Kyrgyz territory, with an introduction by the director of the Hermitage that can be purchased from the museum shop.

Also prominently promoted in the tourist literature are handicrafts such as the traditional felt carpets (*shirdak*) and items belonging to the nomadic lifestyle. In practice, most international visitors travel as part of a tour group, which determines the elements of the heritage product they will come into contact with. Significantly, the travel brochures place considerably more emphasis on the opportunity to experience the nomadic lifestyle and traditions (through home-stays in *yurta*) than on visiting heritage sites.

Incongruities are apparent in the desire to preserve that heritage which is meaningful to the Kyrgyz people and the wider Turkic community whilst creating a heritage tourism product that will help attract the wealthier western markets. Recent attempts to secure World Heritage status have been focused on sites of religious and spiritual significance to the Kyrgyz people, rather than those popular with international tourists, a fact which highlights the importance of sites related to the living heritage. In 1995 Solomon's Mount (*Suleiman-Too*), a large, domed rock on the outskirts of Osh was placed on the list of nominations for UNESCO World Heritage status (see Amambaeva, 2001). The site is thought to have been a place of worship since Neolithic times and comprises features of archaeological interest over a wide time period, including Bronze Age petroglyphs, medieval baths, a cemetery and the ruins of a mausoleum built by Babur, a 16th-century Uzbek khan. The Muslim prophet Solomon was buried here in the 16th-century giving the hill its name and establishing it as an important place of pilgrimage, which it remains. World Heritage status has also been sought for the *Manas Ordo* in the Talas region. Like Solomon's Mount, this site is a collection of natural and historical features, including a sacred mountain (the *Manas-Supa*), an ancient Hun burial ground and a medieval mausoleum. The area is said to be the place where *Manas* lived and died and has enormous spiritual significance for the ethnic Kyrgyz as a site of pilgrimage. Other sites which, in the past, have been evaluated and considered for World Heritage status by UNESCO include the Burana minaret and the petroglyphs at Saymaltash on the northern shore of Lake Issyk-Köl. However, none of these sites has, as yet, been accorded World Heritage status, a mark of distinction which, in all probability, would add to their touristic appeal and extend their renown beyond Central Asia.

It is also significant that funding which has been successfully secured from international sponsors such as the Soros Foundation and the United Nations Development Programme (UNDP) has tended to be earmarked for the development of traditional and contemporary culture, rather than for the preservation of artefacts. Recent projects funded by the UNDP in Kyrgyzstan have included the publication of a catalogue of contemporary painters and the establishment of a Centre for the Development of Traditional and Contemporary Culture. The Soros Foundation has provided funding for the staging of musical events such as the 'Silk Road Melodies' festival held throughout Kyrgyzstan in October 2001 to promote traditional music that was characterised as rudimentary and neglected during the colonial era (Humphrey, 1999).

UNESCO has principally been active in supporting the preservation of the epic poems. In 1995 UNESCO assisted in financing an ostentatious celebration of the *Manas* epos which is estimated to have cost the Kyrgyz government more than US$8 million (Mayhew *et al.*, 2000). In 1997 the UNDP allotted US$150,000 for a related project entitled 'Support for Manaschis and Akyns' to fund the training of the bards who traditionally recite the epics. UNESCO also continues to partially fund two organisations for the promotion of the epos set up at the time of the *Manas* celebrations, although these have been reduced in size and importance due to lack of government funding.[2] A recent achievement has been the transferral of all 65 variants of the *Manas* epos to CD-ROM, which was funded by UNESCO as part of its programme for the preservation of intangible heritage. However, whilst efforts to sustain the tradition of oral histories are well placed, the inability to pay membership subscriptions to the United Nations has placed the future of these efforts in doubt (Okeeva, 2000). UNESCO sponsored efforts to publicise the historic value of epics such as *Manas* to the wider community have experienced little success with the International Year of Manas in 1995 passing largely unnoticed outside of the former CIS countries. Nonetheless, the efforts being made to revive these cultures and traditions seem likely to prolong, if not ensure their survival.

Conclusion

There is evidence that the desire to increase the contribution of tourism to the troubled Kyrgyz economy's growth is affecting the direction of heritage tourism development strategies currently aimed almost exclusively at attracting international visitors. The heritage product being promoted by the State Agency for Tourism and Sports, the WTO and individual tour operators is mainly based on the relics of former civilisations. These civilisations have been accorded their importance due to their connections with the Silk Road and their restoration by Soviet archaeologists during the colonial period. Such sites are arguably more likely to benefit from government funding for the protection and interpretation of heritage due to their potential to generate revenue from international tourism. Meanwhile, the living, cultural traditions of Islam, pan-Turkism and to a lesser extent nomadism are experiencing a renaissance in the wake of Kyrgyz independence. The potential exists to utilise cultural heritage, common to several of the ethnic groups in Kyrgyzstan, as a tool for reducing ethnic tension, particularly in southern areas of the country. However, the exclusion of sites of spiritual and religious interest associated with the common Islamic and Turkic cultural heritage of the Central Asian ethnic groups, both tangible and intangible, from the heritage tourism marketing literature and national tourism development strategies is significant. It is particularly noteworthy since this type of heritage has been included in Kyrgyzstan's submissions to the World Heritage list and applications for international funding for heritage protection. In addition to the potential to use such sites as a tool for nation building and fostering cohesion within and between ethnic groups, the increased attention which comes with World Heritage status could lead to an increase in visitation and revenue from international visitors and ultimately assist in removing many of the economic and socio-cultural barriers to heritage tourism development discussed in this paper.

Correspondence

Any correspondence should be directed to Karen Thompson, Scottish Hotel

School, University of Strathclyde, 94 Cathedral Street, Glasgow G4 0LG
(karen.thompson@strath.ac.uk).

Notes

1. One brochure tells how the open air sculpture museum in Bishkek has been decimated
   since independence by scrap metal thieves.
2. The State Directorate for the Promotion of the Manas Epos and the Manas Heritage
   Organisation are the two NGOs referred to here.

References

Abetekov, A. (1995) The culture of Kyrgyzstan in the age of Manas. In T. Askarov, A.
    Asankanov, T. Omurbekov, A. Abetekov and N. Bekmukhamedova (eds) *'Manas' Epos
    and the World's Epic Heritage* (pp. 11–12). Bishkek: Kyrgyz Republic National Academy
    of Sciences.
Adams, K.M. (1998) Domestic tourism and nation building in South Sulawesi. *Indonesia
    and the Malay World* 26, 77–96.
Akmatova, L. (2001) Personal communication with Ludmilla Akmatova, Kyrgyz State
    Agency for Tourism and Sports, Bishkek, 21 November.
Amambaeva, B. (2001) Sacred mountains of Kyrgyzstan. Unpublished manuscript pre-
    sented at UNESCO seminar, Wakayama City, Japan, September.
Anon (2001) Status of Russian language yet to be confirmed. *Bishkek Observer* (30 October),
    5.
Anderson, J. (1999) *Kyrgyzstan: Central Asia's Island of Democracy?* Amsterdam: OPA.
Asankanov, A. (1995) The Epos Manas and the development of an ethnic ss among the
    Kyrgyz. In T. Askarov, A. Asankanov, T. Omurbekov, A. Abetekov and N.
    Bekmukhamedova (eds) *'Manas' Epos and the World's Epic Heritage* (pp. 27–8). Bishkek:
    Kyrgyz Republic National Academy of Sciences.
Asankanov, A. and Bekmukhamedova, N. (1999) *Akyns and Manaschis: Creators and
    Keepers of the Kyrgyz Peoples' Spiritual Culture*. Bishkek: United Nations Development
    Programme.
Badretdin, S. (2000) Pan-Turkism: Past, present and future. *Tatar Gazette* 3–4. On WWW at
    http://www.peoples.org.ru/tatar/eng_099.html. Accessed 20.01.04.
Bakieva, G. (1999) Islam as a socio-cultural code. In National Commission of the Kyrgyz
    Republic for UNESCO (ed.) *Culture and Religion in Central Asia: Collection of Materials
    UNESCO International Forum* (pp. 63–70). Bishkek: National Commission of the Kyrgyz
    Republic for UNESCO.
Bashiri, I. (1999a) Kyrgyz national identity. On WWW at http://www.iles.umn.edu/
    faculty/bashiri/Kyrgid/kyrgid.htm. Accessed 15.05.02.
Bashiri, I. (1999b) Manas: The Kyrgyz epic. On WWW at http://www.iles.umn.edu/
    faculty/bashiri/manas/manas.htm. Accessed 03.12.01.
BDO Consulting (1996) *Constraints to Tourism Development in Kyrgyzstan*. Amsterdam:
    World Bank/Netherlands TA Trust for Central Asia.
Begimkulov, E.I. (1999) The maintenance and development of the common cultural and
    historical heritage of the peoples of Central Asia. In National Commission of the
    Kyrgyz Republic for UNESCO (ed.) *Culture and Religion in Central Asia:Collection of
    Materials UNESCO International Forum* (pp. 71–4). Bishkek: National Commission of
    the Kyrgyz Republic for UNESCO.
Bichel, A.R. (1997) *Identity/Difference in Central Asia*. New York: ICARP.
Boobbyer, P. (1998) Russian liberal conservatism. In G. Hosking and R. Service (eds)
    Russian Nationalism, Past and Present (pp. 35–54). Basingstoke: Macmillan.
Carney, C.P. and Moran, J.P. (2000) Imagining communities in Central Asia: Nationalism
    and interstate affect in the post-Soviet era. *Asian Affairs: An American Review* 26 (4),
    179–99.
CIA (2002) The World Factbook. On WWW at http://www.odci.gov.cia/publications/
    factbook/kg.html. Accessed 15.05.02.
De Vaus, D.A. (1996) *Surveys in Social Research* (5th edn). London: UCL.

Duncan, P. (1990) The USSR. In M. Watson (ed.) *Contemporary Minority Nationalism* (pp. 152–65). London: Routledge.

Eckford, P.K. (1997) *International Tourism Potential in Issyk-Kul Oblast the Kyrgyz Republic: Report and Analysis*. WTO: Madrid.

Elebaeva, A. (2003) The theory and practice of Ethnonationalism in states of the Central Asian Region. *Ethnichesky Mir* 20, 58–61.

Fairbanks, C.H. (2001) Disillusionment in the Caucasus and central Asia. *Journal of Democracy* 12 (4), 49–56.

Franklin, B. (ed.) (1973) *The Essential Stalin: Major Theoretical Writings 1905–1952*. London: Croom Helm.

Galieva, Z. (1995) The 'Manas' Epos as a historical source In T. Askarov, A. Asankanov, T. Omurbekov, A. Abetekov and N. Bekmukhamedova (eds) *'Manas' Epos and the World's Epic Heritage* (pp. 3–4). Bishkek: Kyrgyz Republic National Academy of Sciences.

Gellner, E. (1994) *Encounters with Nationalism*. Oxford: Blackwell.

Horowitz, D.L. (1985) *Ethnic Groups in Conflict*. Berkeley: University of California Press.

Humphrey, M.A. (1999) Komuz Krisis. *Folk Roots Magazine* 197, 13–17.

Jennings, G. (2001) *Tourism Research*. Milton, Australia: John Wiley.

Kamidov, A. (2002) Brewing ethnic tension causing concern in south Kyrgyzstan. On WWW at http://www.tol.cz/look/wire/article.tpl?IdLanguage=1&IdPublication= 10&NrIssue=533&NrSection=2&NrArticle=7802#author. Accessed 20.01.04.

Kellas, J.G. (1998) *The Politics of Nationalism and Ethnicity* (2nd edn). Basingstoke: MacMillan.

Lewis, D.C. (1999) Ethnicity and religion in Central Asia. In National Commission of the Kyrgyz Republic for UNESCO (ed.) *Culture and Religion in Central Asia: Collection of Materials UNESCO International Forum* (pp. 90–94). Bishkek: National Commission of the Kyrgyz Republic for UNESCO.

Mayhew, G., Plunkett, R. and Richmond, S. (2000) *Central Asia* (2nd edn). London: Lonely Planet.

Megoran, N. (2000a) Language issues feed Kyrgyz nationalism. *Asia Times* (7 June).

Megoran, N. (2000b) Language and ethnicity in Kyrgyzstan. *Eurasia Insight*. On WWW at http://www.eurasianet.org/departments/insight/articles/eav060700.shtml. Accessed 20.05.02.

Mitchell, T. (2001) Making the nation: The politics of heritage in Egypt. In N. AlSayyad (ed.) *Consuming Tradition, Manufacturing Heritage: Global Norms and Urban Forms in the Age of Tourism* (pp. 212–39). London: Routledge.

Musayev, S. (1994) *The Epos 'Manas'*. Bishkek: Kyrgyz Polygraph Kombinat.

Okeeva, A. (2000) Personal communication with Aziza Okeeva, National Commission of the Kyrgyz Republic for UNESCO, Bishkek, 22 November.

Omarov, M.N. (1999) Prospects for the development of Kyrgyzstan towards an open society. In J.C.K. Daly (ed.) *Democratic Processes in Central Asia: Experience and Perspectives* (pp. 20–25). Bishkek: International University of Kyrgyzstan.

Pitchford, S.R. (1995) Ethnic tourism and nationalism in Wales. *Annals of Tourism Research* 22 (1), 35–52.

Pretes, M. (2003) Tourism and nationalism. *Annals of Tourism Research* 30 (1), 125–42.

Saipjanov, A. (2003) Kyrgyzstan statehood festivities a potential source of interethnic tension. *Eurasia Insight*. On WWW at http://www.eurasianet.org/departments/insight/articles/eav082603a.shtml. Accessed 20.01.04.

Smith, A.D. (1981) *The Ethnic Revival in the Modern World*. Cambridge: Cambridge University Press.

Taksanov, A. (2003) Uzbek tourism: More than just medieval architecture. *Times of Central Asia* (23 January).

Touche Ross / International School of Mountaineering (1995) *Kyrgyzstan Tourism Development Project: Final Report*. London: Touche Ross & Co / Gwynedd: International School of Mountaineering.

UNDP (1999) *United Nations Resident Coordinator Report (Kyrgyzstan)*. Bishkek: United Nations Development Program.

Urry, J. (1994) Cultural change and contemporary tourism. *Leisure Studies* 13 (4), 233–8.

World Trade Law, Culture, Heritage and Tourism. Towards a Holistic Conceptual Approach?

James Tunney
Law Division, Dundee Business School, University of Abertay, Dundee

This article argues that law is an important factor in the consideration of the evolution of tourism discourse. Thus it is important for academics to consider the law-tourism connection. But law is a dynamic phenomenon that is experiencing change. Within law, the domain of world trade is increasingly significant. In addition, the conceptualisation of culture and heritage is ongoing and as the law has implications for the development of those concepts, then correspondingly the law-culture and heritage connection should be considered. World trade law in turn has culture and heritage implications. Tourism will be affected by both the evolution of world trade and evolving conceptions of culture and heritage, not least legal ones. Accordingly, as a result of the increasing interpenetration and interconnections of issues, it is submitted that consideration of the four conceptual domains of world trade, law, tourism and culture and heritage, suggests the desirability of a holistic approach to (or awareness of) the consideration of certain issues that may fall into the intellectual space advanced by the potential intersection of these issues. This is especially justifiable in view of the multiplicity of academic viewpoints that studies of tourism embrace. It may be necessary in order to provide options for the solution of legal issues that involve these factors. Thus it is argued that it is important to consider the domain delineated above in a holistic way, recognising that the forces of development act reflexively on each other as a start in order to overcome inevitable epistemological difficulties.

Keywords: world trade law, culture, heritage, tourism, holistic conceptualisation

The Dynamism of Law and the Link with Tourism: Law-tourism

Discussion of issues associated with tourism is necessarily an interdisciplinary endeavour, which must consider law as an important component. While law, lawyers and legal systems are facing much well-deserved criticism (Crier, 2002), it would be a mistake to underestimate their pervasive influence. It should be pointed out that some jurists argue that a lot of legal theory (as opposed to legal reasoning, say, in courts) is vacuous (Posner, 2001). That having been said, domains such as 'travel and tourism law' are especially relevant to tourism studies. Travel law, travel and tourism law, tourism law and sub-groups such as 'holiday law' and 'hotel and catering law' all deal with tourism. Laws in relation to ownership and safeguarding of cultural property may impact on the tourism industries. Issues of liability, such as personal injury, will be foremost in the minds of most managers. Competition law may also dictate the evolution of the structure of the industry. Unsurprisingly, academic tourism literature reveals an increased consciousness of specific legal issues, such as the implications of the *Disability Discrimination Act* (e.g. Miller & Kirk, 2002). New directions, such as what might be termed genetic heritage tourism, give rise to legal issues that are likewise evolving on a parallel trajectory. There have been many other significant cases at national level where travel and tourism issues have been centre stage, as for example over issues of civil rights. In the case of *Heart of Atlanta Motel* (1964), it was held by the US Supreme Court that Congress had power to ban racial discrimination in places of public accommodation, including hotels and motels. The Heart of Atlanta in the 'Heart of Dixie' lost the argument that people are not commerce under the constitution. Within national systems, the context of the clash between travel and tourism and the environment has already given rise to much debate, as shown in another US case of *Sierra Club v. Morton* (1972). This involved a dispute between a tourism facility of Walt Disney Enterprises and the Sierra Club and led to interesting judicial debate, language and reasoning. The conservation group wanted to block the conversion of 80 acres of wilderness into a recreation complex and ski resort. In order to have legal standing to bring the case anyone who was bringing the suit would have to have been directly affected by the action in question. Environmentalists outside the court context sought to bolster their position by seeking to reinterpret the idea of legal standing when taking action on environmental issues (Stone, 1972). This also shows how concepts may move from discourse to discourse. It is worth noting that national legal issues may be decided in the context of state membership of regional legal communities such as the EU. A series of controversial Irish cases that were decided on the basis of principles of EU law have shown the link between rights associated with travel and abortion (*SPUC v. Grogan*, 1991). That link may not have been an obvious one. Legal circumstance often conspires to concoct them. Thus these cases demonstrate how law and travel and tourism may intersect at a national and regional level and are directly relevant to travel and tourism discourse in the widest sense. Law may have direct, immediate and actual implications and sometimes make deeper, theoretical and philosophical contributions. In general, however, the impact of law is sometimes solely conceived to be related to the impact of legal rules. Knowledge of law is generally equated with knowledge of rules. On this level there is obviously a need to understand some of the principal impacts of law on tourism.

But law is also dynamic. Within law, it could be argued that the evolution and impact of 'world trade law' may represent one of the greatest sources of potential conceptual challenge to the landscapes of tourism and tourism studies in the long-run. Critical analysis must test the assumptions underpinning any intellectual construct. As the law-tourism nexus is becoming clear, so is that of law-world trade in parallel. But when one also considers the law-culture and heritage connection, it is clear that a dynamic field of academic debate is being framed. It is argued by certain academics that law is not only about the knowledge of rules (Samuel, 2003). This suggests deeper epistemological and ontological engagements if disciplines are to communicate. This process of communication is also complicated by the contingent and contestable nature of the boundaries that make the delineation quite difficult.

A Contestable Description of the Emergent Conception of 'World Trade Law': Law-world Trade

It is always important to emphasise that law and legal systems may be characterised by conservatism but still manifest dynamism at particular times. At the present time of 'global legal pluralism' it is necessary to elaborate on the meaning of world trade law although the use of the description 'world trade law' would be contested by some legal academics. Nomenclature of subjects within law is not fixed, especially in turbulent times. More well-established terms include 'international economic law' and the legal aspects of international economic relations (see Jackson *et al.*, 2002). International trade law is sometimes contrasted with international economic law in that the former is fairly confined to the narrow context of commercial transactions in many works (e.g. Chuah, 2001). International business law may also be an appropriate term. Wider notions of international trade law are emerging (see e.g. Fletcher *et al.*, 2001). But the emergence of the World Trade Organisation (WTO) as the central economic institution of the world economy is critically significant. The solidity of the Dispute Settling Mechanism (DSM) is a chief distinguishing feature from the previous *General Agreement on Tariffs and Trade* (GATT) system, with greater leverage for the continuing liberalisation of trade. It requires some re-adjustment for lawyers (Ehlermann, 2002) and others. Combined with a new organisational focus and other procedural reforms, the WTO might be said to be at the centre of world trade. The greater shift towards rule-orientation is consistent with a process often described as 'juridification', a term which suggests an ongoing legal crystallisation of trade rules at a world level. Consensus-based systems that prevailed before are ultimately being displaced. However, there has sometimes been a reluctance to admit that trade rules constitute law, especially where there are genuine constitutional restrictions on the exercise of external power, such as in the USA.

If the WTO and its emergent jurisprudence are taken to be at the centre, then the penumbra of world trade law is quite wide. The exact trajectory in the sphere of international law is unclear. International lawyers are reluctant to admit that the exact scope, meaning and import of 'international law' are in a state of flux, not least as a result of events in Iraq. Jurists (e.g. Kahn, 1999) suggest that most international law scholars see their role not as the study of a social practice and belief but, rather, as contributing to the progressive realisation of an international order. The Appellate Body of the WTO itself has sought to clarify the relationship between its rules and the rest of international law. Discussion on issues in relation to international treaties is common. Thus for example in a recent dispute, in relation to United State-Softwood Lumber (2004), discussion on the impact of the *Vienna Convention on the Law of the Treaties* crops up in argument, as is fairly usual. Ultimately there will be a period of reconciliation of both sets of rules. But in some cases, the emerging world trade rules may displace or be perceived to displace other less crystallised international rules.

At the same time, the network of regional legal communities governing the context of operation of industries (such as tourism) could be considered part of the world trade law regime. The core conceptual base of the EC/EU revolves around the attainment of single or common markets based on an evolving treaty construct, which guarantees freedom of movement of the factors of production. The deeper logic of course relates to the attempt to eliminate tensions that derive from purely national constructs of law and associated political dogma through novel legal constructions. The European Court of Justice (ECJ) was given the task of interpreting and applying the law under the treaties. It boldly articulated the nature of the evolving legal community. When given the opportunity, it stressed that the community was a new order in international law, based on a transfer of sovereignty, for which member states had limited their rights (see Weatherill & Beaumont, 1999). The limitation of rights had particular consequences that were quietly revolutionary when viewed *ex ante*. Some might see parallels with the trajectory of development of the GATT agenda, primarily driven by an ingrained institutional commitment sometimes described as involving 'embedded liberalism'. In the tourism context, there is a range of potentially diverse sources of regulation within regional legal communities (such as that of Package Travel in the EU).

The individual natural or legal person may find that such treaties have direct relevance to a situation they find themselves involved in and that no national law is of assistance, or indeed there is a conflicting national law. While the GATT, WTO and EU constructs focus on inter-state relationship, the principles of 'direct effects' may allow individuals to rely on certain provisions of these agreements. This notion was crucial in the context of development of EU law and is also relevant to other international treaties. The *Finance Ministry* case (1973) for example, reveals this in relation to GATT, in so far as the Court of Cassation demonstrated that individuals may be able to argue that the provisions of such international agreements may take precedence over conflicting national provisions in certain circumstances.

But to complicate things further, protection of international business transactions could also be considered as part of world trade law. This requires an awareness or comprehension and consideration of the formation, enforcement of international sales transactions and securities. Similarly, ideas of a new *lex mercatoria* (law merchant) might suggest the advisability of considering the regulation of the trader or merchant as part of any world system. This refers to the idea of a set of customary principle and rules that are widely recognised in international transactions. These are seen to be among the earliest forms of globalisation in the legal field. Communications technology and intellectual property issues are also increasingly regulated at an international level, and have been for over a century. The Council of Europe *Convention on Cybercrime* of 2001 and the *World Intellectual Property Organisation Conventions* (WIPO) of 1996 could be cited (as well as the Trade Related Aspects of Intellectual Property Agreement (TRIPS) that forms part of the WTO framework).

It is interesting to contrast US support of TRIPS and openness to the *Cybercrime Convention*, and its ultimate respect for the recent WTO Steel Subsidies decision on the one hand, with its ambivalence towards the *World Heritage Convention*, hostility to the *Kyoto Protocol* and *International Criminal Court*, and opposition to other UN initiatives. Commercial interests are dictating the construction of international obligations at present, according to some (McGrath, 1996). However, on a longer trajectory and with the possibility of a re-awakening of the US Supreme Court with the 'terrorism' prisoner cases, the exercise of executive power might become a little more contained. In the longer term, the possibility of greater global regulation of competition, which is one of the 'Singapore Issues' in the world trade discussions, may form a critical dimension of world trade. But even if the suggested description of such a field is too wide, or the centrality of trade is contested as a useful and unifying description thereof, it is clear that the emergent system of regulation of trade and international business is an important factor in the evolution of the environment in which other global forces such as tourism must operate.

The impact and consequences of such a *corpus* of law, thus conceived in a general way, is formidable. Key decisions may come from national courts, reflecting and contributing to the evolution of international principles, which contribute to the context of world trade. World trade law thus conceived is obviously of importance in a general way in relation to tourism and tourist industries. While the emphasis of world trade has been on goods, the incorporation of services and IP widens the net. There is a need to consider the triangular network of national, regional and international or world regulation, as decisions may come from a number of places therein. Likewise there is a need to consider the evolution of legal concepts (as well as the impact of existing regulation). Either way, the law-world trade connection parallels the clarification of the law-tourism connection.

The Legal Development of Concepts of Culture and Heritage: Law-culture and Heritage

Culture is a notoriously elusive concept that needs to be defined before it can be discussed in meaningful ways (Tunney, 2001). Does the particular definition used cover old houses, new architecture, dance, music, folk or rap, or perhaps the complexities of notions such as Japanese *kazari* (see Rousmaniere, 2002)? Does it include phenomena that are pro-establishment or anti-establishment, static or dynamic, transient or permanent, commercial or non-commercial, contemporary or antique? What does not constitute culture? Clearly, it should be defined with caution, and if meaningful discourse is to emerge, definitions must be clear and specific. Ultimately, they may depend on the overall context rather than on any absolute sense of meaning.

Notions of 'heritage' may seem more straightforward, but again it is necessary to exercise caution, and the politics of heritage and culture must also be considered (Bianchi & Boniface, 2002). Does it cover genetic heritage, for example? And when both culture and heritage are approached in the context of legal (and especially judicial reasoning) the fluidity tolerated in some disciplines quickly evaporates in vagueness to reveal dangerous shards of competing interests. In general terms, courts must be able to draw on clear, well-defined, operable concepts from the most appropriate literature. Such concepts must be capable of articulation in ways that make them available to judges, with all the nuances and distinct meanings that only become clear in the arena of contest. Binding legal principles and doctrines are more often hammered out in particular court disputes. Where parties have something to fight for, and the resources and will to do so, dispute resolution gives rise to useful legal trajectories for others who follow. Legal principles may represent both a shield and a sword. In many emergent, legal domains, creative lawyers will seek to exploit existing legal doctrines, invent new ones, or catch the wind of a new judicial disposition to resolve disputes. However, access to such legal creativity is nevertheless costly and presupposes a pre-existing constituency of consciousness. In fact, many 'legal positivists' are incredibly hostile to 'judicial activism' and 'judicial legislation', sometimes for good reason. There is also scepticism within law about seeking too much through law and seeking 'cosmic justice' (Sowell, 1999). Indeed, within the law itself, there is a deep dynamic of culture and heritage in its institutions, conduct and practice, which has both positive and negative elements (e.g. Monateri, 2000). Nevertheless, for better or worse, legal process cannot afford the luxury of indecision. Endless philosophical speculation is not available to judges, and the dialectical method can only be preliminary to a conclusion of some type. However, the simple determinacy of rules and propositions are an essential aspect of their demo-cratic legitimacy. Rules are conceived, made and chosen by legislators and judges. At a certain point therefore, there needs to be a degree of pragmatism about the values that advocates of various views seek to promote and about how they might be implemented or preserved in rule-based systems or at least packaged in a way that they can be brought into the debate. It is worth pointing out the different levels from which such legal issues may emerge and be eluci-dated, from the national, regional and world level.

From National to Regional to World Legal Regulation of Culture and Heritage

At national levels, there is a diverse range of legal instruments that reflect political, economic, religious and cultural concerns to a greater or lesser degree. Relevant constitutions, statutes or judicial pronouncements deal with the ownership of natural or physical resources and cultural heritage as well as more specifically with management, commercial exploitation, access and dispute settlement. However, there is arguably no clear and standard legal definition or conception of the meaning of heritage or associated notions of culture. This makes dialogue across nations very difficult and creates ambigu-ities in any quest to distil useful, transposable legal concepts. Within the mosaic of national discourses, both political and legal, there will be deeper debates about the nature of culture and heritage.

Within the USA, for example, hostility to the *World Heritage Convention* has been pronounced. This reflects the previous reluctance of President Reagan and others to accept outside interference and has led to continued arguments that membership is unconstitutional. In contrast to mature legal systems such as the USA, in other countries where legal systems and institutions are imma-ture, little can be gained by examining associated national approaches, as little jurisprudence may exist. By the same token, their perspective may be neglected. In the developed world, for instance, adherence to principles of 'res-titution' and reparations in the context of disputes is arguably one of the most notable trends in national jurisprudence. The successful pursuit of Holocaust claims, along with Native American and Australian Aboriginal efforts at repa-triation of cultural objects, may have contributed to the emergence of a viable principle of restitution and reparation in relation to heritage. Similarly, the greater organisation and sophistication of land claim cases and heritage pursued by indigenous people is significant. The celebrated *Mabo* case (Tunney, 2000a), for example, should be seen as part of the evolution of national jurisprudence in relation to issues of culture and heritage. It was, however, inspired by international law principles. Interestingly, this case, and later cases based upon it, demonstrate how academically diverse any investigation of native title or its destruction would have to be, even though it would ultimately be a legal issue. Since *Mabo*, Australian courts have increasingly settled more abstract claims about heritage. In the *John Bulun Bulun* cases, for example, they were invited to expand the use of copyright to protect traditional values (Blakeney, 1998), and it is possible that elsewhere, too, the evolution of national jurisprudence will settle such major and contested claims as those relating to the Elgin/Parthenon Marbles.

Culture and heritage may be significantly regulated at an intra-regional level, as (for example) in the 1976 *Convention on the Protection of the Archaeological, Historical and Artistic Heritage of the American Nations*, an instrument deriving from the Organisation of American States. Heritage and cultural issues are also regulated by the Council of Europe (Pickard, 2002), and they figure prominently in the separate legal system of the EU. However, focus is often on specific policy to the detriment of judicial evolution. While there are knowledgeable practitioners on every minute aspect of Commission policy in relation to culture, there are far fewer on the role of the judiciary, and it is certainly arguable that most advances in EC/EU law came through the activity of judges (as critics of judicial activism would readily acknowledge). One example is the development of the principle of equal pay, judicially blossoming in the face of executive inertia. Furthermore, culture and heritage interest groups often overlook the relevance of other facets of law, like that of competition, as they may not initially appear to be relevant. In the EU, the protection of culture was inserted in the treaty. But certain academics think that this has been neglected in legal argument (Cunningham, 2001). This may have been because lawyers find it a vague concept and may wait for the context of contest to seek to define it.

Direct Regulation of World Heritage and Culture

Return of cultural treasure involves a plurality of legal considerations and often international trade issues also (Greenfield, 1996). More generally, there is a body of law regulating cultural issues that might be termed world heritage law, revolving around the *World Heritage Convention* and a host of other international and national legislative enactments. From the protection of cultural property during armed conflict, to submarine heritage, and through to the protection of monuments, there is a wide range of international instruments, including *United Nations General Assembly* resolutions. They are more firmly set within the boundaries and formulated rules of international law. Recommendations, declarations and charters on archaeological heritage, excavations and management, protection of cultural heritage, the built environment, historic monuments and towns, and natural heritage, form a web of regulation. As this web of regulation evolves, there is a need for those who wish to shape the evolution of concepts, to actively engage and participate in a widening field.

At the end of 2002, UNESCO celebrated the 30th anniversary of the *World Heritage Convention*. The Convention has been rightly lauded for dealing with both cultural and natural properties. While there are shortcomings in its operations, it has considerable achievements to its credit. However, it is only on the battlefields of competing interest that the robustness of the system will be tested. Opponents of the Convention do not share the same values inspiring those who drove it forward, and may exploit weaknesses in systems not yet tempered through trial. Indeed, it could be argued that people who work to protect culture and heritage may too readily assume others share their values. Sometimes, international rules and regulations are not enough.

The destruction of Buddhist statues in Afghanistan in 2001 and antiquities in Iraq in 2003 sent shock waves through the international heritage community. Indeed, the destruction of heritage in Afghanistan and Iraq, along with the more extreme 'neo-liberal' free market arguments, demonstrates considerable opposition. One question that arose from the Afghanistan statues context was whether heritage could give rise to an international right to intervene in national sovereignty to protect it. Others might also cite mining and oil extraction, transport developments, energy requirements, the motor industry, logging and agriculture, as activities potentially hostile to the preservation of heritage. Such industries can often marshal potent economic arguments, and carry much political leverage, to obtain their own ends. Their power may defeat arguments that are based on longer-term concerns based on universal principles and, more particularly, on notions of the inherent value of culture or heritage.

Indeed, when the *World Heritage Convention* is examined, it is hard to find a coherent rationale that explains to a judge the basis on which the system operates and which can be employed to settle contests. The preamble to the *World Heritage Convention* talks of 'outstanding universal value' and the need for the international community as a whole to participate in a complementary way to the state's role. The philosophical basis of protection seems clear to its advocates. The list system and the *List of World Heritage in Danger* are very specific regimes and easily comprehensible. Such systems can evolve happily through the well-established principles of international law as they apply to international organisations such as UNESCO. The *Operational Guidelines for the Implementation of the World Heritage Convention* are very specific and relatively easily capable of application. Nevertheless judges in certain cases, in Australia for example, have commented on the difficulty of applying more vague general principles, and critics in the United States express indignation when World Heritage notices appear on national monuments. While non-lawyers are fond of the noble phrase and sentiment in international documents, duller, more careful legal articulations may ultimately be more use in specific historical contexts. What happens when there is a dispute between the existing or future designation of a site and some other pressing need? The unfolding regulation of world heritage requires a continual involvement that is alert to the necessary fragility of legal protection.

The experience of indigenous people with the use of legal means to secure the protection of their interests, for example, led to inevitable frustration. Many of their advocates suggested that the legal efforts have been unsuccessful, due to intrinsic difficulties of enforcement (Posey & Dutfield, 1996). As a result of legitimate frustration, such authors sometimes suggested solutions ostensibly based on the idea that the evolution of legal norms at an international level could not be successful. However, unless revolution is taking place, the nature of evolution of law and legal systems requires a long-term commitment of engagement and participation, for those who want to advocate a cause or proposition.

To complicate matters further, it is clear that legal rules are now coming from a wide range of tribunals and courts. Indeed there is such a diverse proliferation of potentially relevant sources that some legitimately would caution against seeing anything like universal principles. Thus for example rulings that might come from tribunals such as the *International Tribunal for the Law of the Sea* are likely to become increasingly important (see ITLOS, 2003). It could be argued that those who want to advocate views about culture and heritage protection, for example, should seek to input and influence such diverse legal evolution. However, it is worth noting that there is evidence in the USA of hostility to the citation of non-US legal authority, particularly before the Supreme Court. Thus there is an emerging debate about the mobility of legal authority. If such a hostile view prevails, then the argument in favour of a more cosmopolitan building of international legal principles will lose out to a nationalist type of legal positivism.

The Subtle Challenge of Culture and Heritage in Particular WTO Contexts: World Trade Law-culture and Heritage

Some contexts bring culture and trade together explicitly in a contemporary sense. For example, the growth in tomb-raiding is related to technology and trade (Beech, 2003), and the link between the environment and trade has also received much attention (Sturm & Ulph, 2002). Regions and nations may compete for heritage 'prizes', as do regional authorities, and nations for ownership of the 'Iceman of the Alps' (Hitchcock, 1999). However, the links between culture and heritage may be subtler. In Europe, numerous cases have been brought by the Commission against member states that are arguably about culture, although they have not been explicitly decided on that basis. Examples include the case about the beer purity laws – the *Reinheitsgebot* (*Commission v. Germany*, 1987), when the European Court of Justice found that restrictions on the use of the word *Bier* in Germany to beverages produced using only barley, hops, yeast and water and the prohibition on the sale of beer with additives were not justifiable under the Treaty of Rome 1957.

Similarly, some decisions by the World Trade Organisation have prompted discussion on the relationship between trade and culture. The *Canadian Periodicals* case gave rise to discussion about the protection of cultural issues in the WTO dispute settlement system (see e.g. Carmody, 2002). Some critics argue that the construct of the WTO rules is not sufficiently sensitive to issues of 'culture'. This is often linked to related perceptions that the issue of protection of health of the consumer is jeopardised by the freedom of trade rules that is guaranteed under the WTO system. The *Beef Hormones* case (EC-Hormones, 1998) is often cited on this point. Similarly, it is argued that national environmental concerns may be difficult to pursue because of multilateral trade rules. One such dispute is the *Shrimp-Turtle* case (United States-Shrimp, 1998), which dealt with regulations pursuant to the US 1973 Endangered Species Act. This Act, that was designed to protect turtles from the negative consequences of shrimp trawling, generated a conflict between national laws and world trade obligations. In like manner, the recurrent issue of dolphins caught in tuna nets has given rise to much heated discussion. The *Banana* cases have not only generated much legal literature, but have impacted on culture and popular discourse (see e.g. Ryle, 2002). In this instance, the argument has been that the freedom to support historic trading links that support small banana producers in the Caribbean is impossible under current trade rules. The consequence of the trading rules therefore is related to other socio-economic issues that are argued to be more subtle than current rules allow for.

Decisions in some of these key cases make it clear that the WTO does not seek to interfere with justifiable national rules. Members can respond and react to the decisions that do not go in their favour in ways that still accomplish the original objectives they sought. This demonstrates the ample ground left for WTO member regulation. However, if decisions about hormones are difficult to make and are also controversial, it can be expected that multi-faceted disputes that arise in relation to tourism, where culture and tourism collide, may be very complex indeed.

World Trade Law-tourism

The policy nexus between culture and heritage and tourism has already been made in certain international instruments, as with the *International Committee of Monuments and Sites (ICOMOS) Charter on Cultural Tourism* 1999. Clearly, the development of tourism is closely associated with the development of world trade and globalisation discourse (Teo, 2002). But then more specific questions arise as to the potential link between the WTO rules and especially the DSM and the evolution of tourism issues. It can be expected that national rules in relation to the ownership of heritage sites and of cultural property, the provision of electronic services and the protection of Intellectual Property will arise, in ways that impact directly on tourism industries.

Two issues are crucial in the debate over the legal ramifications of tourism's role in world trade. The first relates to the direct impact of the WTO on tourism in particular contexts (Wang & Qu, 2002). Writers such as Paton (2003) have argued that it is necessary to clarify and define travel and tourism under the *General Agreement on Trade in Services* (GATS). Since the inception of the WTO, there has been doubt about the relationship between world trade rules and other international legal instruments on the protection of the environment. A similar uncertainty should exist about the exact relationships of international instruments on culture, heritage and cultural tourism. There is an emerging focus on the implications of GATS on telecommunications, financial services and education. This is happening in relation to travel and tourism also.

Secondly, there is a greater challenge, which relates to the need to construct a hierarchy of principles to explain and translate insights from the academic literature on tourism and values emerging from tourist experience into principles that can at least inform judicial debate. Judges and legislators need to make choices in deciding cases and in making law respectively. In the making of those choices they need to draw upon options from the academic community, that may achieve the goals they think are necessary to settle disputes or to achieve legislative goals. In the world trade context, it is necessary that the academic literature and the policy choices be spelt out in some coherent way so that the genuine factors in particular disputes can be teased out in relation to tourism. The complexity of issues appertaining to culture and heritage require much examination and explanation even to be expressed in legal terms. Tourism discourse that deals explicitly with culture and heritage contexts can help provide some clarity so that legal decisions that can be expected to occur in the next few decades, particularly as they arise in world trade law contexts, can at least take the full range of considerations into account.

Tourism-culture and Heritage

Much tourism discussion is implicitly about issues of culture and heritage. If the definitions of culture and heritage are as potentially wide as they may be when used in anthropology, for example, then it is arguably the case that tourism issues may become inextricably linked to conceptions of culture and heritage. Particular issues that could be readily in the realm of tourism studies create issues that are increasingly being recognised as having some connection with cultural and heritage discourse. Competition over scarce natural resources and recreational amenities may lead to disputes, as when the increased popularity of surfing results in 'surf rage', efforts at self-regulation, and discussion as to whether or not legal regulation is needed (Fickling, 2003). Badgers that could be 'natural heritage', can threaten cultural heritage, as embodied in megalithic sites or Roman remains (Jowitt, 2004). Confrontation may invoke contrasting opinions from different perspectives by museum curators, scientists and indigenous people (Harris, 2003). Increased tourism may threaten cultural heritage through infrastructure changes (Douglas, 2003). If tourism fails to deliver the anticipated benefits, there may be a reaction against conservation efforts (Itano, 2003). The main point is that tourism, visitor attractions and sites will probably give rise to a number of issues that come within the domain of culture and heritage, depending on how those concepts are defined.

Tentatively Towards Holistic Conceptualisation: The Whole Field of Studies

Thus we may imagine a square whose internal space is bounded by law, world trade, culture and heritage and tourism. Within that space there is a great arena that will witness debates in future decades. It is argued here that it would be useful if academics were able to provide a panoramic view of the relevant forces, the strategic interests, the potential outcomes and the possible options. Lawyers and business advisers need to have a panoramic perspective of legal regulation as it becomes more complex (Tunney, 2002). In like manner, the different platforms in tourism scholarship (Jafari, 1990) need to reflect changing contexts. Clarity of choice is important, since the field of tourism studies is interdisciplinary, albeit with its own unique specialists. As a consequence, for instance, issues such as the inter-relationships of image, identity and culture (Cronin & O'Connor, 2003) engender reasonably diverse exploration.

Pragmatism as advocated by such philosophers as William James (James, 1955) might be sometimes a more useful strategic approach to the evolution of cultural discourse within law, than mere pious aspirationalism, however intellectually piquant that may be. Some may believe that lawyers will not confront the attempt to define culture. That would be mistaken. It is not merely a theoretical issue. Rightly or wrongly, and irrespective of how courts approach the issue, 'culture' has been quite explicitly inserted into the EC Treaty and is now a legal concept. Studies of tourism and studies of the role of law within tourism may equally benefit from the overlap. Academic focus on cultural tourism (McKercher *et al.*, 2002) may give precise definitions of cultural context that may ultimately prove relevant in legal debates.

Indeed, law itself is changing, as Nader emphasises (2002: 230):

> Schools of thought are blurred, and multiple mirrors combine to enlarge both the strategies of research and the recognition of common objectives, one of which is an understanding of the relationship of global to local as well as of locals to locals. Microlevel fragments and dislocations are now integrated with macrolevel questions that involve law but go beyond law.

Primarily as a result of global forces, law is undergoing re-conceptualisation. International law itself now comes from many sites and locations (Higgins, 2003). Such a context requires awareness of interconnecting forces, particularly at international level, as can be seen, for example, in theories of international relations or in migration studies. However, lawyers have been able to avoid much discussion about epistemology in their domain. Thus they are often weak in the explanation of the construct of knowledge in law. There has been greater interest recently. In that context, Samuel examines what he terms as the schemes of intelligibility in the social sciences and argues that the greatest dichotomy therein is between the 'holistic' and 'atomistic' view of society (Samuel, 2003).

At the same time, re-conceptualisation is also an emergent theme in tourism discourse, which sometimes requires wider forms of analysis, as in the need for an enhanced focus on community involvement (Hardy *et al.*, 2000). In tourism studies there is evidence of theoretical convergence (Apostolakis, 2003), which partly reflects technological and regulatory convergence, as in studies of ecotourism (Herath, 2002). Similarly, the harmonisation of legal systems leads to conceptual integration, which needs unifying perspectives to assist interpretation (Tunney, 1999).

Given the challenges ahead, one academic approach to where tourism, culture and heritage issues may meet in legal contexts may be to look at them in a way that recognises that they are reflexive and thus interdependent in certain conditions. Equally, it is appropriate to aim simply at more accurate predictions on complex issues by a greater awareness of contributory factors. A lawyer, for example, might ask whether a US court would allow the consequences of designation of World Heritage Site of the Old City of Havana to stand, particularly if faced with a returning pre-revolutionary property owner – an issue that might arise even without 'regime change'.

The pervasive nature of tourism will increasingly figure in world trade law disputes. At the same time, there is discontent with forces of globalisation. Already there is discontent with international institutions (Danaher, 2001), and the association of globalisation with world trade has led to an exponential increase in criticism. There are many diverse bases for criticism and much discontent (Stiglitz, 2002). The anti-globalisation critique is itself subject to critique (Legrain, 2002). Within that spectrum of arguments there are debates about the nature and role of free trade and questions about the implications of such debates for the work of disciplines such as economics. For example, some commentators such as Carmody fear that free trade and its associated efficiency promotes homogeneity and jeopardise deep human values (2002). To deal with the tensions, economists such as Throsby (2001) call for a greater 'human-centred' notion of economics. He argues that the battle to obtain or retain economic power conflicts with the assertion of cultural identity, and that a deeper understanding of the relationship between economics and culture is needed to improve matters. Whatever the outcome of these debates, there may be an increased academic challenge to engage with more domains than they may have wanted to.

Faced with such conflicting claims over the nature and impacts of globalisation and disciplinary flux in law and elsewhere there may at least be an argument to corroborate that it might be preferable to adopt a holistic approach to the study of some issues associated with tourism. Basically, such an analytical approach treats the whole as greater than the sum of its own parts, and can be profitably applied to world trade, culture, law and tourism. Such an approach may help to facilitate dialogue across disciplines in order to merely define what the issues and options are when approached both in a macro and a micro way.

Tourism may become a major focus for opposition for example by local communities or groups, or other forces of anti-globalisation. Such a danger may suggest the benefit of seeking holistic solutions, which may need sometimes to re-conceptualise doctrine and discourse. A narrow, formalist legal reading of complex disputes may lead to unbalanced decision-making. Interdisciplinary contacts need to be more sophisticated and deeper. As well as welcome specific studies on law (such as Callander & Page, 2003) deeper opportunities exist. The very re-shaping of existing paradigms must recognise the phenomenon of law in a wider sense than it often has hitherto. One of the simple ways to do this as an academic is to engage with contemporary legal discourse (as manifest in legal and interdisciplinary legal literature). There is little evidence of that, if one examines the references used in much academic tourism discourse or the subject matter of contemporary PhDs. Likewise, there is little evidence of non-law study of particular disputes that might prove hugely important to those involved in culture and heritage domains. Lawyers may have little need, incentive or desire to venture far beyond their own discipline and indeed may have a strong incentive to maintain disciplinary exclusivity. What use would a wider philosophical base provide? To take one example, although the literature on local communities in tourism has grown significantly, they are still relatively invisible in regimes of legal protection, because insights are not fed into legal contexts. If one examines what might be termed 'travel law' and looks at a range of contexts such as Article 81 and 82 of the EC Treaty, the rules on Package Travel, consumer credit and consumer regulation, the dominant conception is that of a vulnerable traveller *qua* consumer, directly and indirectly. But non-law literature demonstrates that the host community is probably the more vulnerable now. If the argument in favour of recognition of the local community is to work, then they have to be made visible and it needs to be articulated in ways that can be legislated and made justiciable. Otherwise, the persistence of what this author has called 'the ghost-host community syndrome' will not change. This predominantly pro-traveller law is subject to the striking exception of the DVT case (2003) in the UK and other similar ones around the world, which arguably generated relatively little academic attention. Likewise, the incorporation of debate on genetic contexts into the work of UNESCO demonstrates the conceptual proximity hitherto separate contexts. Where might a holistic approach be applicable? A particular doctrinal development that heritage could link up with more is the development of 'global public goods' discourse (Kaul *et al.*, 2003). This chimes with the direction of the World Bank (2002). The World Tourism Organisation's '*Global Code of Ethics for Tourism*' may have some influence on the emergence of legal principles and practices in the travel and tourism context. Particularly neglected domains of tourism such as 'social tourism' may become popular again. If the argument in favour of a holistic approach seems light and abstract, then practical reasons such as the increased involvement of museums in the business of foreign tourism may make it seem more relevant. There may be greater disciplinary mobility. This requires some simple approaches in order to build bridges. Such approaches may yield unanticipated benefits. Otherwise adequate analyses of, say, space tourism or Antarctic tourism will not be forthcoming. The notion of parallax could be used to describe the idea that different standpoints of a phenomenon will give different perspectives at least.

Conclusion: Looking Across the Whole Field

A space that is bounded by rough intellectual fences of concepts of culture and heritage, world trade, tourism and law needs to be explored to help identify the shifting, dynamic interactions. Tourism and heritage are complex human phenomena reflexively bound up with legal systems. The inherent proximity of issues of culture and heritage to tourism and the reflexive relationship between them (as well as with law) means that there is in reality a complex multi-layered dialogue. In world trade regulation, one danger is that the dialectical process of evolution will shift in favour of potentially dominant trade paradigms in the absence of more sophisticated counter-weight doctrines. A holistic disciplinary approach that includes sophisticated legal inputs could be part of a pragmatic solution that offers options. Failure to do so may create a momentum of opposition that will not only threaten a negative impact on world trade, but also the tourism industries.

Correspondence

Any correspondence should be directed to James Tunney, Dundee Business School, Old College, University of Abertay, Dundee DD1 1HG (J.Tunney@ tay.ac.uk).

References

Apostolakis, A. (2003) The convergence process in heritage tourism. *Annals of Tourism Research* 30 (4), 795–812.
Beech, H. (2003) Stealing beauty. *Time* (3 November), 48–56.
Bianchi, R. and Boniface, P. (2002) The politics of world heritage. *International Journal of Heritage Studies* 8 (2), 79–80.
Blakeney, M. (1998) Communal intellectual property rights of indigenous peoples in cultural expressions. *Journal of World Intellectual Property* 1 (6), 985–1002.
Callander, M. and Page, S.J. (2003) Managing risk in adventure tourism operations in New

Zealand: A review of the legal case history and potential for litigation. *Tourism Management* 24 (1) (February), 13–23.

Carmody, C. (2002) When 'cultural identity was not at issue': Thinking about Canada – certain measures concerning periodicals. *Law and Policy in International Business* 30 (2), 231–320.

Chuah, J.C.T. (2001) *Law of International Trade* (2nd edn). London: Sweet and Maxwell.

Commission v Germany, Case 178/84 [1987] ECR 1227, [1988] 1 CMLR 780.

Cronin, M. and O'Connor, B. (2003) *Irish Tourism: Image. Culture and Identity.* Clevedon: Channel View.

Crier, C. (2002) *The Case Against Lawyers.* New York: Broadway.

Cunningham, C. (2001) In defence of member state culture: The unrealised potential of Article 151(4) of the EC Treaty and the consequences for EC cultural policy. *Cornell International Law Journal* 34 (1), 119–63.

Danaher, K. (2001) *Ten Reasons to Abolish the IMF and World Bank.* New York: Seven Stories.

Deep Vein Thrombosis, Air Travel Group Litigation (2003) 1 All E.R. 935, Nelson J. High Court of Justice Queens Bench Division.

EC-Hormones (1998) *European Communities – Measures concerning Meat and Meat Products.* WT/DS26/AB/R.

Douglas, E. (2003) Ring road threatens sacred slopes of pilgrims. *Observer* (14 September), 23.

Ehlermann, C-D. (2002) Six years on the bench of the 'World Trade Court'. *Journal of World Trade* 36 (4), 605–39.

Fickling, D. (2003) Turning the tide on surf rage down under. *Guardian* (11 November), 14.

Finance Ministry v Manifattura Lane, Marzotto SpA (1973) *International Law Reports.* Vol. 77, 551 (1988).

Fletcher, I., Mistelis, L. and Cremona, M. (eds) (2001) *Foundations and Perspectives of International Trade Law.* London: Sweet and Maxwell.

Greenfield, J. (1996) *The Return of Cultural Treasures.* Cambridge: Cambridge University Press.

Hardy A., Beeton, J.S. and Pearson, L. (2002) Sustainable tourism: An overview of the concept and its position in relation to conceptualisation of tourism. *Journal of Sustainable Tourism* 10 (6), 475–91.

Harris, P. (2003) Aborigines clash with scientists over bones. *Observer* (1 June), 13.

Heart of Atlanta Motel v United States (1964) 379 US 241.

Herath, G. (2002) Research methodologies for planning ecotourism and nature conservation. *Tourism Economics* 8 (1), 77–101.

Higgins, R. (2003) The ICJ, the ECJ and the integrity of international law. *International Comparative Law Quarterly* 52, 1–20.

Hitchcock, M. (1999) Tourism and ethnicity; situational perspectives. *International Journal of Tourism Research* 1, 17–32.

Itano, N. (2003) Lions prey to backlash by Kenya's tribesmen. *Scotland on Sunday* (9 November), 24.

International Tribunal on the Law of the Sea (ITLOS) (2003) Cases reported on WWW at http://www.itlos.org. Accessed 24.03.04.

Jackson, J., Davey, W.J. and Sykes, A.O. (2002) *Legal Problems of International Economic Relations: Cases, Materials and Text* (4th edn). St Paul, MN: West Group.

Jafari, J. (1990) Research and scholarship: The basis of tourism education. *Journal of Tourism Studies* 1 (1), 33–41.

James, W. (1955) *Pragmatism and Four Essays from the Meaning of Truth.* New York: Meridian.

Jowitt, J. (2004) Tunnelling badgers endanger Britain's trove of hidden relics. *Observer* (4 January), 6.

Kahn P.W. (1999) *The Cultural Study of Law: Reconstructing Legal Scholarship.* Chicago: University of Chicago Press.

Kaul, I., Conceição, P., Le Joulven, K. and Menduza, R.U. (eds) (2003) *Providing Global Public Goods: Managing Globalization.* Oxford: Oxford University Press/UNDP.

Legrain, P. (2002) *Open World: The Truth About Globalisation.* London: Abacus.

Luisi and Carbone v Ministero del Tesero, Cases 286/82, 26/83 [1984] ECR 377, [1985] 3 CMLR 52.

Martinez, O. (1999) *Neo-liberalism in Crisis*. Madrid: Instituto Cubano del Libro.

McGrath, M. (1996) The patent provisions in TRIPs: Protecting reasonable remuneration for services rendered –or the latest development in western colonialism 7. EIPR 398.

McKercher, B., Ho, P.S.Y., du Cros, H. and Chow So-Ming, B. (2002) Activities-based segmentation of the cultural tourism market. *Journal of Travel and Tourism Marketing* 12 (1), 23–44.

Miller, G.A. and Kirk, E. (2002) The Disability Discrimination Act: Time for the stick. *Journal of Sustainable Tourism* 10 (1) 82–8.

Monateri P. (2000) Black Gaius: A quest for the multicultural origins of the western legal tradition. *Hastings Law Journal* 51, 479.

Nader, L. (2002) *The Life of the Law: Anthropological Projects*. Berkeley: University of California Press.

Nash, D. (1996) *Anthropology of Tourism*. Oxford: Pergamon.

Paton, T (2003) The impact of the GATS on the provision of international travel and tourism services. *International Trade Law and Regulation* 9 (3), 77–87.

Pickard. R. (2002) A comparative review of policy for the protection of the architectural heritage of Europe. *International Journal of Heritage Studies* 8 (4), 349–63.

Posey, D. and Dutfield, G. (1996) *Beyond Intellectual Property: Towards Traditional Resource Rights for Indigenous Peoples and Local Communities* (pp. 117–18). Ottawa: International Development Research Centre.

Posner, R.A. (2001) *Frontiers of Legal Theory*. London: Harvard University Press.

Rousmaniere, N. (ed.) (2002) *Arts of Kazari: Japan on Display, 15th–19th Centuries*. London: British Museum.

Ryle, S. (2002) Banana war leaves the Caribbean a casualty. *Observer* (24 November), 7.

Samuel, G. (2003) *Epistemology and Method in Law* (p. 318). Aldershot: Ashgate.

Sierra Club v. Morton (1972) 405 US 727.

Sowell, T. (1999) *The Quest for Cosmic Justice*. New York: Free Press.

SPUC Ireland Ltd v Grogan [1991] ECR I-4685, [1991] 3 CMLR 849.

Stiglitz, J. (2002) *Globalization and its Discontents*. London: Allen Lane.

Stone, C.D. (1972) Should trees have standing? Towards Legal Rights for Natural Objects, *Southern California Law Review* 45, 450.

Sturm. D and Ulph A. (2002) Environment and trade: The implications of imperfect information and political economy. *World Trade Review* 1 (3), 235–56.

Teo, P. (2002) Striking a balance for sustainable tourism: Implications of the discourse on globalisation. *Journal of Sustainable Tourism* 10 (6), 459–74.

Throsby, D. (2001) *Economics and Culture*. Cambridge: Cambridge University Press.

Tunney, J. (1998) The need for strategic awareness of EU law for HTSFs. *High Technology Small Firms Conference Proceedings* (vol. 1) (pp. 31–40). Enschede.

Tunney, J. (1999) The future convergence of legal concepts in the age of cyberspace. *Proceedings of 1st Asia-Pacific Conference on Cyberlaw*.

Tunney, J. (2001) Is culture the cuckoo's egg in the competition law nest? *European Competition Law Review* 5 (May).

Tunney, J. (2000a) Native title and the search for justice: Mabo (1992). In E. O'Dell (ed.) *Leading Cases of the Twentieth Century* (pp. 445–66). Dublin: Round Hall.

Tunney J. (2002) Conceptions of justice in 'The Field'. *Dublin University Law Journal* 24 199–235.

United States-Softwood Lumber (2004) United States – Investigation of the International Trade Commission in softwood lumber from Canada, WT/DS277/R.

United States-Shrimp (1998) United States – import prohibition of certain shrimp and shrimp products. WT/DS58/AB/R.

Wang and Qu (2002) Impacts of accession to WTO on China's travel industry. *Journal of Travel and Tourism Marketing* 12 (10), 63–80.

Weatherill, S. and Beaumont, P. (1999) *EU Law*. London: Penguin.

World Bank (2002) *World Development Report 2003: Sustainable Development in a Dynamic World*. Washington, DC: World Bank.

An Observation Station[1] for Culture and Tourism in Vietnam: A Forum for World Heritage and Public Participation

Tomke Lask and Stefan Herold
Laboratory of Anthropology of Communication (LAC), University of Liege, Belgium

World Heritage is increasingly approached in an international context and it seems appropriate for the protection of World Heritage sites in our globalised world. However, we should question whether or not the global aspects are not over-emphasised, leaving behind local and national interests. Increasing the number of stakeholders in the selection process of World Heritage sites, especially those mostly excluded from any decision-making process, seems to be a promising approach. It enlarges the debate and facilitates consensus at all levels on how to promote and to protect World Heritage. The creation of an observation station, together with a new local selection system of cultural heritage sites, a kind of participatory budget of cultural heritage, would be an important step in integrating more civic perception into World Heritage policy.

Keywords: culture, tourism, Vietnam, world heritage sites, conservation

Introduction

The growing internationalisation of all sectors of modern life has led to the establishment of international standards and facilitates economic and, to a lesser extent, cultural exchange. Many international institutions, for example, the UN, WHO, IMF and UNESCO, provide the structure for an internationally acceptable common ground for cooperation. At first sight, in such a globalised world, it seems appropriate that World Heritage Sites should be subject to international constraints, but it is also relevant to ask how far the international system, based on the expertise of an equally international elite, is not over-emphasising the global aspects, to the detriment of local and national interests. Put differently, it is at least arguable that there would be an improvement in the selection and protection of World Heritage Sites (cultural or natural) if there were more public participation in the official selection procedure. After all, public participation is relevant because only sites that are supported by the local population will become sustainable.

Public participation is clearly a bigger problem in countries where civil society is poorly organised and generally absent from national decision-making processes. Reasons for the lack of civil action are wide-ranging, and include a weakness in democratic traditions, and a preoccupation with poverty and the daily fight for survival. However, despite such understandable concerns, it is suggested here that including those stakeholders hitherto excluded from decision making over World Heritage has value, and this paper offers a concrete proposition for change in this dimension of the politics of World Heritage.

World Heritage Sites: Places of Cultural Exchange?

At a recent ASEF[2] seminar in Hanoi in November 2001 on 'Cultural Heritage, Man and Tourism', delegates addressed the difficulties of imagining what people from other cultures would appreciate, what would not interest them and, finally, what might interest them but which should nevertheless be kept inaccessible for the sake of local culture and the well-being of the local community (Hitchcock, 2002). The debate showed clearly that the destination areas of tourism are conscious constructions of images to be sold, involving a selection of elements to be displayed for sale. The crux of the problem is how and what to choose. The purported primary motivation of intercultural exchange for tourists (as often portrayed in tourist brochures), is not really the aim of this construction (Hitchcock, 2000: 6). However, if these destination areas are to be sustainable, they must satisfy both the expectations of the tourists and the economic expectations of host populations. In any case, the venue at which tourism occurs is, at least sometimes, evocative of a kind of theme park (Zukin, 1993) where everyone can enact their own desires without entering the real world of the other. Are sites labelled 'World Heritage' any less susceptible to this commercial display and, if so, what makes the difference?

During the Hanoi seminar, and drawing on a previous analysis of authenticity and souvenirs (Hitchcock, 2002: 71ff.), a different kind of tourism destination area was evoked. It involved an abstract space where mutual exchange in culture and arts was possible, and where different cultural influences could lead to the creation of something new. Tourism would thus become a way of contacting another culture and exposing oneself to its cultural influences. This notion of tourism destinations as meeting points or zones that contribute to creativity and help to open up minds by cultural exchange is quite seductive, and may be contrasted with MacCannell's more negative notion of 'empty meeting grounds' (1992). These new scenarios of tourism enable individuals to enrich their experience through encountering the 'other', rather than settling for the more usual self-reflexive tourist experience where individual identity is reinforced through exposure to cultural diversity (see Barth, 1969). They rather represent a no man's land where, at every instance, cross-cultural communication must be invented (Clifford, 1997: 192–4; Lask, 2002: 16–28; Sahlins, 1989).

World Heritage sites can and should function as places of genuine exchange because, in theory, at least, they are universally and culturally significant. They should facilitate visitor understanding of cultural universality as well as cultural diversity, an aim expressed in the adoption of the Universal Declaration on Cultural Diversity and its Action Plan during the 31st session of UNESCO's General Conference in October 2001 (UNESCO, 2002).

As with other dimensions of culture, World Heritage is an invention (Anderson, 1995; Hobsbawm & Ranger, 1997), and comprehensive participation in the construction of this invention is necessary to assure its sustainability. However, such participation is not assured, and will vary across World Heritage Sites, every one of which is unique. Nevertheless, a start would be made with the establishment of a forum, a 'free zone', where information on the political, economic and social aspects of tourism and World Heritage could be freely exchanged. The consequent involvement of populations in or around heritage sites would enhance both their commitment to the World Heritage Site and the cultural 'authenticity' of the site itself. This kind of forum might provide the opportunity to elaborate sustainable policies for international cooperation on cultural tourism, and seems a more promising territory of tourism than that normally associated with UNESCO, where diplomacy often predominates. At the very least, the possibility is worth investigation, and an independent approach to culture and tourism by an observation station might bear fruit.

Observing What and for Whom?

Public authorities generally value tourism most for the economic benefits it brings to a country or region. Indeed, as the World Tourism Organisation's Declarations at Buenos Aires (WTO, 1995) and Bali (WTO, 1996) indicated, tourism is considered the most important global economic activity. However, while tourist expenditure and the tourist 'gaze' (Urry, 2000) have an impact on intangible cultural heritage, and may be important contributors to social change, the gaze local people return is usually omitted from most social scientific studies, even though such gazes are complementary and are equally relevant to any comprehensive understanding of tourist encounters. Indeed, a one-sided economic approach to tourism development fails to take into account the middle and long-term disadvantages, and while economists may claim they can construe its social and cultural impacts, linking everything to the economic sphere is too narrow.

This can be seen, for example, in the recent collaboration of the Walloon Region of Belgium with the Quebec Region in Canada (General Commissioner on Tourism of the Walloon Region, interview, April 2001). It is perhaps to be expected that when two state agencies undertake such a project, and follow the standard approach to the problem, economic aspects are accorded priority and other issues thus become secondary. Similar trends are evident in some regional observatories in France (Côte d'Azur, Alsace, Île-de-France, Languedoc, Roussillon, Rhône Alpes), in Quebec and Portugal.[3]

By contrast, use of the observation station necessitates a trans-disciplinary approach to problem resolving and analysis from the outset, and facilitates an integrated analysis of tourism's impact on local and national social structures. Without denying the economic and ecological aspects of tourism, the observation station prioritises tourism's role in cultural change and cultural diversity, and is thus distinguished from more economic-orientated 'observatories' that have previously focused on tourist development.

It is argued here that interdisciplinary studies of tourists in destination areas will contribute to a better understanding of their impact and facilitate measures to enhance intercultural communication. At the same time, the observation station comes to represent a symbolic space for cultural and scientific exchange, which can be summarised in the following five basic functions. First, it collects collect data, both directly and indirectly relating to tourism, which can then be made accessible to many kinds of users. Secondly, it brings together and makes available expertise on tourism's varied relationships to policy-making and policy-implementation, economics and other social sciences. Thirdly, by adopting an interdisciplinary approach to tourism, the dynamic processes of tourism development can be monitored, problems avoided, and solutions developed. Indeed, the observation station could take on the role of an independent observer of development projects linked directly or indirectly to tourism, with a particular interest in the sustainability of tourism over the long term. Finally, it could also offer independent audits on the efficiency and impact of local development projects and contribute to the continued analysis of international political conceptions of development and its concrete policy (Escobar, 1995; Stavenhagen, 1985).

Such functions could occur only if there were continual observation and analysis of the impact of international, state or NGO-projects *in situ*, and understanding the success and failure of development policies and evaluating them from the perspectives of numerous disciplines would necessitate continuous information exchange and networking, whereby information on hitherto isolated development projects and policies would be brought together on a continuous basis.

All such activities would be of limited value unless they were translated and transmitted in ways that could offer cross-cultural interpretations of the different values, conceptions and *Weltanschauungen* emerging from various tourist developments involving residents and tourists, and unless such interaction were situated in a wider context, where the focus would be on the sustainability of any tourist enterprise.

In these ways, an observation station would facilitate analysis of present situations and assist in the accumulation of expertise in the long-term study of tourism's impacts on local populations. At the same time, both macro and micro aspects of tourism development would be considered, and social changes with negative effects might be detected in advance. If this did occur, measures could be introduced that would prevent or minimise crises in tourism development.

Clearly, such observation stations could not be established immediately on a worldwide basis. However, it may be that several pilot projects, in different countries, would provide useful indications of the value of this idea, preferably where international tourism has been introduced only recently. Such a pilot project would be appropriate in Vietnam, for instance, for tourism really only started in that country a decade or so ago, and its social and cultural impacts could be monitored almost from the beginning.

A Pilot Experience in Vietnam

The Convention Concerning the Protection of the World's Cultural and Natural Heritage (popularly known as the World Heritage Convention) was adopted in 1972 by the General Conference of UNESCO, and its primary aim is to conserve cultural and natural sites that are selected by the statutory body of the convention, the World Heritage Committee. Since then, the Vietnamese National Assembly has ratified the convention and in October 1987 the Vietnamese government officially acknowledged its adherence. At the time of writing there were five World Heritage Sites in Vietnam: Ha Long Bay, the complex of Hue monuments, Hoi An ancient town, My Son sanctuary and (from July 2003) the national park of Phong Nha-Ke Bang.

Any appreciation of how the World Heritage Convention is locally applied needs to be based on a broad understanding of the key political features of

Vietnam. Most importantly, it is still a socialist country with strongly centralised political structures. The leading political institution is the Communist Party, and the key instrument for promoting the Party's aims is the Vietnam Fatherland's Front, membership of which includes the nation's political parties, trade unions and social organisations. In recent years, the most important development was in 1986, when the Sixth Party Congress adopted the policy of *Doi Moi* (renovation/ renewal) to implement progressively more market economy reforms.

Central government also exerts an influence at cultural levels, as indicated in the role of the Ministry of Culture and Information as co-organiser of the 2001 ASEF seminar, and it was clear the Ministry was very interested in the emergence of cultural tourism as the most important economic activity in Vietnam.

According to the Director of the Vietnamese National UNESCO Committee (Personal communication through Zenon Kowal, official representative of the Walloon/Brussels Region of Belgium in Hanoi, 21 November 2003), Vietnam is anxious to apply the World Heritage Convention. Culture is of major importance in Vietnam and as well as adopting the Convention, national laws have been enacted to protect tangible and intangible heritage. However, detailed application of such laws is still to occur and the position of ethnic minorities, which are potentially of great interest to tourists, is especially problematic. During the war with the United States, many allied themselves with the USA, and after the war they were repressed and subjected to a policy of Vietnamisation. As a result of *Doi Moi*, they have shared in the wider opportunities for political representation, but central government has accorded them no special status or protection. While declarations of goodwill towards them by central government are numerous, the gap between intention and realisation remains large.

According to the Director, central government is clear on how to protect World Heritage Sites in Vietnam, and numerous institutions and organisations are said to specialise in this domain. However, such certainty may not be found at provincial level, which are also powerful administrative units. Here, local institutions and processes need to be created and the budget allocated by central government to the provinces for such purposes should be increased. As a result, funds for the protection and maintenance of the World Heritage Sites come primarily from tourism, but as local authorities exploit them financially, the sites become over-commercialised and disfigured. In fact, protection has been replaced by commercial exploitation.

Tourism, World Heritage Sites and Conservation in Vietnam

Tourism is relatively new to Vietnam, and while the country was opened to tourist activities in 1988, it is only since 1995 that tourism has become a major tool for development, under the Vietnamese National Administration of Tourism (VNAT). As its websites indicate (VNAT 2002a, 2002b, 2002c), since the early 1990s there has been a substantial increase in tourism arrivals. In 1990, 250,000 foreign tourists visited the country. Seven years later there were more than 1.7 million, and by 2001 the number had increased to more than 2.3 million. They were catered for by 3000 hotels, 300 inbound travel agencies, and more than 1000 travel agencies worldwide (Pham Tu, Vice Chairman of the National Administration of Tourism, personal communication, April 2001). Similar increases are recorded in domestic tourist numbers, which increased from 1 million in 1990 to 8.5 million in 1997.

While the Vietnamese government continues to define tourism as primarily an economic phenomenon, it is aware of potential social and cultural impacts, and has tabled legislation to guarantee respect for individual tourists and tourist groups, and to facilitate the economic development of tourism (Vietnamese Government, 1999a). In June 2001 the National Assembly also introduced the Law on Cultural Heritage (Vietnamese Government, 2001). However, such laws are not very specific. The Law on Cultural Heritage, for example, focuses primarily on defining tangible or intangible cultural heritage, historical-cultural sites, scenic landscapes, relics and antiquities, whereas cultural tourism policies and strategies should be designed to avoid common problems of mass tourism, and seek instead a balanced and sustainable use of heritage for the benefit of existing and future generations (Council of Europe, Committee of Ministers, 1996).

Problems become evident when the focus moves to individual World Heritage Sites. Ha Long Bay, for example, first became a World Heritage Site in 1994, under Criterion 3 of the Convention, and in 2000 was further inscribed under Criterion 1 because of its universal geological value as the most extensive and best-known example of marine-invaded tower *karst* and one of the most important areas of *fengcong* and *fenglin karst* in the world (UNESCO, 2000). However, with no special staff for site management, and little control of visitors or activities along its borders, the spectacular limestone island caves and quaint coastal villages are fast deteriorating, becoming crowded, tacky and polluted. Additionally, from an environmental point of view, Ha Long Bay has always been a high-impact area. The most serious problem has been coal mining and the storage and transport of coal in coastal waters. Also, mangroves, a key feature of the bay's special character and habitat, have apparently been sacrificed in the construction of hotels and the development of a sandy beach. In fact, the need for environmental standards is obvious and the lesson that tourism does not have to lead to haphazard development is still to be learned here.

Problems of a different kind emerge in Hué, where the most pressing question is whether or not to rebuild the imperial city, as more than 70% of its buildings were destroyed during the Vietnam War (UNESCO, 1998). From a European point of view, such reconstruction might be considered inauthentic, especially if modern materials were to be used. Such issues are of less concern to the Vietnamese, who are more inclined to ask who wants to live in such reconstructed and 'old fashioned' houses.

In Hanoi, other problems can be found. During the 2001 ASEF seminar in Hanoi, it was noted that small hotels were increasing in every part of the old town, and could not be controlled through existing legislation, as laws concerning private and public ownership of land and property often overlapped and were contradictory (Pandolfi, 2001: 29–32). Whereas the state, as a local authority, possessed the land, the houses, apartments and shops were owned by numerous private persons, often occupants of houses that were subdivided into many different units. Furthermore, whereas the authorities lacked the requisite funds to purchase properties, Vietnamese from the south were able to do so, but their subsequent conversion of old houses into hotels was altering the character and charm of the old quarter and might even affect its attractiveness for tourism.

Remedial Measures and Problems

An unspoiled natural, cultural and human environment is fundamental for the development of tourism, and rational management of tourism may indeed help protect and develop the physical environment and cultural heritage, and improve the overall quality of life. This should include effective measures to inform and educate tourists, both domestic and international, to preserve, conserve and respect the natural, cultural and human environment of destination areas. Following the report of the World Commission on Environment and Development, popularly known as the Brundtland Report (World Commission on Environment and Development, 1987), and UNEP's work on the environment (UN, 1987), the World Conference on Sustainable Tourism recognised 'economic and social cohesion among the people of the world as a fundamental principle of sustainable development', and underlined the need 'to promote measures that permit a more equitable distribution of the benefits and burdens of tourism' (WCST, 1995). This implies a change in consumption patterns and the introduction of pricing methods, which allow environmental costs to be integrated into tourism.

Other international declarations are also relevant to tourism's socio-cultural and environmental impacts. These include the Manila Declaration on World Tourism (WTO, 1980), the Acapulco Document (WTO, 1982), the Tourist Code and Tourism Bill of Rights (WTO, 1985), and The Hague Declaration on Tourism (WTO, 1989), which refer to the Universal Declaration of Human Rights and, in particular, to Article 24, which states that 'everyone has the right to rest and leisure, including reasonable limitation of working hours and holidays with pay' (UN, 1948). They also cite Article 7 of the International Covenant on Economic, Social and Cultural Rights (UN, 1966a), by which states undertake to ensure, for everyone, 'rest, leisure, reasonable limitation of working hours and periodic holidays with pay, as well as remuneration for public holidays', and Article 12 of the International Covenant on Civil and Political Rights (UN, 1966b), which states that: 'Everyone shall be free to leave any country, including his own'.

Vietnam's own tourism legislation is yet to transform international recommendations and conventions into national laws. However, some efforts have been made and the government has launched the 1999–2000 State Tourism Action Programme for the next few years, entitled 'Vietnam – a destination for the new millennium' (Vietnamese Government, 1999b). It recognises that Vietnamese tourism is at a relatively formative stage, and (as written in the CPV CC 8th Plenum resolution) aims to develop a programme to overcome weaknesses and open a new page of development 'step by step to make our country a high level tourism and trade-service centre in the region' (VNAT, 2002c). More generally, though, while the Ordinance on Tourism (Article 7) promises to guarantee the respect of all the international Conventions already signed or to be signed in future by Vietnam, none of the recommendations in the above declarations have been specifically adopted in Vietnam. Indeed, until 2004 Vietnam lacked any concrete action plan on tourism, even though it recognised the need to protect and restore its cultural heritage for future generations.

However, decrees and laws derived from international Charters and recommendations of WTO or UNESCO will not be enough in a society where a large proportion of the population interprets the laws rather loosely. For example and according to an official of the Vietnam National Administration of Tourism, interviewed by the authors in November 2001 only about 20% of Vietnamese ask for official permission before commencing construction work. It will be an uphill struggle to convince Vietnamese that laws do not only regulate or control to one's disadvantage, but might also be for the general good. It might also be necessary to convince people, perhaps through the educational system, that their active support in protecting cultural heritage sites will be a crucial complement to the existing legislation.

Following the directives of the Council of Europe (1995) to member states, the attainment of sustainable tourism implies promotion of 'every form of development, of urban planning, of tourist activity that respects the environment, preserves natural and cultural resources in the long term, and is socially and economically acceptable and fair'. However, it is no easy matter to translate this general imperative into specific contexts. Are there recognised cultural and social criteria to be followed? And where are the systematic studies of tourism's impact on local population to verify whether or not such 'respect' is being accorded? Understanding the mechanisms that nourish tourist-local interaction at World Heritage Sites, as well as at other tourism destination areas, 'will contribute to site preservation and help resolve latent conflicts. In Vietnam, as elsewhere, tourism seems to be an inevitable and increasingly important economic activity, and therefore merits urgent political and economic attention. The consequences should be studied, measured, and the results applied, to improve policies and develop more productive and mutually respectful cross-cultural practices in tourist destination areas.

The Role of the Observation Station

It is in such a context that, again, the prospect of a pilot observation station has a clear appeal. This is not a single, stand-alone initiative to assist one or more specific partners at a precise moment, but rather a project involving steady and sustained cooperation among researchers, advisers, decision makers and (especially) those who make heritage a living item: the ordinary people.

The precise form it is to take will be a matter of negotiation, but lessons might be learned from public participation mechanisms that were created in developing countries, often for other purposes, but whose practices might be adapted to develop World Heritage policy in general. One such example is the Participatory Budget, established in 1989 in Porto Alegre (Brazil). The Participatory Budget is a community-based decision-making process in which residents establish criteria for resource allocation, present their priorities regarding government expenditures and ultimately determine the municipal budget (see Andreatta, 1995).

Over 15 years, from 1989 to 2004, this decision-making process has been a worthwhile tool for creating trust between the public service and the community and in fostering a sense of social responsibility in the public service and in government management. The transparency of the procedures and the budget allocations contributed largely to the success of the participatory budget in Brazil, and more than 70 Brazilian cities adopted this system of basic democracy for local administration, as well as many other cities in Latin America, and even some in Europe – for example, Mons in Belgium. Applying such policies to World Heritage Sites would involve residents, perhaps change their attitudes, and could help make World Heritage policy lively and sustainable.

Before the Participatory Budget can be launched properly, the urban space must be divided into administrative regions. This is done through the cooperation of civil society, local residents and other associations, for example, NGOs, whose combined 'indigenous knowledge' (Sillitoe, 2002: 1–23) of urban space is fundamental during this process. As a consequence, the final result does not necessarily correspond to the city's pre-existing administrative units. The next step is to decide on the priorities in every administrative region. Anyone can participate in meetings, on the assumption that they live in the region and might be considered an expert on his or her living space. Those who want to participate but cannot be present can vote on the appropriate Internet site, provided a prior registration has been conducted. At the next level of the decision process, elected representatives of every region must first reach a consensus concerning their priorities, which they then present to the mayor who – while not being required to accept it in its totality, is required to explain why parts are rejected. Once an agreement is reached, it is published with all the financial details and a timetable, enabling citizens to verify, at any time, what really has been done in his or her region. Finally, at the end of the year, the mayor must justify any deviation from the established schedule to the representatives.

Citizens are encouraged to attend meetings, and child-care services are provided so that parents, especially single mothers, can participate. Technical staff of the city administration attend as consultants, commenting on the feasibility and the costs of proposals made by citizens. At every level of the decision-making process, the meetings are held in public, even where decisions are made only by mandated representatives, thus enabling observers to decide whether or not their representatives are carrying out their work satisfactorily. If they are perceived not to be doing so, they might not be re-elected the following year.

The Participatory Budget takes at least two years before its first concrete application, requiring a year for the administrative division and another to establish the priority list. From then on, the realisation of one Participatory Budget occurs in parallel with negotiations for the following year. In Brazil, the Participatory Budget focuses on such basic needs as canalisation, pavements, and public transportation, but in other social and economic contexts the focus will be on other topics. In principle, the mechanism can be adapted to the process of establishing World Heritage lists, and Vietnam should prove a good candidate. It is a well organised society and, with the existing civil organisation and the addition of new forms of civil society, for example, NGOs, the definition and maintenance of World Heritage Sites would certainly be enhanced through expanded citizen participation in the debate and the decision process. Once people have debated the value and the importance of their heritage to the world, they are more likely to accord more respect to their own cultural heritage and ensure that tourists also respect it. An observation station could be the independent mechanism in helping organise this process and supporting local participation and decision-making by making available its international expertise on tourism and related issues.

Conclusion

The creation of an observation station, together with a new and local system of selecting cultural heritage sites, would be an important step in introducing greater public participation into World Heritage policy. By establishing a broad database of independently assembled information, accessible to all, it would encourage a better understanding of the complex interaction between local residents and tourists, and of the changes arising from World Heritage listing. Economic information might also be included, especially on investment in the local economy and the eventual impact of World Heritage listing on social structures. The observation station could also provide more objective information on tourism's impact than decision-makers usually receive, and in a context which makes it less likely that it will be ignored, for fear that knowledge of tourism's negative impacts might create local resistance against tourism development (Tosun, 2002: 247–51). Over a long term, the observation station would offer insights of great value to politicians and local administrators and, as a consequence, contribute to the construction of sustainable tourism. Such a neutral space for information, research and exchange, in the interests of better protection of World Heritage Sites and/or other tourist places, is innovative in that it not only facilitates administration and policy formation, but also facilitates the integration of public participation in local decision-making on national heritage.

One caveat is especially in order. Continual reference to globalisation can too easily lead to searches for single solutions to global problems, and the implementation of the World Heritage Convention is a case in point. However, international agencies like UNESCO should beware of adopting a 'one size should fit all' maxim and should recognise, instead, that ultimately a case-by-case approach is likely to be more successful. As anthropologists have long recognised, administrative styles and policy-making imperatives are as diverse as cultures and social systems, and are as deserving of respect. Through the operation of an observation station for culture and tourism, local, national and international interests can come together more effectively and sympathetically in developing a more sustainable and (locally-grounded) sustainable world heritage policy. And this would be no mean achievement.

Correspondence

Any correspondence should be directed to Dr Tomke Lask at (tclask@ulg.ac.be) or Stefan Herold at (stefan.herold@ulg.ac.be).

Notes

1. The official term created and applied by UNESCO for such an institution of integrated observation and research, is 'observatory' (UNESCO, 2002: 21). However, the term 'observation station' is preferred because UNESCO also refers to a global network of several 'Observatories on Cultural Diversity' (UNESCO, 2002: 21).
2. The Asia-Europe Foundation was established in February 1997 by members of the Asia-Europe Meeting (ASEM). It is based in Singapore and reports to a Board of 26 governors comprising members of the 25 ASEM countries and the European Commission. Its mission is to build bridges between the civil societies of Asia and Europe through promoting cultural, intellectual and personal exchanges between the two world regions.
3. See: http://mrw.wallonie.be/dgee/cgt/otw/Index.htm, http://www.Belgique-

tourisme.nethttp://www.tourisme.gouv.qc.ca, http://www.tourisme.ont.asso.fr, http://www. touriscope. com, http://www.tourism-alsace.com/fr/observatoire. html, http://www.paris-ile-de-France.com, http://www.sunfrance.net/observatoire/ index.php3, http://www.rhonealpes- ort.com, http://www.atl-turismolisboa.pt. Accessed 05.04.

References

Anderson, B. (1995) *Imagined Communities*. London and New York: Verso.

Andreatta, H. (1995) *Participative Budget Porto Alegre*. Porto Alegre: Municipal Department of Culture.

Barth, F. (1969) Introduction. In F. Barth (ed.) *Ethnic Groups and Boundaries* (pp. 9–38). Bergen, Oslo and London: Norwegian University Press, George Allen & Unwin.

Clifford, J. (1997) Museums as contact zones. In J. Clifford (ed.) *Routes. Travel and Translation in the Late Twentieth Century* (pp. 188–219). Cambridge, MA and London: Harvard University Press.

Council of Europe, Committee of Ministers (1995) *Recommendation R (95) 10 to Member States on a Sustainable Tourist Development Policy in Protected Areas*. Strasbourg.

Council of Europe, Committee of Ministers (1996) *Final Declaration and Resolutions*. Fourth European Conference of Ministers responsible for the cultural heritage of the states party to the European Cultural Convention, Helsinki, May.

Escobar, A. (1995) *Encountering Development. The Making and Unmaking of the Third World*. Princeton: Princeton University Press.

Hitchcock, M. (2000) Introduction. In M. Hitchcock and K. Teague (eds) *Souvenirs: The Material Culture of Tourism* (pp.1–17). Aldershot: Ashgate.

Hitchcock, M. (2002) Souvenirs, cultural heritage and development. In Ministry of Culture and Information of Vietnam, Walloon Brussels Region, Asia-Europe Foundation, Laboratory of Anthropology of Communication (University of Liege, Belgium) (eds) *Cultural Heritage, Man and Tourism. Report of the Asia–Europe Seminar Hanoi (Vietnam) 5–7 November 2001* (pp. 71–80). Liege: CRD.

Hobsbawm, E. and Ranger, T. (1997) *The Invention of Tradition*. Cambridge: Cambridge University Press.

Lask, T. (2002) *'Wir Waren doch Immer Freunde in der Schule'. Einführung in die Anthropologie der Grenzräume. Europäisches Grenzverständnis am Beispiel Leidingens*. Saarbrücken: Röhrig Universitätsverlag.

MacCannell, D. (1992) *Empty Meeting Grounds*. London and New York: Routledge.

Pandolfi, L. (2001) Quelques caractéristiques juridiques, économiques et sociales du patrimoine urbain de Hanoi. In Ministry of Culture and Information of Vietnam, Walloon Brussels Region, Asia-Europe Foundation, Laboratory of Anthropology of Communication (University of Liege, Belgium) (eds) *Cultural Heritage, Man and Tourism. Report of the Asia-Europe Seminar Hanoi (Vietnam) 5–7 November 2001* (pp. 29–32). Liege: CRD.

Sahlins, P. (1989) *Boundaries: The Making of France and Spain in the Pyrenees*. Berkeley and Oxford: University of California Press.

Sillitoe, P. (2002) Participant observation to participatory development: Making anthropology work. In P. Sillitoe, A. Bicker and J. Pottier (eds) *Participating in Development. Approaches to Indigenous knowledge* (pp. 1–23). London and New York: Routledge.

Stavenhagen, R. (1985) Etnodesenvolvimento: Uma dimensão ignorada no pensamento desenvolvimentista. *Anuário Antropológico* 84, 13–56.

Tosun, C. (2002) Host perceptions of impacts. A comparative tourism study. *Annals of Tourism Research* 29 (1), 231–53.

UN (1948) *Universal Declaration of Human Rights*. Adopted and proclaimed by the United Nations General Assembly resolution 217 A (III) (December).

UN (1966a) *International Covenant on Economic, Social and Cultural Rights*. Adopted and opened for signature, ratification and accession by the United Nations General Assembly resolution 2200A (XXI), December.

UN (1966b) *International Covenant on Civil and Political Rights*. Adopted and opened for signature, ratification and accession by the United Nations General Assembly resolution 2200A (XXI), December.

UN (1987) *United Nations Environment Programme. The Environmental Perspective to the Year 2000 and Beyond.* 96th plenary meeting of the United Nations General Assembly, December.

UNESCO (1998) *Hué, Ville 'Patrimoine Mondial'. Diagnostic Juridique et Urbain. Recommandations Réglementaires.* Hué, Paris and Lille: Province and City of Hué, World Cultural Heritage Centre of UNESCO, Lille Métropole.

UNESCO (2000) *Report of the 24th World Heritage Committee Session (November – December 2000).* Cairns: UNESCO.

UNESCO (2002) Cultural diversity: A pool of ideas for implementation. In UNESCO (ed.) *Universal Declaration on Cultural Diversity. Cultural Diversity Series* 1 (pp. 17–59). Paris: UNESCO.

Urry, J. (2000) *The Tourist Gaze. Leisure and Travel in Contemporary Societies.* London: Sage.

Vietnamese Government (1999a) *Ordinance on Tourism No 02L/CTN.* Hanoi: President of the Socialist Republic of Vietnam.

Vietnamese Government (1999b) *1999–2000 State Tourism Action Programme for the Next Few Years. 'Vietnam – a Destination for the New Millennium'.* Principally accepted by Prime Minister on official document No36/CP KTTH, January. Hanoi.

Vietnamese Government (2001) *Bill on Cultural Heritage.* Ninth session of the Vietnamese National Assembly, June. Hanoi.

Vietnamese National Administration of Tourism (VNAT) (2002a) On WWW at http://www.vietnamtourism.com/e_pages/tourist/general/sltk_1990_1992.htm. Accessed 31.08.02.

Vietnamese National Administration of Tourism (VNAT) (2002b) On WWW at http://www.vietnamtourism.com/e_pages/tourist/general/sltk_1993_1999.htm. Accessed 31.08.02.

Vietnamese National Administration of Tourism (2002c) On WWW at http://64.247.21.245/vietnamtourism/dulich/cthd_quocgia/fr_ctrinh.htm. Accessed 31.08.02.

World Commission on Environment and Development (WCED) (1987) *Our Common Future: World Commission on Environment and Development.* Oxford: Oxford University Press.

World Conference on Sustainable Tourism (WCST) (1995) *Charter for Sustainable Tourism.* World Conference on Sustainable Tourism, Lanzarote, April.

WTO (World Tourism Organisation) (1980) *Manila Declaration on World Tourism.* World Tourism Conference, Manila, September–October.

WTO (1982) *Acapulco Document.* World Tourism meeting convened by WTO, Acapulco, August.

WTO (1985) *Tourist Code and Tourism Bill of Rights.* General Assembly of WTO, Sofia, September.

WTO (1989) *The Hague Declaration on Tourism.* Inter-Parliamentary Conference on Tourism of the Inter-Parliamentary Union (IPU), WTO and the Netherlands Inter-Parliamentary Group, The Hague, April.

WTO (1995) *Buenos Aires Declaration.* Fiftieth session of the Executive Council of WTO, Buenos Aires, May.

WTO (1996) *Bali Declaration on Tourism.* Second international forum on Parliaments and local authorities: Tourism policy-markers Bali, September.

Zukin, S. (1993) *Landscapes of Power. From Detroit to Disney World.* Berkley and Oxford: University of California Press.

Websites

http://www.vietnamtourism.com/e_pages/tourist/general/sltk_1990_1992.htm. Accessed 04.05.04.

http://www.vietnamtourism.com/e_pages/tourist/general/sltk_1993_1999.htm. Accessed 04.05.04.

http://64.247.21.245/vietnamtourism/dulich/cthd_quocgia/fr_ctrinh.htm. Accessed 04.05.04.

http://mrw.wallonie.be/dgee/cgt/otw/Index.htm. Accessed 04.05.04.

http://www.Belgique-tourisme.nethttp://www.tourisme.gouv.qc.ca. Accessed 04.05.04.

http://www.tourisme.ont.asso.fr. Accessed 04.05.04.

http://www.touriscope.com. Accessed 04.05.04.

http://www.tourism-alsace.com/fr/observatoire.html. Accessed 04.05.04.

http://www.paris-ile-de-France.com. Accessed 04.05.04.

http://www.sunfrance.net/observatoire/index.php3. Accessed 04.05.04.

http://www.rhonealpes-ort.com. Accessed 04.05.04.

http://www.atl-turismolisboa.pt. Accessed 04.05.04.

Commentary
The Meanings and Effectiveness of World Heritage Designation in the USA

Kevin Williams
Department of Geography, Lancaster University, Lancaster, UK

The USA played a pivotal role in developing the idea of the World Heritage Convention just over 30 years ago. This paper begins by examining the history of the World Heritage Convention's practical application in the USA and goes on to discuss the Convention's present-day application at Yellowstone National Park, Great Smoky Mountains National Park and the national scale. It may be concluded that although there is a high level of compliance with the requirements of the World Heritage Convention, numerous issues need to be resolved to ensure that World Heritage Site designation remains an effective protection tool for sites of international importance.

Keywords: world heritage designation, USA

Introduction

In the late 1960s and early 1970s, the United States of America provided a great deal of momentum for the idea of World Heritage. This was prompted by President Nixon's support for the concept of a World Heritage Trust, an idea developed by Joseph Fisher and Russell Train. As a consequence, on 7 December 1973 the USA became one of the first State Parties to sign up to the Convention. The late 1970s and 1980s subsequently saw the nomination of a number of sites, including Yellowstone and the Grand Canyon, even though in 1984 the Reagan Administration withdrew from UNESCO, however, the administration opted to remain active in the area of World Heritage (Yeager, 1999).

After the listing of these early sites, in the 1990s the number of nominations rapidly decreased. In May 1990, too, the Tentative List was published by the Department of the Interior, in cooperation with the Federal Interagency Panel for World Heritage, and was subsequently updated in 1992. The 1992 list, which identified 50 potential sites (United States National Park Service, 1998), was prepared by the Federal Interagency Panel for World Heritage, which is advised and chaired by the Assistant Secretary for Fish, Wildlife and Parks, and is staffed by the National Park Service.

The American nomination process is voluntary, and is clearly laid out in Title IV of the Historic Preservation Act Amendments of 1980 and 36 CFR Part 73. It requires that each proposal must have a defined boundary and that the relevant committees of the House and Senate are notified of all pending proposals and, again, when the Department of the Interior has decided to nominate a property. The use of Congressional input has worked effectively, and members comment favourably on proposed sites within their own states. Indeed, no site has been nominated unless it received support from local government and the state's Congressional delegation (Yeager, 1999: 6).

The World Heritage Convention has been promoted at numerous World Heritage Sites across the USA. World Heritage designations add value to the sites, which have been embraced by many areas in the USA, and one positive economic outcome of designation is increased tourism, especially foreign tourism. Between 1990 and 1995, for example, foreign visitation to American World Heritage sites increased by 9.4%, whereas over the same period foreign visitors to all national parks increased by 4.2% (Yeager, 1999: 3), which suggests that World Heritage designation attracts foreign visitors, especially those with specific interests, who want to learn about and visit such sites (Yeager, 1999: 3).

World Heritage designation has also been used to facilitate international cooperation with Canada on mountain rescue, managing traffic and rescue operations on the Alesk River at the trans-boundary World Heritage Sites of Wrangell-St Elias and Glacier Bay. The World Heritage designation has also been used to attract corporate funding to World Heritage Sites. For example, the Reagan Administration used the designation of the Statue of Liberty to attract private sector funding for its restoration in the 1980s.

Despite the positive impacts of World Heritage designation, it has been remarked that, although the USA has been an active member of the World Heritage Convention since its inception, the vast majority of visitors to national parks have no idea that they are visiting a World Heritage Site. Wilkinson has compared World Heritage to a great atlas sitting unopened on the bookshelf, and suggests that the 'time has arrived for us to take a look at the pages inside' (Wilkinson, 1996: 36), while Cook (in Wilkinson, 1996: 38) has also commented on the lack of promotion of World Heritage in the USA compared to other countries.

He also suggests that, as the Convention is given greater publicity, perhaps through the controversies that World Heritage listing may generate, public awareness will increase, and that while 'some people are going to love World Heritage . . . others won't take too kindly to it' (Cook, in Wilkinson, 1996: 38).

This latter comment is particular pertinent to attempts to enshrine the American Land Sovereignty Protection Act (ALSPA) in American law, a major issue affecting the application of the World Heritage Convention in the USA over the last few years. The aim behind this proposed legislation is to increase public consultation before sites are nominated to UNESCO's World Heritage list. However, it has been argued that the ALSPA legislation was introduced for reasons other than public consultation. Pomerance (1997: 198) argues that ALSPA is based on the mistaken belief that the World Heritage Convention impacts on US sovereignty and private land rights. Therefore, it is claimed that the debate surrounding ALSPA has been couched in terms which suggested United Nations exerts an influence over US parks and monuments (Congressional Research Service, 2000: 3).

The Research

The study consisted of face-to-face semi-structured interviews between March 2001 and March 2002 with members of government departments, government agencies and Non-Governmental Organisations (NGOs) at national level and at the Yellowstone National Park and Great Smoky Mountain National Park. The study utilised purposive and snowball sampling techniques. It began by using a purposive sampling strategy through the identification of key interviewees at the regional and national scale. Interviewees were selected through Internet searches, informal telephone enquiries and through references made by other interviewees. However, as research progressed, snowball sampling became increasingly used as interviewees identified through the purposive sampling strategy recommended other potential interviewees to the author.

The author sought to gain the views of those at the regional and national scale of a number of facets of the World Heritage concept. Thus, the interview schedule was divided into six sections concerning the meanings of heritage, tentative lists, publicity and education, management, monitoring issues and the future of the World Heritage Convention.

The results of the research indicate that reasons for nominating sites for World Heritage status include the desire for recognition, publicity, protection and economic benefits. Interviewees at the Yellowstone and Great Smoky Mountain National Parks, for example, considered such sites to be of international significance, a view reflected in the fact that both sites were nominated under all four World Heritage criteria. In addition, World Heritage designation provides site managers with a degree of leverage in terms of finance, site protection and management resources. For example World Heritage listing has acted as a catalyst in bringing disparate interest groups together in the wider Great Smoky Mountain region to plan at a regional as opposed to local scale. A further example is seen in the use of the World Heritage Convention's reactive (or public) monitoring system at Yellowstone National Park by 14 environmental groups. Their pressure resulted in a visit to the site by the World Heritage Committee, and to Yellowstone National Park being placed on the List of World Heritage in Danger. This illustrates how public monitoring can democratise an otherwise political top down process and, therefore, democratise site protection. The public can thus play an important part in the monitoring of World Heritage sites by writing directly to the World Heritage Committee, which allows them to raise the issue with the State Party in question (Prott, 1991: 18).

However, despite the use of the World Heritage Convention by groups at Yellowstone, it is noteworthy that those interviewed in the Yellowstone region considered the World Heritage Committee a distant entity because of the hierarchical process for communicating with it through Washington. Despite this lack of communication between those at the top and bottom of the World Heritage structure, however, interviewees held favourable views of the World Heritage Committee.

In the light of the perceived benefits of the World Heritage Convention, it is surprising that the American Tentative List was last updated in 1992, a process that occurred without any public consultation. This lack of consultation and the abeyant nature of the Tentative List was reflected in an ignorance of the Tentative List process at both Yellowstone and the Great Smoky Mountains. The failure to review the Tentative List may also explain the belief amongst interviewees that the majority of the population in the USA is ignorant and confused by the Convention. Indeed, from the author's informal discussions with park rangers, staff at both sites were also found to be ignorant of the World Heritage site designation. One rationale put forward by those formally interviewed was that park rangers receive no specific training on the subject of World Heritage.

Ignorance and confusion have been reinforced by anti-United Nations sentiments expressed by such groups as the Wise Use Movement. Indeed, because of the complexity of the topic, the development of ALSPA in Congress, and through fear of a hostile reaction, World Heritage designation has received little publicity in the USA. Administrators at Yellowstone National Park and regional NGOs, for example, believed that anti-UN sentiment continued in the area following the World Heritage Committee's visit in 1996. And anti-UN feelings emerged when the Great Smoky Mountains National Park advertised its International Biosphere status on its signage, even though its World Heritage status was not advertised.

It seems, then, that ignorance leads to reduced publicity which, in turn, perpetuates more ignorance. It is a situation that is likely to continue until a publicity strategy is specifically developed to inform the public, which at both sites is currently faced with evidence of multiple designations, all of which compete for the public's attention. At the time of writing, for example, few visitor interpretation facilities at either site deal specifically with World Heritage listing. However, while there are no specific programmes at Yellowstone National Park on World Heritage status, International Biosphere and World Heritage plaques are prominently displayed in the movie theatre, and rangers distribute leaflets if asked about the designation, which in practice rarely occurs.

Conclusion

Research and analysis indicate several key themes. First, there is evidence that World Heritage Site designation provides economic benefits and leverage at site level. Secondly, though, it seems that the future of the World Heritage Convention in the USA is contingent on the development of a new Tentative List, which utilises an open and transparent methodology through public consultation. With this in mind, it is recommended that an approach similar to that used in the UK during 1998–1999 is applied in the USA, and state legislatures encouraged to identify potential sites within their own area. In this way, an element of local pride in heritage would be introduced, and local people would be encouraged to become involved with their heritage. Finally, there is an urgent need for increased public education on the meaning and implications of World Heritage designation. This must occur if widespread ignorance of the World Heritage concept among the general public, NGOs and government agencies is to be removed.

Acknowledgements

This research is one element of a larger research project funded by the Lancaster University, Department of Geography, Rural Studentship award.

Correspondence

Any correspondence should be directed to Dr Kevin Williams, Department of Geography, Lancaster University, Lancaster LA1 4YB, UK (k.williams@lancaster.ac.uk).

References

Congressional Research Service (2000) *World Heritage Convention and U.S. National Parks.* 96-395 Washington, DC: National Council for Science and the Environment.

Pomerance, R. (1997) *Testimony to Committee of Resources Hearing on H.R. 901, 10 June.* Washington. On WWW at http://www.commdocs.house.gov/committees/ resources. Accessed 23.01.01.

Prott, L.V. (1991) The genesis and philosophy of the World Heritage Convention. In P. Burman, J. Fawcett, B. Feilden and Lord Kennet (eds) *Managing World Heritage Sites in Britain* (pp. 1–19). York: Institute of Advanced Architectural Studies, University of York and ICOMOS.

United States National Park Service (1998) *World Heritage Sites in the US.* On WWW at http://www.cr.nps.gov/worldheritage. Accessed 14.08.00.

Wilkinson, T. (1996) Global warning – the designation of Yellowstone: One of the first World Heritage sites. *National Parks* 70 (3–4), 34–40.

Yeager, B. (1999) Statement of Brooks B. Yeager, Deputy Assistant Secretary for Policy and International Affairs, Department of the Interior, before the House Committee on Resources regarding, H.R. 883, the American Land Sovereignty Protection Act, March 18. On WWW at http://www.nps.gov/legal/testimony/106th/alsover. Accessed 23.01.01.

Commentary
Managing the Cedars of Lebanon: Botanical Gardens or Living Forests?

Myra Shackley

Centre for Tourism and Visitor Management, Nottingham Trent University, UK

Lebanon receives about 750,000 visitors a year, attracted by a diverse tourism portfolio with an increasing emphasis on cultural and ecotourism. It was once covered in cedar forest, with the great trees still acting both as metaphor and brand for the country. Today, there are several areas where cedars may still be seen, the most important being the Chouf Reserve, in the Jabal el Barouk mountains near the Bekaa valley, and the famous cedars of the Quadisha valley in north Lebanon (a World Heritage Site since 1998), near the town of Becharre, the centre of Lebanon's ski industry. This paper examines the management of the isolated grove of giant cedar trees at Becharre which has become a sterile botanical garden, and compares it with the living forests of the Chouf Cedar Reserve. The fundamental question being asked here is whether or not World Heritage designation of this natural resource has had conservation benefits, and if such benefits outweigh diminished experience quality for visitors.

Keywords: tourism, Lebanon, cedars, world heritage list

Introduction

The Lebanese cedar (*Cedrus libani*) can grow to an immense size and live to a great age. It is the very symbol of Lebanon, used both as brand and metaphor, representing the great antiquity of Lebanon and symbolising continuity between a glorious past and an uncertain present. Over the past decade since the ending of the civil war Lebanon has expended effort not only in preserving and extending its ancient cedar forests, but also in planting new ones. The country is using cedar trees as symbols of reconstruction, wholeness and greenness, a new variation on the infamous Green Line which once divided Christian from Muslim Beirut. Lebanon is keen to regain its role as a major player in Middle Eastern tourism, utilising a diversified product base that includes ecotourism within its residual cedar forests. Only 2% of Lebanon's original cedar forest cover remains today, but there are several areas where cedars may still be seen. The most important is the Chouf Reserve, in the Jabal el Barouk mountains near the Bekaa valley, and the famous cedars of the Quadisha valley in north Lebanon, near the town of Becharre, the centre of Lebanon's ski industry.

In 1998, the Becharre cedars were inscribed on the World Heritage list as part of *'Ouadi Qadisha (the Holy Valley) and the Forest of the Cedars of God (Horsh Arz el-Rab)* under criteria C(iii)(iv). The Qadisha valley had been the home of monastic communities since the earliest years of Christianity, with the remaining cedar trees being survivors of a sacred forest that formed one of the most highly prized building materials of the ancient world. This fieldwork-based paper examines the management of this culturally significant isolated stand of trees that has become a sterile botanical garden, and compares it with the living forests of the Chouf Cedar Reserve. The issue addressed is the contribution World Heritage designation has made both to the preservation of the cedars and the nature of the visitor experience.

Tourism in Lebanon

Tourism in Lebanon has a chequered history, and today its future is again in doubt after the terrible events of September 2001. This was yet another blow to the country's tourism industry which, having begun to recover from the effects of the civil war, declined once again with the collapse of the Arab-Israeli peace process and subsequent *intifada*. Lebanon receives large numbers of seasonal international visitors from the Gulf States, arriving to escape the extreme heat in summer and to take advantage of the opportunity to ski in winter. However, it has also developed a growing cultural tourism market from Europe, as well as a limited market for USA visitors aided by the decision, taken in 1999 by the US State Department, to remove Lebanon from its travel blacklist.

New developments in Lebanese tourism include the promotion of the cruise business based at the port of Beirut (Thomas, 2001), which has some positive impact on the country's visitor attractions, as cruise passengers are offered day trips including excursions to Beirut, Baalbeck and the Cedars of Becharre (World Bank, 2001). Beirut, is home to half the population of Lebanon and now has a cluster of top class luxury hotels and many franchised hotel operations at different levels. It has once again become a fast moving cosmopolitan city with a fine waterfront and fascinating re-development of its historic centre around spectacular archaeological sites (Berriane, 1997; Pearce & Mourator, 1998).

In 2000, Lebanon welcomed 741,648 visitors, with a peak in July-August because of arrivals from the Gulf (Ministry of Tourism, 2001). Beirut is an expensive destination, there is little provision for hostelers or backpackers, and the cost of daily living is high. However, the Lebanese tourism industry is actually profiting from the current crisis in the Middle East, partly because Arab states are re-directing investment funding from American and European banks to Lebanon. It is also partly due to the already healthy growth in Gulf tourists (many of whom own second homes in Beirut) and is likely to increase as Arabs become reluctant to travel. The resumption of military activity on the southern border near Palestinian strongholds could end this trend.

Although Arab visitors are usually not interested in ecotourism or cultural tourism, the opposite is true for European visitors and Lebanon is especially popular with French speakers. It also receives substantial numbers of German visitors (mostly interested in culture and nature) as are the English, Spanish and Italians. Many European tour operators are now developing tours of Lebanon, sometimes in combination with Syria, and business travel to Lebanon increases steadily.

The Lebanese Environment

The quality of both cultural sites and the natural environment is a key factor in developing new Lebanese tourism products, and unfortunately the effect of the war continues to be evident in the Lebanese countryside, even after a decade of peace (Miksell, 1969). Many reconstruction projects have stopped or slowed down when funds became scarce, and Lebanon's environment, ravaged by 15 years of anarchy, remains desperately fragile. This places additional emphasis on 'flagship' environmental projects, such as those associated with the Cedars, which boost confidence, demonstrate that peace has really arrived and contribute very positive images to incoming international visitors.

The war resulted in substantial deforestation and accelerated soil erosion. Illegal quarries proliferated and continue to operate. In the south, especially in the Chouf region, much of the countryside was mined and even today travellers are warned not to stray from well-marked paths. It is in this very countryside that the Chouf Cedar Reserve, the largest Reserve in Lebanon, has been constructed. Curiously, it was the presence of mines in the Chouf that actually protected the Reserve area from environmental damage to the new plantations of cedars which had been started in the 1960s. During the war, the country lacked any basic services, a legacy which survives in the practice of dumping waste by the roadside, even on tourist routes to the Cedar Reserves. Water supplies and sewage remain a problem, and by the mid-1990s Lebanon did not have a single functional waste treatment plant. Even such protected areas as the Qadisha valley have been inappropriately developed with high-rise housing stock, although this practice theoretically stopped as a result of WHS designation in 1998.

Against this inauspicious background, Lebanon is trying to develop an effective new nature-based tourism industry which is aided by the growth of a number of environmental NGOs, pressure groups and volunteer organisations who oppose poor planning and encourage positive developments. The Chouf and Becharre committees are good examples of this process, and Lebanon now has a number of environmental tour operators encouraging trekking travel and promoting environmentally sensitive leisure activities. The first of many ecolodges was established in the Bekaa valley a few years ago. Although Lebanon technically has 31 areas protected by ministerial decrees, only its three formal Nature Reserves are actually being protected, largely because they receive funding from a variety of NGOs and international organisations as well as the Lebanese government. The most important of these NGOs is probably 'The Green Line', a non-political organisation promoting environmentally sound development. It is effectively Lebanon's 'Greenpeace', based on scientific foundations, and started in 1991 to popularise environmental awareness and contribute to the development of a scientific framework for sustainable environmental management policy. It was named after the infamous 'Green Line' which divided Christian from Muslim Beirut during the civil war which, although dismantled by 1991, remains a physical and psychological scar on the city and the country. Since 1992, environmental issues have assumed far greater prominence in Lebanon with the creation of Nature Reserves in Tripoli, Horst Ehden and, later, in the Chouf, partly financed by the UN acting through the Ministry of the Environment. The Chouf Cedar Reserve is the largest of these, followed by the Horst Ehden Nature Reserve not far from Becharre, which also includes cedars as well as a wide variety of indigenous plants. The third Reserve, Palm Island, is off the coast of Tripoli and is an important nesting place for turtles and Mediterranean monk seals.

The History and Distribution of Cedars in Lebanon

Lebanon was once covered in cedar forests, which for nearly three millennia

(2600 BC–AD 138) supplied the lumber needs of the Middle East, especially for ship timbers and other building materials (Masri, 1995). The Lebanese cedar appears in history as early as the Epic of Gilgamesh, written in the 2nd millennium BC, and cedar resin was widely used for ship caulking, in the preparation of oils, salves and ointments and medicines, and in Egyptian embalming. Cedar wood was exported through the ports of Sidon and Tyre, and logs were felled in the mountains and sent downstream as rafts for export by Phoenician traders (Harden, 1963), who conveyed the wood to ports in Egypt and elsewhere.

Greek historians comment on the strength and beauty of Lebanese cedars, a first choice for building projects in the ancient world when cost was no option. Cedar wood is durable, as demonstrated by roof timbers at the temple of Artemis in Ephesus, which lasted 400 years. It is aromatic, takes a good polish (making it favoured by cabinetmakers), grows with a straight grain, and is easy to work.

Perhaps the most famous trading relationship in history was built around a deal between King Solomon and Hiram of Tyre, his neighbour, for the latter to provide Solomon with cedar wood for the building of the Second Temple in Jerusalem (amply documented in 2 Chronicles 11.3) around 520 BC.

The desirability of this raw material in a region not well supplied with wood was not unrelated to the repeated conquests of Lebanon by neighbouring powers (Bealsz, 1965; Hitti, 1967; Meiggs, 1982; Miksell, 1969; Rowton, 1967). Cedar wood was traded by ship because of the dangers involved in land-based routes and, more recently, cedar timbers were used to construct the first Muslim fleet at Acre and Tyre in AD 645, with the forests exploited throughout the Crusades. Druze villages used cedar wood for domestic purposes until recently, contributing to the deforestation of Lebanon. Unlike pine, cedar is delicate and slow growing and although it seems probable that ancient woodsmen practised sustainable cutting, continually increasing demand during the last millennium, combined with slow growth and deforestation, has reduced the once-magnificent forests to the few small remnants which can be seen today.

Even in remote antiquity the cedar groves of Lebanon were controlled by laws and directives intended both to control the lumber trade and maximise profits. Today's controls are very different but the motive is curiously similar. Stands of cedar trees are found at a number of locations in Lebanon, with the largest at the Cedars of Chouf Reserve, in the Jabal el Barouk mountains, whose eastern flank slopes to the Bekaa valley. However, the best known and most visited cedars are in the area around the beautiful Qadisha valley in north Lebanon, near the town of Becharre, the centre of Lebanon's ski industry. These two cedars forest remnants are the only stands accessible to tourists, but the vast majority of visitors gain their impressions of Lebanese cedars from Becharre, not Chouf, which is perceived by tour operators to be too near the Israeli border (and in Druze country) for comfort.

The Becharre Cedars

In 1998 the Becharre cedars entered the World Heritage list as '*Ouadi Qadisha (the Holy Valley) and the Forest of the Cedars of God (Horsh Arz el-Rab)* under criteria C(iii)(iv). However, protection for the Becharre grove started much earlier, during the reign of the Roman emperor Hadrian, when the great cedar forests of

Lebanon were already much diminished in area. Hadrian had the boundaries of the imperial forests marked by stones bearing inscriptions (two of which are on display in the museum of the American University of Beirut).

In the post-Roman period, the cedars were used as domestic fuel and for lime-burning kilns, and there was extensive medieval cedar forest clearance. This was extended in the 19th century under the Ottoman Empire and completed during World War II by British troops, who used cedarwood to build the railway between Tripoli and Haifa. In 1550, Becharre had 28 trees over 1000 years old, in 1660 there were 22, and in 1696 only 16. Today there are supposed to be 12, but current forest literature mentions only four. Miksell (1969) notes that at the end of the 17th century a total of 400 trees stood within the grove, which was enclosed by a stone wall in 1876 to protect young cedar saplings from grazing by goats. More recently, in 1985, the Committee of the Friends of the Cedars was formed to deal with damage and disease in the grove, using modern woodland management techniques (Tourism Development Council of Becharre, 2000).

Occasionally, visitor access to the grove is restricted in winter when snow is melting to restrict root damage. The Becharre cedars, or *Horsh Arz el Rab* (Cedars of God) include many trees of a great age in a walled grove set anomalously outside a ski resort at the foot of a mountain slope, that was once terraced but is now heavily eroded and over-grazed by herds of goats. A few straggler trees are to be found outside the wall, but from the top of the pass the small size of the grove and its isolation within a desolate, treeless landscape is quite striking. The isolation of the grove emphasises the fragility of Lebanon's cedar forests, and the immense environmental changes that have taken place in this area during the last two millennia.

The Becharre grove includes about 375 cedars of great age; four are thought to be over 1500 years old and have reached heights of 35m, with trunks between 12 and14m around. The trees are impressive, with straight trunks and flat, fanlike, horizontal branches. The grove does include many young trees that are planted to gradually replenish it, but cedar is slow growing and a tree needs to be at least 40 before it can produce fertile seed. Becharre problems include insect damage and tree decay, combined with an absence of vital bird species. The high density of trees means competition for food, light and water. Graffiti, lichen, soil erosion, seedling grazing by goats, lightning strikes and soil impoverishment are all being researched by the 'Friends of the Cedars' committee, and a nursery for a new 200 hectare forest has been started to 'transform the cedarstand into an eco-museum' (Masri, 1995: 8).

Although precise statistics are not kept, the grove received approximately 200,000 visitors in 2000 (20% of total visitors to Lebanon) and visitor numbers are increasing yearly. It is accessed immediately from the main road via a smart new entry / exit post, policed by members of the Committee of Friends of the Cedars, who ask for a voluntary donation on entry. This is a new policy, replacing a previously compulsory admission charge. For the visitor, the grove presents a curiously unreal experience. In order to protect the trees, on arrival they are warned to stick to marked paths, and not to drink, eat, smoke or leave litter. Some 3km of paths have been laid out through the 102 hectare enclosed area, marked by a post every few metres with two hemp ropes between, in an attempt to give a natural look. The paths are sandy, and covered with cedar needles, but the resulting effect is not friendly, giving visitors the impression that both they and the trees are fiercely regimented. Paths within the grove are unsuitable for the elderly or disabled, or for small children, and the grove is afflicted with incessant Middle Eastern pop music emanating from the lively complex of souvenir shops and cafes which has sprung up near its entrance. The effect produced is not of a well-preserved forest grove but of a sterile tree museum. While forest management techniques are much in evidence, the environment, far from giving the visitor a taste of what it would have been like in the original ancient forests, conveys the impression of an over-managed botanical garden. The grove has preserved the trees, but without their spirit of place.

Chouf Cedar Reserve

The Chouf mountains of central south Lebanon can be reached within a one to two hour drive of Beirut. The steep, hilly region is being rapidly urbanised after its agricultural base was diminished as a result of forced displacement and internal migration during the civil war 1975–1991. The Chouf is Druze country, and the Chouf Cedar Reserve (as well as many other projects) is an initiative of Walid Jumblatt, the Druze leader, who maintained a policy of intensive tree planting and forest guard supervision even during the war. The area that is now the Chouf Reserve was once intensively grazed by goats, and was also subject to commercial cedar cutting which continued until 1960, when the Lebanese forestry department began reforestation. Terraces were created and cedars planted around the remains of the ancient forest, including a core 52 hectares in the Ain Zhalta region, which was heavily damaged during Israeli army occupation by shrapnel, arson and permanent habitat destruction arising from intense compaction by heavy machinery and road construction.

In July 1996, the Cedars of Chouf were designated as a Natural Reserve, not only for protection but also to create new employment opportunities and promote nature-based tourism. The Chouf Cedar Society was formed in 1994 to manage the Reserve, which covers 5% of the entire country with a total area of 50,000 hectares, surrounded by a 500m wide buffer zone. It borders on nine villages with a population of 50,000 and whose municipal lands lie within the jurisdiction of the reserve (Al Chouf Cedar Society, 2001). As is common in Lebanon, the villages are scruffy and polluted, piles of rubbish lie in corners and on the roadside, local pine trees have had all accessible branches removed for firewood and there is a pervasive smell of sewage. In such a context, the pristine Reserve comes as something of a surprise.

The Reserve's management team, with Walid Jumblatt as President, operates under the auspices of the Protected Areas project of the Ministry of the Environment, in collaboration with the United Nations Development Programme and the World Conservation Union (IUCN), with financial backing from the Global Environment Facility. Visitor revenue assists in fund generation, as does the excellent shop and visitor centre maintained by the Society, which sells not only small pre-potted cedar trees (each with a certificate of authenticity) but also local produce, honey, preserves and herbs and many cedar-based products. Presentation and product standards are professional, giving the impression of a contemporary, sustainable organisation complemented by a good website (http://www.shoufcedar.org). In addition, the Reserve is actively forming partnerships with oversees institutions and universities to expand its research base, and has developed a Research and Monitoring centre at nearby Moukhtara. Cedars need more research because they are suffering from air and water pollution, the effects of soil erosion, plant pathologies including fungal diseases whose control is critical in regeneration and reforestation projects. The sheer size of the Reserve, its strategic location in the heart of Lebanon, and the biological diversity of its different ecosystems make it of great significance. It includes six cedar forests, the three most significant being Barouk (400 hectares), Maasar al Shouf (six hectares) and Ain Zhalta (100 hectares). Of these, the last is most visited. It boasts the highest self-regenerating stand of cedars in Lebanon, as well as 200 species of birds and 26 of mammals (six of which are on the IUCN Red List) including porcupine, wolf, caracal lynx and mountain gazelle. Although there are some cultural sites within the reserve boundaries, including a shrine and relics of Prophet Ayoub (Job) and the Druze Sha'wane, the area has nothing like the cultural significance of the Qadisha valley.

On a clear day, visitors to the Chouf Reserve can see Cyprus, but visitation is seasonal (as it is in Becharre) and in winter the Reserve is blanketed in 10m of snow. In 2000 about 30,000 people visited the Chouf Cedar Reserve, an increase over the 20,000 who came in 1999. On weekdays, an average of 30 visitors, accompanied by a guide, walk through the forest and observe both old growth and newly planted trees. No unaccompanied visiting or camping is permitted. Visitors are shown the results of vandalism by the Israeli army, including burnt trees, and have a chance of spotting some of the Reserve's unusual wildlife. Admission costs £L10,000 (£L,5000 if vehicle transport not required)[1] and the reserve employs around 25 people. Landscapes are spectacular, high mist-clad slopes of perfect quietness that are curiously timeless. Indeed, one would not be surprised to see King Hiram's lumberjacks coming round the corner to cut trees for Solomon's temple. The quietness and beauty of the Reserve is in marked contrast to the frenetic activity of Beirut and the noisy commoditisation of Becharre. Future plans for the Chouf Reserve include only such compatible activities as trekking, riding and cycling routes, with ski touring in the winter, and themed walks based on such topics as astronomy and local mammals.

Comment and Conclusion

Although it is included within the same World Heritage cultural landscape, the Becharre Cedar Reserve is at the apex of the 50km long Qadisha valley, a long way from the spectacular Christian Maronite monasteries and hermit caves of the lower reaches of the deep gorge. The cedars are associated with this landscape not only geographically but also psychologically, and the cedar is perceived as sacred, largely because of frequent references to it in the Bible. Today, despite the geographical proximity, there is really no other relationship between the sites of the lower Qadisha valley and the Becharre Reserve. It is difficult to see what positive effect World Heritage designation has had on the Qadisha valley, except bringing it to the attention of cultural tour operators to engender a new and more positive vision of Lebanon. However, local people claim that there are discernible improvements in the quality of the Qadisha environment, including better controls over building and garbage, but this is certainly not discernible to the casual visitor. Sewage is still pumped into the river from the villages, but a new waste-water treatment plan has been devised which is being operated in parallel with environmental regulations such as access and hunting restrictions.

There is a marked contrast between the artificial environment of the Becharre cedars, under World Heritage protection, and the mountaintop of the Chouf Cedar Reserve that is a designated Nature Reserve. Both are protected areas, but they protect and display their included cedars in very different ways. Although the Chouf Reserve does not contain such grand trees, it has preserved them in a real mountain forest environment, whereas the Becharre cedars are an isolated pocket, a mere appendage to a ski resort. In the Chouf, the Visitor Centre sells carefully chosen and sustainably packaged high quality local produce. By contrast, the roadside stalls in Becharre sell a wide variety of cedar kitsch, some of it religious with engraved verses from the Psalms that mention the cedars, but most are poorly made and some are not even of cedar. At Becharre, the cedars have become commoditised outside the grove, even if not inside. As a national monument, it is a great disappointment, reducing the cedar icon and national symbol to a mess of cheap souvenirs.

Quite the opposite image is presented at Chouf, where young, keen student guides are anxious to show visitors the wonders of their forest, the new trees, the new walking and bike trails, and the wonderful views. While Chouf displays an acceptable (if over-optimistic) view of the Lebanon of the future, Becharre presents a fossilised and commoditised version of its past.

Correspondence

Any correspondence should be directed to Myra Shackley at the Centre for Tourism and Visitor Management, Nottingham Trent University, Burton Street, Nottingham NG1 4BU, UK (myra.shackley@ntu.ac.uk).

Note

1. At the time of writing (mid-January 2004) UK £1.00 = £ Lebanese 2800

References

Al Chouf Cedar Society (2001) *Al-Shouf Cedar Reserve.* Beirut: Al Chouf Cedar Society.
Bealsz, E.W. (1965) The remnant cedar forests of Lebanon. *Journal of Ecology* 53, 27–36.
Berriane, M.(1997) *Tourisme, Culture et Développement dans la Région Arabe.* Rabat: UNESCO.
Harden, D. (1963) *The Phoenicians.* New York: Prager.
Hitti, P.K. (1967) *Lebanon in History.* London: Macmillan.
Masri, R. (1995) The cedars of Lebanon: Significance, awareness and management of the *Cedrus Libani* in Lebanon. Text of a lecture, on WWW at http://almashriq.hiof.no/lebanon/300/360/363/363.7/trasncript.html) Accessed 05.07.01.
Meiggs, R.(1982) *Trees and Timber in the Ancient Mediterranean.* Oxford: Clarendon.
Miksell, M. (1969) The deforestation of Mt Lebanon. *Geographical Review* 59 (1), 13.
Ministry of Tourism (2001) Tourist arrivals by nationality. Unpublished statistics. Ministry of Tourism, Beirut.
Pearce, D. and Mourator, S.(1998) *Economic and Financial Analysis for Cultural Heritage Projects.* London: Centre for Social and Economic Research on the Global Environment (CSEGE), University College, London.
Rowton, M.B. (1967) The woodlands of ancient western Asia. *Journal of Near Eastern Studies* 26, 5–19.

Thomas, K. (2001) Palestinian crisis and Lebanon cruise season. *Middle East Travel* (September/October), 6

Tourism Development Council of Becharre (2000) *Tourism in the Besharre region - the Cedars*. Becharre: Tourism Development Council of Becharre.

World Bank (2001) *Cultural Heritage and Development: A Framework for Action in the Middle East and North Africa*. Orientations in Development Series Reports. Washington: World Bank.

Commentary
Including the Outsiders: The Contribution of Guides to Integrated Heritage Tourism Management in Cusco, Southern Peru

Gemma McGrath
The University of the Arts, London College of Communication

Over the last decade many archaeological sites in Peru have become important tourist attractions. However, despite the growth in tourism, visitor management and interpretation at the sites are limited and, at times, non-existent. The mainstay of interpretative supply in Peru is the tour guide, and three types of guide were identified in this research: those with university degrees, others with vocational training, and untrained 'local guides' from the local indigenous population living near the archaeological sites. All three types of guide were present at the Cusco region case study sites of Raqchi and Ollantaytambo. Recommendations focus on ways that local guides could be brought into the tourist system to enable their participation, both economic and social, in the tourism developing on their doorstep.

Keywords: tour guides, heritage tourism, visitor management, Cusco, Peru

Introduction

One of the aims of the research was to assess the level of integration at national, regional, and local level between archaeology and tourism within Peru. It also aimed to explore the extent to which the tour guide could be a bridge between the site, the local people and the visitor. It was found, to a large extent, that the quality of this bridge depended on the training provided to guides. The research was undertaken in two phases between the years 2000 and 2001. Phase 1 used Raqchi as a case study area, while Phase 2 focused on the site of Ollantaytambo. Both are Inca sites and both are now established on the Cusco tourist circuit. As Figure 1 shows, Raqchi is on the road to Bolivia and Ollantaytambo is in the Sacred Valley of the Incas.

Peru

Since the time of the sun-worshipping Incas, the land of gold has fuelled the imagination of Europeans (Jenkins, 2000). This vast country still holds tremendous fascination as Peru has truly spectacular landscapes across three distinct and contrasting environments: an immense desert coastline, vast tracks of tropical rainforest, and the Andes. There are also three main ethnic groups in Peru. The first are Indian, living primarily in the highlands, but also found in the jungle. The second group is the *mestizo* population (the result of the mix between Peru's native population and the Spanish and other Europeans), found in different geographical environments, but mainly in the urban centres. The third main ethnic group is the black population, which is mainly found in the coastal areas of the country. There is also a very small white population, again, mainly resident

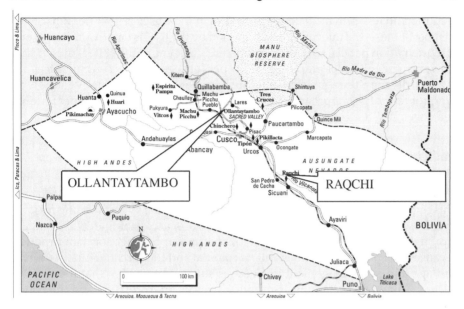

Figure 1 Map of Cusco Region, Peru
Source: Jenkins, D. (2000) *The Rough Guide to Peru*, p. 105. This map is extracted, with permission, from *The Rough Guide to Peru*.

in the urban centres. This ethnic variety contributes to the country's 'human heritage' which is of interest to the visitor.

Tourism in Peru

In 1970, Peru received 133,546 international visitors. As a result of economic and political turmoil, there were significant troughs in the 1980s and early 1990s, but over the past decade there has been a steady increase in arrivals. In 1994, a sharp increase to 386,120 was recorded and was largely attributed to the improved economic conditions brought about by the capture of Guzman, the head of the Maoist terrorist group, the Shining Path (Pacific Consultants International, 1999). By 2000, the one million target was achieved, two years ahead of schedule. Most visitors are in the ABC socioeconomic categories, permanently residing mainly in North America, Germany, France, Spain, United Kingdom, Israel, Argentina, Chile and Brazil.

Until 2003, tourism in Peru was under the jurisdiction of the Ministry of Tourism, Industry and International Commerce (MITINCI). In 2003, in order to denote the new importance now afforded to tourism in Peru, the Ministry of Foreign Trade and Tourism (MINCETUR) was formed, enabling greater attention to be given to tourism.

Archaeology in Peru

Because of the Inca culture and its empire (along with the remains of many of its lesser known pre-Inca cultures), Peru has more archaeological sites than any other South American country. The INC (Instituto Nacional de Cultural) has identified no fewer than 36,000 known sites in the Cusco region (Jenkins, 2000). At most of these, the interpretation provided by the INC is largely limited to map and orientation panels, with on-site museums at some of the better-known sites. However, the INC does employ gate-keepers at sites to collect entrance fees and as a security measure against looters. Such low levels of interpretative supply are symptomatic of the approach to heritage tourism planning commonly found in less developed areas (Hall & McArthur, 1996; Pond, 1993).

Heritage Tourism Management in Cusco

The city of Cusco, known to the Incas as the 'navel of the world', was their imperial capital and the most important place of pilgrimage in South America. This remains the case for contemporary tourists, and the overwhelming majority of visitors to Peru go to Cusco because it is the most accessible gateway to Machu Picchu. It also offers visitors a wealth of spectacular heritage tourism products, because of its natural resources and its colonial and Inca architecture. However, heritage tourism management in Cusco is still 'traditional' in that it prioritises the archaeological site and its excavation over its interpretation and the people involved in it, be they locals or visitors.

Two key factors, in particular, have determined the lack of development of the archaeological sites and their failure to cope with visitor numbers. One is the structure and the other is the culture of both the INC and MITINCI. The central-ised structure of these organisations, and their respective cultures of traditional resource management, constrain responsiveness to, and the inclusion of, site stakeholders.

By contrast, there is much to be said for focusing on the context of archaeologi-cal sites. As Hall and McArthur indicate, a modern approach to heritage tourism management allows tourism to work in the interests of conservation:

> When visitors have a satisfying experience they come closer to supporting the philosophy of the site's management. The more visitors support management, the easier it becomes to manage heritage. (Hall & McArthur, 1996: 4)

When visitors and local communities are placed at the centre of the tourism expe-rience, the virtuous circle described above can become a possibility.

Raqchi and Ollantaytambo

The village of Raqchi, with some 80 households, was the Inca ritual centre and a pilgrimage site dedicated to Viracocha, their creator god. Today, its residents make a precarious living producing pottery during the dry season and working in agriculture on their limited land during the wet season. In addition, local guides take visitors on tours of the site.

The Institute of Archaeology at University College London has run its Raqchi project over the last six years, and its aim is to facilitate better under-standing of the Andean way of life to visitors, largely through improved inter-pretation. In 2001, with the Institute's cooperation, 12 tour guides were interviewed. Most expressed a need for further training to improve their tour guiding of the site, and identified constraints on their access to formal training in Cusco.

According to Jenkins (2000: 146), legend has it:

> ... that Ollantay was a rebel Inca general who took arms against Pachacutec over the affections of the Lord Inca's daughter, and the town of Ollantay-tambo is unique in that it maintains its original Inca trapezoidal shape.

The archaeological site itself is an impressive fortress cut out of the mountain-side. As a strategic protection for the entrance to the Urubamba Valley, it was successful in that it is said to be the only stronghold in the region to have resisted persistent attacks by the Spanish.

Ollantaytambo has been on the tourist circuit for much longer than Raqchi, and is a destination on a package offered to visitors, involving a day trip to the Sacred Valley of the Incas, which also takes in Chinchero and Pisac on market days. At Ollantaytambo, tourism development, and awareness of its importance among local residents, is more marked than in Raqchi. Local guides are better established, and accommodation and restaurant facilities more widespread. Improvements have also been made in the quality of interpretative media available at the refurbished museum, a project developed for the community that is also open to tourists, although visitor levels have been low. In part, this is due to the fact that most visitors arrive as part of a day-trip to the Sacred Valley, which runs to an already-tight schedule.

The Role of the Guide

Like other service 'products', tour guiding is characterised by inseparability, intangibility, variability and labour intensity (Booms & Bitner, 1980). This makes every encounter with visitors 'live', unpredictable and a new challenge, even though the terrain will be well-trodden by the guide.

According to Cohen (1985), one of the key roles of the guide is to be a 'mediator' between the destination and the visitor, and a high level of interpretative skill is needed for a destination to become intelligible to visitors. Cohen talks of interpretation in its literal form, building on Tilden's principles (1957) in a manner which emphasises that the language and narrative of the destination need to be converted by the guide, whose task is ' . . . the translation of the strangeness of a foreign culture into a cultural-idiom familiar to the visitor' (Cohen, 1985: 10).

Key words here are 'foreign' and 'familiar', and the guide must move visitors from the foreign to the familiar by bringing the place to life in a way that is interesting and that makes sense to the visitor. To achieve such intelligibility, which is especially important for destinations that differ significantly from the visitor's country of origin, ' . . . interpretation, and not mere dissemination of information, is the distinguishing communicative function of the trained tourist guide' (Cohen, 1985: 15).

Another key word here is 'trained', as the quality of interpretation may depend considerably on different types of guide and the training they have received. However, as the following section indicates, how guides are trained in Cusco varies considerably.

Types of Guide and Training Routes

In the Cusco region, the title *guía* (guide) is used quite loosely, and may refer to a university graduate who is an Inca history specialist, or an untrained adventure guide who knows the terrain and can offer visitors safety, guidance and companionship on treks or rafting. This latter type is Cohen's 'pathfinder', whereas he would classify the former as a 'mentor' guide (Cohen, 1985).

In fact, many of the problems reported to the Ministry of Tourism about poor guiding apparently occur when agencies use non-specialist guides, the pathfinders, to take tourists rafting in the morning and sightseeing in the afternoon. Whereas the guide may provide excellent service during the first part of the day, he may fail to deliver appropriate guiding in the second part of the day, an indication that, in the second context, the wrong type of guide has perhaps been employed. In fact, it is not uncommon for 'pathfinder' guides to be used when 'mentor' guides with specialist knowledge are really required, and research revealed that the drive to reduce costs has increased in Cusco as more travel agencies compete for business. As a result, the visitor experience and service quality becomes compromised.

'Official guides' have usually trained in Cusco, taking a degree in archaeology or tourism at the university, or following a more vocational course in tourism for guiding at a college. From interviews held during this research with guides with both types of training, it was clear that there is a perceived hierarchy about the different training routes. College guides believed that the academic background of university guides was inappropriate to achieve proficiency in such areas as group management, communication skills and visitor orientation. For their part, university guides felt that college guides were inadequately trained in culture, history, archaeology and architecture of the region. In short, the two formal training routes for those wishing to pursue careers as guides focus on separate but key components needed for the professional guide's role.

A third type of guide is known as *guía* local, or local guide, to differentiate them from *guía* official (the official guides). Local guides usually live near sites that are tourist attractions and provide guiding services to independent tourists who have not arrived with their own guide. They have not usually received any formal training. Instead, their information is derived from myth and legend passed down from the locality and from watching official guides at work. In addition, local guides are from the indigenous population, while official guides are usually from the *mestizo* population of the country.

At Raqchi and Ollantaytambo, local guides tout for tourists to make extra income and to participate in tourism on their doorstep. Sometimes they will be hired by official guides to provide extra information about the place but also to add 'local colour'. As van den Berghe notes,

> In ethnic tourism, the native is not merely 'there' to provide services, he is an integral part of the exotic spectacle, an actor whose 'quaint' behaviour, dress and artefacts are themselves significant attractions. (van den Berghe, 1980: 338)

In this way, official and local guides do work together, but overt power relations come into play in such encounters.

The different routes to the profession of guiding in Peru may be an influencing factor on the variability in service provision. Through visitor–guide encounters, demand meets supply in a very local and concrete way and, as such, expectations may either be met or thwarted by the experience.

Conclusion

The lack of integration between the INC and the MITINCI is a major weakness in the overall development of tourism management in Peru and leads to a lack of 'internal marketing' in Peru's heritage tourism strategy. Currently, the provision of guides in the Cusco region is unreliable. There are star performers, but some guides are quite deficient in the skills and basic facts required for competent guiding. Clearly, there are good arguments for adopting a modern integrated approach to heritage management. The use of local guides, trained to some degree to work independently or to complement the work of the official guides, can facilitate tourism's positive impacts, and would be one way of redistributing income to poorer areas. And the inclusion of those currently at the periphery of the tourism industry, such as these local guides, would provide a sustainable solution to some of the current problems identified in the research undertaken.

More specifically, if those living in the rural areas of Cusco region cannot afford to go to the urban centres where guide training is provided, it should be delivered in the rural areas. This could be through workshops, which would introduce the wider aspects of tourism to those already working with tourists, for example, as guides, souvenir sellers, or accommodation providers, but who themselves have yet to be tourists (Blanton, 1981). Such a process would also go some way to include those currently excluded from the existing tourism system. By gaining a deeper understanding of the nature of the tourism industry and the motives of tourists, local communities would thus be empowered to participate more efficiently and profitably in tourism, which would then become a more appropriate development option for them.

Correspondence

Any correspondence should be directed to Gemma McGrath, The University of the Arts, London College of Communication, School of Marketing, London SE1 5SB (g.mcgrath@lcc.arts.ac.uk).

Acknowledgements

The author would like to thank Bill Sillar at the Institute of Archaeology for his collaboration in this research, the Anglo-Peruvian Society for its financial support, and all those people in Peru who gave their time to help with the first stage of the project.

References

Blanton, D. (1981) Tourism training in developing countries: The social and cultural dimension. *Annals of Tourism Research* 8 (1), 116–33.
Booms, B. and Bitner, M. (1980) New management tools for the successful tourism manager. *Annals of Tourism Research* 7 (3), 337–52.

Cohen, E. (1985) The tourist guide: The origins, structure, and dynamics of a role. *Annals of Tourism Research* 12, 5–29.

Hall, C.M. and McArthur, S. (1996) *Heritage Management in Australia: The Human Dimension*. Oxford: Oxford University Press.

Jenkins, D. (2000) *The Rough Guide to Peru*. London: Rough Guides, Penguin.

MITINCI and Pacific Consultants International (1999) *Peru Master Plan*. Tokyo: Pacific Consultants International.

Pond, K. (1993) *The Professional Guide: Dynamics of Tour Guiding*. New York: Van Nostrand Reinhold.

Tilden, F. (1957) *Interpreting our Heritage*. Chapel Hill: University of North Carolina Press.

van den Berghe, P. (1980) Tourism as Ethnic Relations. *Ethnic and Racial Studies* 3, 375–92.

Commentary
Locating Global Legacies in Tana Toraja, Indonesia

Kathleen M. Adams
Loyola University, Chicago

In 2001, the picturesque Toraja village of Ke´te´ Kesu´ was nominated for candidacy as
a UNESCO World Heritage Site. Situated in the South Sulawesi highlands in Indonesia, this hamlet is home to rice farmers, wood carvers, tourist vendors, government
workers and sporadically-visiting anthropologists. Drawing on long-term anthropological field research in the village, I suggest that while world heritage sites may entail
what UNESCO terms *'genius loci'*, they are, rarely the unchanging embodiments of
tradition they are imagined to be. The paper illustrates how heritage landscapes such as
Ke'te' Kesu' are, to some extent, products of local responses and and engagements with
regional, national and global political, cultural and economic dynamics. Ultimately, I
argue that the emergence of UNESCO world heritage sites is not a 'natural' process, but
rather one borne out of complex exchanges, competitions and collaborations between
local groups, as well as national and international entities.

Keywords: UNESCO, World Heritage Site, Toraja, Indonesia

In early 2001, the picturesque Sa'dan Toraja village of Ke´te´ Kesu´ was nominated for candidacy as a UNESCO World Heritage Site. Situated in the highlands
of South Sulawesi, Indonesia, this hamlet is home to rice farmers, wood carvers,
tourist vendors, government workers and periodic visiting anthropologists.
When I first learned of this nomination I, too, shared in the jubilation of Ke´te´
Kesu´'s inhabitants. In the mid-1980s, while conducting dissertation research on
tourism, ethnic and artistic change in Tana Toraja, I resided in this highland
village for several years. In subsequent years I have regularly returned to Ke´te´
Kesu´ to visit Toraja friends and update my research. These years of research
experience in Ke´te´ Kesu´ have rendered me an emphatic supporter of the
hamlet's inclusion on the list of World Heritage Sites, as it is clearly a striking
landscape upon which ancestral memories have been inscribed and enacted. As I
deepened my inquiries into the candidacy and its ramifications, however, it
became increasingly clear that UNESCO's underlying notions concerning World
Heritage Sites embodied certain assumptions that often contrast markedly with
the actualities of the sites in question.[1]

Central to UNESCO language about heritage sites are notions concerning
preservation and assumptions that these 'traditional' sites are at risk of being
assaulted by contemporary influences. Drawing on the case of Ke´te´ Kesu´ as
illustration, I argue that the so-called 'heritage landscapes' UNESCO strives to
preserve from transformative external forces frequently are products of local
responses to and engagements with regional, national, and global political,
cultural and economic dynamics. That is, many of UNESCO's heritage sites are
hardly the unchanging embodiments of tradition they are imagined to be. In fact,
it may well be that it is precisely this history of (over-looked) discourse with the

wider world that enables World Heritage Sites to gain UNESCO attention and pre-eminence. In short, drawing on the case of Ke'te' Kesu', I suggest that the emergence of heritage sites is not a 'natural' process, but rather one borne out of complex exchanges, competitions, and collaborations between local groups, as well as national and international entities.

In examining the Toraja case, I wish to underscore that the ancestral houses (known as *tongkonan*) that comprise the village of Ke'te' Kesu' embody an unrivalled richness of indigenous ideas concerning heritage, ancestry, and mythic history (cf. Adams, 1998; Nooy-Palm, 1979, 1986; Waterson, 1995). However, the hamlet itself is also very much a product of the Dutch colonial past. Moreover, in the course of its evolution over the past century, Ke'te' Kesu' has been shaped by other processes and institutions that stretch far beyond the local. While local actors and rivalries between local elites are salient to understanding Ke'te Kesu''s trajectory to candidacy as a World Heritage site, a more informed analysis requires situating this particular cultural landscape into a larger national and global context.

As I chronicle in a recent article (Adams, 2003), the physical layout of the hamlet of Ke'te' Kesu' was born out of the colonial process. At the turn of the last century, the four ancestral houses that comprise the heart of the village were scattered on various peaks, miles from the current site. With the arrival of Dutch colonial forces in 1906, the advantages of concentrating ancestral houses near Dutch colonial headquarters were clear to the aristocratic founder of Ke'te' Kesu'. By 1927, this founder had relocated these scattered houses to their current site, thereby ensuring the longevity of the Kesu' name in the new Dutch era. By the mid-20th century, Indonesian national independence threatened to erase the prominence of the Kesu' name, as local districts were reshaped and renamed by new government bureaucrats. This threat of administrative erasure of the Kesu' name prompted Kesu' elites to search for alternative means to ensure the continued prestige of their heritage. International tourism and foreign and domestic social science researchers became avenues for Ke'te' Kesu''s survival. In a similar vein, as Kesu'ers gained in experience outside the region, the western institutions of museums and libraries were embraced as supplementary avenues for fortifying Kesu' heritage (see Adams, 1995). Finally, as the Asian economic crisis reached Tana Toraja and Indonesian political stability eroded in the late 1990s, Kesu'ers explored new non-touristic avenues to promote their economic survival and simultaneously their heritage: through marketing modern utilitarian wooden objects embellished with carved Toraja motifs nationally and internationally, Kesu'ers' livelihood and involvement in producing traditional symbols was assured. In short, while certainly a '*genius loci*', Ke'te' Kesu' is not the static and unchanging embodiment of tradition imagined by UNESCO.

Rather, Ke'te' Kesu' is the product of a long interplay between the local, the national and the global. Likewise, Ke'te' Kesu'ers are reshaping and rethinking their notions about heritage, as they encounter multiple forces from within, around, and beyond the nation. Examining Ke'te' Kesu''s ascendance to candidacy as a World Heritage site offers insights into the process of cultural objectification, as we come to better appreciate the complex roles of local and international players in promoting this dynamic locale. I believe that the Ke'te' Kesu''s story is not a unique tale in the annals of UNESCO World Heritage sites.

Rather, it would seem that most locales that successfully gain candidacy for UNESCO World Heritage site status are places that have undergone similar trajectories, where local, national and international forces have conspired, wittingly and unwittingly, to project these 'endangered' sites onto the global stage.

Correspondence

Any correspondence should be directed to Kathleen Adams at Loyola University, Chicago (kadams@luc.edu).

Notes

1. This disjuncture is the focus of a longer research paper published in *Indonesia and the Malay World* (Adams, 2003).

References

Adams, K.M. (1995) Making-up the Toraja? The appropriation of tourism, anthropology, and museums for politics in Upland Sulawesi, Indonesia. *Ethnology* 34 (4), 143–53.

Adams, K.M. (1998) More than an ethnic marker: Toraja art as identity negotiator. *American Ethnologist* 25 (3), 327–51.

Adams, K. M. (2003) The politics of heritage in Tana Toraja, Indonesia: Interplaying the local and the global. *Indonesia and the Malay World* 89 (31), 91–107.

Nooy-Palm, C.H.M. (1979) *The Sa'dan Toraja: A Study of their Social Life and Religion* (vol. 1). The Hague: Martinnus Nijhoff.

Nooy-Palm, C.H.M. (1986) *The Sa'dan Toraja: A Study of their Social Life and Religion* (vol. 2). *Rituals of the East and West*. Dordrecht, Holland and Cinnaminson, USA: Foris.

Waterson, R. (1995) Houses and hierarchies in island Southeast Asia. In J. Carsten and S. Hugh-Jones (eds) *About the House: Levi-Strauss and Beyond* (pp. 47–68). Cambridge: Cambridge University Press.

Commentary
Global Heritage and Local Problems: Some Examples from Indonesia

Geoffrey Wall and Heather Black
Faculty of Environmental Studies, University of Waterloo, Canada

This article examines what happens to those who live in and around monuments as a result of World Heritage designation. Using the examples of Borobudur and Prambanan in Indonesia as study sites, it is argued that the values that local people attach to heritage are often different from, although not necessarily less important than, the values ascribed by international agencies, government officials, tourism developers and others. However, their perspectives are often not adequately represented or respected by other participants in the planning and management of sites, to the detriment of both the plans and the people. The tendency to adopt top-down, rational comprehensive planning procedures has resulted in the disenfranchisement of local people, giving greater prominence to expressions of national, 'official' culture and nationalism at the expense of local culture. It has tended to freeze sites and displace human activities, effectively excluding local people from their own heritage.

Keywords: world heritage, Indonesia

Introduction

World Heritage sites constitute extreme examples of global–local interactions and the stakeholders involved in their selection, designation, planning and management are many and varied. They involve the United Nations, governmental organisations at all levels from global to local, and residents who live in and around the sites. They are visited by international and domestic tourists, and attract entrepreneurs, again both international and local, that cater to their needs. These stakeholders are involved in World Heritage sites in different roles and for varied reasons and they are impacted by heritage designation in different ways. They ascribe different values to the sites and have differential access to power over the management of the sites as well as over their own relationships to the sites.

The above situations prompt numerous important questions. They include: Whose heritage is at stake? Who owns culture? How should heritage sites and their surroundings be planned? Whose interests should receive priority in the planning process? What trade-offs are acceptable when conservation, authenticity, tourism promotion and economic development are involved? And what are the needs, opportunities and rights of local people living in and around the heritage places?

This commentary focuses on the last question and is concerned with what happens to those who live in the shadows of monumental sites when they are accorded World Heritage status. It is argued that the values local people attach to heritage are often different from, although not necessarily less important than, the values ascribed by art historians, archaeologists, government officials, tourism developers and others. However, their perspectives are often not adequately represented or respected by other participants in the planning and management of sites, to the detriment of both the plans and the people.

Study Sites

The empirical part of this research focuses on two sites in Indonesia. The characteristics of Indonesia are pertinent to the investigation. First, Indonesia is a developing country that has experienced many economic and political challenges in recent years. Secondly, it is a fragmented country. Not only is it an archipelago of over 1500 islands, but also it exhibits great cultural diversity, so much so that forging a coherent national identity has been an ongoing concern and 'Unity in diversity' is the national slogan.

Two sites were selected as the objects of investigation: Borobudur and Prambaban. Both are located near and to the north of the city of Yogyakarta. Both are magnificent monuments and UNESCO World Heritage sites. The former is a magnificent stupa, probably dating from the 8th century, and is often called the largest Buddhist monument in the world. Prambaban was completed in AD 856 and consists of more than 50 temple sites of predominantly Hindu, but also some Buddhist, origins. Both sites have been extensively restored, a process still in progress, particularly at Prambanan.

Formal designation as a World Heritage site requires the preparation and international acceptance of a plan. Master plans were drafted in 1974 and implemented over the following decade. A major consequence is that both sites have become archaeological parks and, in this process, many local people have been displaced. Both sites are important destinations for domestic and international tourists.

The religious contexts are worthy of note. Three of the world's great religions are represented here, for these Buddhist and Hindu relics are found in what is now the largest Moslem country in the world. Furthermore, the beliefs of many local residents incorporate aspects of ancestor worship and animism.

Methods

Plans for the sites were reviewed and the extent of their implementation was assessed through on-site observation. Interviews were conducted with three types of respondents: key actors who had been involved in the planning process, local people in and around the sites, and individuals who had been displaced by the creation of the archaeological parks. Further information on the research procedures is available in Black (1997).

Results

Space does not permit the detailed presentation of all of the results of the studies. Rather, a number of the highlights will be presented briefly. Although events in Borobudur occurred prior to those in Prambanan, and there is evidence that lessons learned at the first site were applied at the second, no attempt will be made here to distinguish the processes applied in the two sites.

The archaeological parks have been implemented successfully, the monuments are well protected, conservation efforts are ongoing and, at least until the onset of the Asian economic crisis and political turmoil in Indonesia disrupted tourism flows, there has been substantial growth in tourism. However, it is argued that outside the parks plans have been less successful. Indeed, the master plan was prepared without the knowledge or input of local people. Later, land was expropriated from those living within what became the archaeological park, resettlement areas were prepared, and people were forced to move.

Much could be written about the opinions and lifestyle changes of the displaced residents. A simple comparison of land use maps of the original settlement with those of new settlements, with their rigid lines of identical homes and scant provision for animals or informal gatherings, are a visual representation of some of the changes (Black & Wall, 2001). And when entrance to the site was restricted, the sale of drinks, snacks and souvenirs to tourists became more difficult unless a booth was rented and paid for. As one informant indicated:

> Somehow, people have to feel that this park and this city belong to them: they need to feel ownership. When you have to buy a ticket to see the monuments, even though the price is very small, you don't feel that those monuments belong to you and you don't belong to those monuments either. There is no sense of interdependence and that is emphasised by things like admittance fees.

The manipulation of culture can also be seen at another level. Borobudur and Prambanan are promoted to Indonesians and the rest of the world as symbols of Indonesian identity. Prambanan, a predominantly Hindu site, hosts a 'sound and light' show which documents the building of the temples. The dancers perform to the slow beat of Javanese gamelan (percussion) in contrast to the lively beat of Balinese (Hindu) gamelan. A Balinese companion at the performance derided the dancers with the words 'Look at these Javanese pretending to be Balinese!' For her it was an example of cultural appropriation by a dominant group. However, the reality is that, despite hundreds of years of Islam, dance dramas based on the Hindu epics have a continuity in Javanese culture, and the Ramayana and Mahabharata have been performed to the accompaniment of Javanese gamelan for many centuries. Furthermore, the dances at Prambanan were choreographed especially with tourists in mind, adding a further layer of complexity.

Discussion

A top-down approach to planning was adopted in which government officials and international consultants imposed what they considered best on an unsuspecting local population. Furthermore, the planners, who lived in very different circumstances, tried to anticipate the needs of local people rather than to consult with them about their hopes and fears. As a consequence, the spiritual value of the monuments to local people was underestimated for they and their families had grown up in the shadows of the monuments and had a close affinity with them.

Although the cases are now several decades old, they are not unusual or extreme, and people still vividly remember the circumstances surrounding displacement and live with the consequences. While it is acknowledged that greater efforts are now usually made to involve concerned and affected publics, it is suggested that heritage professionals have been slow to learn from the rural development community concerning the merits of public participation, equitable resource distribution and local involvement in decision making and in the distribution of benefits. Certainly, poverty may have made some local people threats to the sites as they sold artefacts and used temple stones for building materials. However, few government officials and planners have recognised that local residents actually have something positive to offer: they have stories to tell about their site; their cultural expressions can be employed to animate the sites; their families have been informal guardians of the site for generations, and they can still care for the site if they are allowed to and are taught how to do so.

As indicated above, culture is a contested domain. In World Heritage sites, a global culture often displaces local culture. If you are not from central Java, do you feel that Borobudur and Prambaban are truly part of your heritage? Or do you feel that they are part of someone else's heritage which, if you are fortunate, you may be able to experience and share?

Conclusion

Formal designation as a World Heritage site requires preparation and international acceptance of a plan. The tendency to adopt top-down, rational comprehensive planning procedures has resulted in the disenfranchisement of local people whose ancestors have lived with and been guardians of the sites, sometimes for centuries. This process has tended to give greater prominence to expressions of national, 'official' culture and nationalism at the expense of local culture. It has tended to freeze sites and displace human activities that were previously ongoing at and around them, surrounding them with a *cordon sanitaire* that effectively excludes local people from their own heritage.

The builders of the monuments are dead and the ways in which they expressed their culture, if not dead, are re-created and displayed for the tourist gaze. That culture, as the builders of the monuments knew it, no longer exists. The continuity lies in what humans value and the fact that local people look up to the monuments as they go about their daily activities. The relationships between hosts and guests continue. The continuity of that relationship can be enhanced through the implementation of a constructive and creative planning process that incorporates the knowledge, skills and desires of local people, leading to more secure monument preservation, a more 'authentic' tourism experience, and improved life opportunities for those living in the shadows of the monuments.

Correspondence

Any correspondence should be directed to Geoffrey Wall at the Faculty of Environmental Studies, University of Waterloo, Waterloo, Ontario N2L 3G1, Canada (gwall@fes.uwaterloo.ca).

References

Black, H. (1997) Monumental problems: Cultural heritage and communities in Indonesia and Thailand. Unpublished MA Thesis, School of Planning, University of Waterloo.
Black, H. and Wall, G. (2001) Global-local interrelationships in UNESCO World Heritage sites. In P. Teo, T.C. Chang and H.K. Chong (eds) *Interconnected Worlds: Tourism in Southeast Asia* (pp. 121–36). Amsterdam: Elsevier.

Commentary
Creating and Recreating Heritage in Singapore

Kim Jane Saunders

Department of Business and Service Sector Management, London Metropolitan University, London, UK

The aim of this paper is to examine the extent to which public planning and policy have created a 'national' identity for Singapore since its independence in 1965, the importance of heritage to contemporary Singapore, and how heritage is marketed to Singaporeans and visitors. Over the last 30 years Singapore has striven to create itself as one of the most modern and successful of the ASEAN nations, but this may have been at the cost of its indigenous cultures and authentic heritage. Many of the craft industries common in the late 1970s and 1980s have been lost, and while the Singapore Tourism Board promotes Chinatown, Little India and Kampong Glam as 'pockets of individuality' in Singapore's multicultural society, souvenirs currently on sale were made in China, India, Malaysia and Indonesia. By contrast, the enduring image of 'Singapore Girl' for Singapore Airlines led to an entire souvenir culture and a batik clad 'Singapore Girl' Barbie Doll.

Keywords: heritage, Singapore, culture, identity

Introduction

In 1965 Singapore had to create an identity for itself as an independent nation and its policy makers looked to the heritage and culture of the time to plan the future. Today, Singapore continues to re-create and re-invent its communal, national and global identity through policies of social engineering (Ooi, 2002: 202–3) and by packaging and marketing heritage to its citizens and visitors. While the creation of the nation's identity and the re-invention of its heritage draws some criticism from Singaporeans and non-Singaporeans alike, there are lessons to be learned from what the country has achieved and how it has achieved it.

What is Singapore's role in world and regional heritage? Geographically and historically,[1] Singapore is the gateway to Southeast Asia and is well placed as an air and sea hub in the region. Economically, it is one of ASEAN's biggest Tigers. Politically, it is one of the most stable countries in the region, and culturally it is as diverse as many of its neighbours.[2] However, like many new and rapidly industrialised countries, it has suffered the disadvantage of having sacrificed some indigenous culture and history in the name of modernisation.

Singapore has no World Heritage sites and yet heritage is the key to its contemporary political and social identity and it is well placed to provide access to World Heritage sites within the region. In an age of mass transport, with bigger planes (500 passengers), and ships with 1500–2500 passengers, it may well be necessary to limit the number of tourists to a destination. Should the idea of a quota system for visiting World Heritage sites become reality,[3] visitors would require a convenient inter-regional stopover. In this scenario,

Singapore might function as an educational and arts appreciation hub, offering cultural or educational tourism opportunities to enhance the visitors' experience.

What is Singapore's National Heritage and Why is it Important?

Historically, Singapore's heritage and pre-independence history has been shaped by an early indigenous history which was essentially Malay. Its trading history involved Chinese, Indians and Arabs, followed by British colonialism (1819–1942), the Japanese Occupation (1942–45), the postcolonial period (1946–63) and union with Malaya (1963–65). Its heritage is therefore drawn from Chinese traders, sojourners and migrants, and from indigenous Malays (Daud, 1999: 35), Indians, Peranakans,[4] Eurasians and others. However, following the split with Malaysia and independence in 1965, Singapore had to create a new nation overnight. Diversities had to be put aside in favour of shared traditions and commonalties. In 1965, the creation of 'Malaysian Malaysia' required the creation of 'Singaporean Singapore' (Wee, 2002: 135), but what did Singaporean Singapore mean?

Singapore's identity has been shaped and moulded by its government's policies. Culturally (and collectively) Singaporeans espouse Confucian Asian values (Ooi, 2002: 14) and, within a multi-racial, multi-lingual and multi-religious democratic society, citizens must abide by the nation's shared values.[5] In Singapore, for example, 'heritage has important social, economic and political purposes for the State. It binds Singapore and it sells it' (Yeoh & Kong, 1999: 144). As in many Asian cities, this heritage is 'characterised as . . . living rather than . . . monumental,' but while 'change is accepted as a way of life associated with advancement . . . living heritage is not easily appreciated' (Lee Lai Choo, 1999: 182). It is in this context that Singapore has largely concentrated on creating and recreating 'tangible heritage' through its historical and cultural legacies and a sense of values carried by the people. Its 'intangible heritage' is drawn from the recognition of a cultural identity being moulded from the past through the Malay, Chinese and Indian cultures, and the encouragement of an art/cultural and lifestyle experience in a modern context, which encompasses local, regional and international elements. These include cultural cuisine, the traditional Sam Sui soup restaurant, the Imperial Herbal Restaurant, Analakshmi, Indian vegetarian restaurant and Nonya cuisine.

Singapore's Changing Image: Creating Singapore – Cultural Planning and Policy Making

Singapore's image has changed over the last four decades for citizens and visitors. The development of Singapore into Asia's premier 'Garden City' was initiated in 1963 and directed by Mr Lee Kuan Yew, Singapore's first Prime Minister from 1959, and founding Father of contemporary Singapore. He instigated a policy of 'greening' the city, which was followed in 1979 by the 'colouring' of Singapore. The 1970s and 1980s were also dominated by comprehensive building schemes of the Housing Development Board, which provided affordable high-rise housing to replace shophouses and *kampongs* (traditional settlements) and accommodate the majority of the population.

During the processes of nation building, industrialisation and economic development, Singapore was also promoting itself as a tourism destination, offering instant access to Asian cultures, peoples, festivals and cuisine, and much of Singapore's planning continues to be themed in this way. The Merlion (a mythical lion's head with a fish tail) was created in 1972 as the tourism symbol for Singapore. Singapore was marketed as 'Instant Asia', 'Surprising Singapore' and 'New Asia – Singapore' in time for the millennium. As Ooi contends (2002: 148), the creation of these new identities is directly related to the government's overall vision for the nation.

In 1985, the Singapore Tourism Promotion Board (STPB), which in 1997 was renamed the Singapore Tourist Board (STB), decided to focus on 'Surprising Singapore', contrasting modern and traditional, western and eastern exotic in marketing Singapore as a destination with a unique cultural heritage. During the 1980s, the spotlight was on cultural consciousness (Chang & Yeoh, 2001) and Chinatown, the Singapore River, Fort Canning, Haw Par Villa (The Tiger Balm Gardens) and the Colonial district (Civic District) were all deemed worthy of conservation and re-development.

In 1996, there was a move away from 'Surprising Singapore' to 'New Asia – Singapore, which was promoted as a tourism capital, destination, hub and business centre (Chang & Yeo, 2001: 281). Ooi argues that, by instigating this change, the tourism authorities were providing Singapore with a new identity:

> The Singaporean authorities have literally re-invented their product identity with new messages and new images. The STB and other state agencies have also introduced New Asia – Singapore as a way of life for Singaporeans themselves. (Ooi, 2002: 148)

The change is reflected in souvenir T-shirts available for sale. During the 1980s, 'Fine City' T-shirts, referring to Singapore's very strict rules and regulations (Ooi, 2002: 151) gave way to neon-coloured beach style souvenirs that suggest a fun-loving Tropical Island city, thus echoing STB's conception of Singapore as 'the most surprising tropical island on earth'.

Having established political, economic and social stability in Singapore and laid down foundations for national education and values during the 1970s, 1980s and early 1990s, political attention has recently turned to pursuit of the aesthetic. The focus is the creation of a regional arts hub and encouragement of creativity and entrepreneurship. In 2000, for instance, the government announced that in the 21st century it wished to turn Singapore into a global arts city (MITA, 2000), which would spearhead an Asian renaissance and strengthen national identity through the appreciation of heritage.

Strategically, Singapore is well placed as a gateway to Asia (MITA, 2000: 35) and, in effect, it has re-created itself as a focal regional point for technology, science, tourism, the arts and transport. For instance, tourism is now a major source of foreign exchange. In 2000, it brought in S$6 billion, and in 2002 it attracted 7 million visitors, double the arrivals figures of the 1970s. Most Asian visitors came from Indonesia, Japan, Malaysia, China and South Korea, while non-Asians were primarily from Australia, the UK and the USA. Cruise ship arrivals, in particular, have increased, and in 2000 the Singapore Cruise Centre handled 47 Cruise ships and 898,000 passengers (MITA, 2001).

The Role of Government in Creating Identity and Marketing Heritage

The Singapore Tourism Board (STB), which in 1997 replaced the Singapore Tourism Promotion Board (STPB) of 1964, is responsible for the development and promotion of tourism in Singapore, and its mission is to establish Singapore as a tourism hub. The STB controls the tourism industry in Singapore and its functions include training tour guides and licensing travel agencies (Ooi, 2002: 156).

The STB works closely with the Ministry of Information for the Arts (MITA) and other government bodies. In the early 1990s, the STPB realised that some of the vanishing trades of Singapore were of interest to visitors. Since then, there have been numerous major preservation projects, including the designation of traditional tea merchants and herbalists in Chinatown as authentic trades. As a consequence, some traditional craft people have been able to remain in business, even though the STB has been criticised for not doing enough to preserve other activities or communities (Lee Lai Choo, 1999: 183; Sullivan, 1993: 284)

One of the STPB's most significant contributions to Singapore's heritage was its support in 1994 for the preservation and renovation of Raffles Hotel. Confronted with a proposal from the Urban Redevelopment Board to pull it down, the STPB argued strongly for its restoration, suggesting that:

> Singaporeans were becoming bonded with historical Singapore. A beautifully restored Raffles would (once again) become a treasured tourist icon, the restored building would be seen as a positive signal about the sensitive artistic side of a maturing global city. (Batey, 2002: 163)

Such projects have their critics. It has been argued that tourism has led to Disneyfication. Chinatown, for example, has been pedestrianised, and Smith Street has become a 'Food Alley'. Visitors go to Chinatown in search of Chinese-ness, much as people go to Little India in search of Indian authenticity (Ooi, 2002: 35). However, visitors to Chinatown include Chinese Singaporeans, who flock to queue for *Bac Hwa* (a specialty BBQ meat) at Chinese New Year. They eat in the hawker centres, and shop daily at the local open markets (wet markets), held under apartments built by the Housing Development Board, where fresh produce is cheaper than the supermarkets.

Now that Singapore's scientific and technological aspirations have been met, government attention and finance has turned to the arts, and the Ministry for Information and the Arts (MITA) plays an important role in promoting 'heritage'. It comprises five statutory boards: the National Heritage Board (NHB), the National Arts Council (NAC), the Singapore Broadcasting Authority (SBA), the National Libraries Board (NLB) and the Public Monuments Board (PMB). MITA's mission is 'to inform, educate and entertain, to make Singapore into a hub city of the world and build a society that is economically dynamic, socially cohesive and culturally vibrant' (MITA, 2001: 31). A recent and much-praised example of MITA's initiative is 'The Esplanade, Theatres on the Bay', which opened in October 2002.

Museums, too, have an important role to play. With conservation areas, they are considered 'vital to national identity and to making Singaporean citizens aware of their multi-faced history' (Alvin Tan Peng Hong, 1999: 111). Elsewhere, it has been argued that they are 'cultural memory banks' (Wibisono, 2000: 189). This is certainly true of museums in Singapore. In 1993 MITA and the STB formed the National Heritage Board (NHB), bringing together the National Museum, the National Archives and the Oral History Department. Now a statutory board under MITA, the NHB's role is to preserve, present and promote the cultural heritage of Singapore. It works closely with the Ministry of Education, and also manages the Singapore History Museum (SHM) (formally the National Museum), the Singapore Arts Museum (SAM), which was formed with the collections of the former National Gallery (part of the old National Museum), and the Asian Civilisations Museum (ACM). As a recent example of its initiative, Singapore's Asian collections were housed in the ACM's Empress Place Building (EPB) and re-opened to the public in March 2003 after renovation. The NHB also encompasses the Children's Discovery Gallery, the National Archives (NAS), the Heritage Conservation Centre (HCC) and the National Museum Shop.

Other government organisations are also involved in promoting the arts and Singapore's 'heritage'. The National Arts Council (NAC), the national funding agency, was formed in 1991 'to develop Singapore as a distinctive global city for the arts' and to become 'an integral part of the lives of the people of Singapore'. Similarly, the Urban Redevelopment Authority (URA), the national planning authority for Singapore and the national conservation authority, seeks to conserve the past and, through its activities, to reunite citizens with their roots (Yeoh & Kong, 1999: 141). As an example of such a remit, the URA has tried to re-create the atmosphere of historical Singapore and simultaneously achieve long-term commercial viability by re-inventing and recreating past heritage, as in its promotion of the Chinese Heritage Centre in Chinatown in July 2002.

How is Heritage Marketed in Singapore and Globally?

As part of creating an identity for independent Singapore, identity also had to be created for the national airline. Originally part of MSA (Malaysia, Singapore Airlines), the national flag carrier had to fly the flag for the new nation. Ian Batey's advertising campaign for Singapore Airlines (SIA) led to the enduring 'Singapore Girl: A Great Way to Fly' and, as a result, Singapore Girl was incorporated into local culture and has come to represent Singapore and Singaporeans abroad. Clad in Pierre Balmain designer blue batik-patterned, Malay-style *sarong kebaya*, 'Singapore Girl' was introduced in 1972 and the style of the uniform has remained unchanged. Indeed, it spawned a complete range of imitations. Not only are copies of the *sarong kebaya* for sale, but also there is a wide range of batik accessories.

The image of 'Singapore Girl' is a still a significant contribution to Singapore's global image. As Batey contends, 'traditionally an image of an airline is only as strong as the image of its country . . . which in 1972 was seen by the west as a third world city state with creaky rickshaws and flooded streets' (Batey, 2002: 118–19). Graceful in her traditional Malay style batik (*sarong kebaya*), with a warm and welcoming smile, 'Singapore Girl' was the international face of Singapore. She personified the hospitable traditions of the east and represented a modern cosmopolitan nation with a brand new national airline. Her claim to fame was further advanced in 1991, when her wax effigy was unveiled at Madame

Tussaud's Museum, in London, thus becoming the first commercial image to be an exhibit. She also inspired her very own Barbie Doll, as Mattel manufactures a genuine batik-clad Singapore Airlines Barbie for Singapore Airlines. In short, she became and remains a global icon for a modern Singapore which is yet rooted in a multi-cultural Asian past.

Souvenirs from Singapore: Heritage and Material Culture

In Singapore, there is little opportunity to promote the development of local ethnic handicrafts because hardly anything is produced locally. However, Blue Ginger City Batik, Royal Ming Porcelain, and Tiger Balm are a few examples of authentic Singapore-made items. Three decades ago, the situation was different, and Sullivan (1993) documented many of the traditional arts and crafts peculiar to Singapore in the 1970s. By the 1990s, many had sadly disappeared or were disappearing. The Singapore handicraft centre at Chinatown point, constructed in the early 1980s, was intended to provide a retail outlet for some of Singapore's endangered crafts that were being displaced by urban redevelopment, but many of the items now sold there originate in China, Indonesia or Malaysia. Nearby, Yue Hwa Chinese Products Emporium has a much wider range of Chinese products.

In their Official Monthly Guide, the STB (November 2001) suggests that visitors shop for 'art and heritage gifts' and 'Singaporean memorabilia' but the choice of items produced in Singapore remains limited. However, authentic batik from Indonesia and Malaysia is available, as are hand-woven silk shawls from Thailand. There are also some products 'inspired by Singapore's heritage' (STB, 2001: 80), including Straits Chinese-style porcelain and jewellery made by RISIS. At Singapore's airport, Duty Free Shops (DFS Galleria), have created a multi-ethnic shopping experience, where Chinese and Indian handicrafts are available, along with the ubiquitous range of Singapore Airlines-style batik goods. These have become synonymous with Singapore's identity and are reflected in its souvenir market, even though some critics consider the Chinese souvenirs to be caricatures of Chinese culture (Ooi, 2002: 35).

The Marketing of Heritage to 'Hosts' and 'Guests'

As indicated in the comprehensive guides produced and regularly updated by the STB, the STB and the NHB market Singapore's heritage very thoroughly to locals and visitors. By fusing modernity and the exotic Asia, Singapore tries to fuse an indigenous existence with a new identity (Ooi, 2002: 144). It is an experience that seems to divide tourists into those who enjoy the sanitised instant Asia experience, which does not involve getting the camera wet, and those who seek authentic Asia. However, despite the re-development, re-creation and destination branding and packaging, Singapore does indeed have authentic experiences to offer, for many of the festivals in multi-cultural Singapore offer an opportunity to join locals in celebration. These include the Taoist Festival of the Hungry Ghosts, *Thimiti* (Tamil Fire walking), Chinese New Year, the Hindu festivals of *Thaipusam* and *Deepvali*, and the Malay *Hari Raya* (STB, 2001: 107–9).

For Singaporeans, national and cultural heritage have always been, and still are, very important to their sense of identity and to their sense of belonging.

Through heritage, they are anchored in time and space, nationally and regionally. Mindful of the potential threat to national unity and nation building that could emerge from a nation of migrants with diverse ethnic and cultural roots, government policy has focused on the development of the common good. However, having moved from Third World to First World status, economically and politically, Singapore can now celebrate its cosmopolitan status through its multi-cultural heritage. All Chinese, Malay, and Indian holidays and festivals are observed and celebrated, the nation's museums represent the main cultures within Singapore, and dedicated heritage centres for every group highlight the important contributions they have made to the Republic of Singapore. In short, cultural diversity is integral to the shared heritage of the nation.

However, as Singapore matures as a nation and its citizens gain confidence in their cultural identity, there are likely to be more questions and challenges to national policies. Recognising this, the Remaking of Singapore committee has launched a dot.gov website to encourage public debate on public policies (*Straits Times*, 6 June 2002).

Conclusion

> Singapore's National Monuments:
> No Ancient ruins, no vast temple complexes,
> No world wonders.
> But, without them, Singapore would be bereft.
> (www.heritagehub.com.sg national treasures 2002)

Unlike Malacca, another of the Straits Settlements, along with Penang, Singapore does not have a World Heritage site. However, as the opening quote from the heritagehub website shows, heritage is important to Singapore and is valued despite initial sacrifices. Singapore is surprising and it continues to surprise, and it has succeeded in creating a national and a communal identity for an ethnically diverse and multi-racial society, largely descended from immigrants. It has united its diversity through shared values, and rules and the common good prevail over that of the individual. Such is the price of success. However, Singapore has never lost sight of its ethnic and cultural roots and heritage. It has been contended that to continue to succeed, Singapore must maintain a high standard of living, political stability and harmonious relations among ethnic groups (Quah, 1990: 19). As many in Singapore recognise, this requires that it preserve and nurture what it can, while continuing to re-create and re-invent where necessary.

Correspondence

Any correspondence should be directed to Kim Jane Saunders at London Metropolitan University, International Institute for Culture, Tourism and Development, Stapleton House, 277–281 Holloway Road, London N7 8HN, UK (kjsaunders@pacific.net.sg).

Notes

1. The Republic of Singapore is an island city state of 606.7 square kilometres, with 63 offshore islands. It has commanded a strategic location for maritime trade for centu-

ries. Sir Thomas Raffles secured a trading base for the British East India Company in 1819. When planning the town of Singapore in 1822, he grouped migrants according to their ethnic origins and the names of these areas remain part of contemporary Singapore. Bugis Street, Arab Street, China Town, Little India, Kampong Java and Kampong Glam all indicate the origins of these early immigrants.
2. The population is approximately 4 million, including 800,000 foreigners (MITA, 2001). There are three main ethnic groups: the Chinese account for 76.8% of the population, the Malays 13.9% and the Indians 7.9%. Others are 2.4% (MITA, 2001). Singapore is also home to foreign workers from neighbouring Malaysia, Thailand, Indonesia, the Philippines, Myanmar and Sri Lanka. The national language is Malay and the official languages are Malay, Mandarin, Tamil and English. A 'Speak mandarin' campaign has been in place since 1979 in an effort to unify the Chinese community linguistically. The main religions of the country are Buddhism, Islam, Christianity, Taoism and Hinduism.
3. The Kingdom of Bhutan, for instance, controls the number of visitors to the country to protect its culture and heritage.
4. The Peranakan culture is a unique blend of Chinese and Malay cultures. In the Straits Settlements, the cross-culture of Chinese traders who married locally became known as the *Nonya Baba* culture.
5. Every Singapore citizen must abide by the Nation's Shared Values which are: Nation before Community, Society above the Self; Family as the basic unit of society; Community support, and respect for the individual and Racial and Religious Harmony (MITA, 2001: 12).

References

Alvin Tan Peng Hong (1999) Two imaginings: The past in present Singapore. In K-W. Kwok, C.G. Kwa, L. Kong and B. Yeoh (eds) *Our Place in Time: Exploring Heritage and Memory in Singapore* (pp. 111–31). Singapore: Singapore Heritage Society.

Batey, I. (2002) *Asian Branding – A Great Way to Fly*. Singapore: Prentice Hall.

Chang, T.C. and Yeo, P. (2001) *From Rhetoric to Reality: Cultural Heritage and Tourism in Singapore*. In L. Low and D.M. Johnston (eds) *Singapore Inc. Public Policy Options in the Third Millennium* (pp. 273–303). Singapore: Asia Pacific.

Daud, R. (1999) *Commentary: A Malay Perspective*. In K-W. Kwok, C.G. Kwa, L. Kong, and B. Yeoh (eds) *Our Place in Time: Exploring Heritage and Memory in Singapore* (pp. 34–7). Singapore: Singapore Heritage Society.

Kwok, K-W., Kwa, C.G., Kong, L. and Yeoh, B. (eds) (1999) *Our Place in Time: Exploring Heritage and Memory in Singapore*. Singapore: Singapore Heritage Society.

Lee Lai Choo, M. (1999) Heritage and planning. In K-W. Kwok, C.G. Kwa, L. Kong and B. Yeoh (eds) *Our Place in Time: Exploring Heritage and Memory in Singapore* (pp. 175–89). Singapore: Singapore Heritage Society.

MITA (2000) *Renaissance City Report: Culture and the Arts in Renaissance Singapore*. Singapore: MITA.

MITA (Ministry of Information and the Arts) (2001) *Singapore Facts and Pictures 2001*. Singapore: MITA.

Ooi, C.S. (2002) *Cultural Tourism and Tourism Cultures*. Copenhagen: Copenhagen Business School.

Quah, J.S. (ed.) (1990) *In Search of Singapore's National Values*. Singapore: Times Academic.

STB (Singapore Tourism Board) (2001) *Singapore – New Asia Official Guide (November)*. Singapore: STB.

Sullivan, M. (1993) *Can Survive La: Cottage Industries in High-rise Singapore* (2nd edn). Singapore: Graham Brash.

Tay, A. (2002) Surprising Singapore. *Silverkris Inflight Magazine* (February).

Wee, C.J.W-L. (2002) From universal to local culture: The state ethnic identity, and capitalism in Singapore. In C.J.W.-L. Wee (ed.) *Local Cultures and the New Asia: The State, Culture and Capitalism in Southeast Asia* (pp. 129–57). Singapore: Institute of Southeast Asian Studies.

Wibisono, P. (2000) Textile exhibition issues in Indonesian museums. In M. Hitchcock and

W. Nuriyanti (eds) *Building on Batik: The Globalization of a Craft Community* (pp. 189–96). Aldershot: Ashgate, University of North London.

Yeoh, B. and Kong, L. (1999) The notion of place in the construction of history, nostalgia and heritage. In K-W. Kwok, C.G. Kwa, L. Kong and B. Yeoh (eds) *Our Place in Time: Exploring Heritage and Memory in Singapore* (pp. 132–51). Singapore: Singapore Heritage Society.

Yew, L.K. (2000) *From Third World to First: The Singapore Story 1965–2000*. Singapore: Times Media.

Commentary
Wunderkammer 02: An Exhibition of Art, Craft and Souvenirs from World Heritage Sites in Tasmania and Far North Queensland

David L. Hume
Plimsoll Gallery, University of Tasmania, Hobart, Australia.

With its focus on the regions of Tasmania and Far North Queensland, this exhibition (30 August – 20 September 2002) examines the objects and artworks collected today in the tradition of the *Wunderkammer*. It brings together artists and craft people who, in some way, have engaged with the tourist aesthetic and economy of souvenirs. Central to this project is a study of the representation of place culture and heritage through the agency of tourist art and souvenirs.

Keywords: *Wunderkammer*, World Heritage sites, Tasmania, Far North Queensland, souvenirs

This commentary is an extract from Graburn's continuing research that focuses on two key World Heritage Sites in Australia and explores the politics of representation through an exhibition of tourist art and related art media.

In the process of gathering exhibits for *Wunderkammer 02* artworks were sought that initially address Graburn's (1976: 15) notion of how such sites are integrated into the broader global geography, while at the same time, they differentiate themselves through the identification of unique features. Natural craft materials speak, firstly, to the differentiating action of Graburn's equation, and the minor species timber crafts present a tidy and popular example. In chamber 1, the viewer is presented with contrasting timberwork and other natural fibre arts that demonstrate the qualities of Huon Pine, Black Heart Sassafras, Blackwood and Myrtle from Tasmania and the complex patterns of Spalted Mango, Cedar and Purple Gidgee from Far North Queensland.

During the past 30 years environmental concerns have seen an altering perception of this timber resource and the development of new modes of exploitation and consumption which, in turn, have created a new range of dilemmas that have manifested themselves in increased tourist traffic and new forms of environmental degradation.

The forestry heritage of these two regions is now principally represented in the arts and crafts and, whereas the timber was exploited in earlier periods for large-scale timber projects, now the timber is utilised for the provision of crafted artefacts for the tourist industry. In the case of timber and natural fibre souvenirs, the artist must look outside of the gazetted area for his or her material resources and extrapolate a connection with the destination. In this way, just as Huon pine has come to represent not just its very specific environmental conditions, but the entirety of Tasmania, so too, hard arid zone timbers like

Figure 1 Vessel, Purple Gidgee. Artist unknown. (*Source*: Daintree Timber Museum and Gallery)

Purple Gidgee have become associated with the qualities of the Daintree Rainforest.

Tasmanian Blackwood was a favoured timber for 1920s souvenir maker R. Shott. Samples of his work have been preserved in the Queen Victoria Museum and Gallery, Launceston and provide a starting point for Tasmanian timber souvenirs. Included in *Wunderkammer 02* are familiar souvenir forms from the Shott Collection, such as condiment sets, candlestick holders, carved maps of Tasmania, together with a small boomerang that clearly aspires to integrate Tasmania as part of Australia, through a form that is not typical of indigenous Tasmanians. Next to these we can view the continuation of this tradition in contemporary works from Tasmanian wood craftsmen, Peter Meure and Peter

Figure 2 R. Shot and son, *Blackwood key ring and Blackwood boomerang*. Collection of the Queen Victoria Museum and Art Gallery, Launceston, Tasmania, Australia

Mahler, works that may be contrasted to similar contributions from Graham
Davies of Daintree Village.

Tasmanian woodcrafts are dominated by minor species native timber,
while there is a commitment in the Far North Queensland to the development
of new timbers for the craft market. This development has seen the recognition of non-indigenous species as valuable craft timbers, like Mango wood,
which is enhanced through a spalting process that engages with the tropical
climate in the development of figurative swirls and contour-like patterns,
deposited onto the timber through the encouragement of certain bacteria. In
this development we are able to see a clear similarity with Tasmania's prized
Blackheart Sassafras, that develops its distinct dark centre through the agency
of micro bacteria.

The exploration of new natural media has, in part, been provoked by the short-
age of traditional craft materials that has resulted from the untouchable status of
the site. Most artists and crafts people, such as Graham Davis from Daintree
village, respect this status and are quick to point out 'that you don't want to go
ripping stuff out of the park'. (private conversation) In similar circumstances,
Lola Greeno points to the need for the indigenous Palawa community of Tasmania to keep secret the location of the beaches from which she and other practitioners of the ancient art of shell necklace-making gather their materials. In the
example of these exquisite necklaces we can see an engagement with the environment that stretches beyond the understanding aspired to by the makers of many
other exhibits in this show.

Following European settlement, these necklaces were purchased as souvenirs
by visitors to Tasmania until around 1930 (Kleinert & Neale, 2000). After this
period their popularity as souvenirs declined. Today, through the efforts of
Greeno and a small band of Palawa artists, the practice has survived as fine art;
with the replacement of wallaby sinew with nylon twine the only alteration to the
traditional practice. Shell necklaces recently made available to tourists demonstrate the flexible design qualities of this art in Tasmania. The art of indigenous
nations from Far North Queensland is also represented in this exhibition;
however, here, changes in form and media are more pronounced. Indeed, we can
detect a deliberate response to the tourist industry in the shape of Mukunji's
rainmakers; dot painted Burnie beans, thread on a leather thong.

Both World Heritage destinations, at either end of Australia, present artists
and crafts people working in and around their environs with an enormous
wealth of form and imagery from which to develop and create representations of
the sites. Some artists obtain remnant materials from the periphery of the sites

Figure 3 Shell necklace, Artist unknown. Collection of the Tasmanian Museum and
Art Gallery, Australia

Figure 4 Henri Hunsinger, *In the Tropics*. Print on paper. Courtesy of the Artist

Figure 5 Maria MacDermott, *Lake St Clair (series)* 2001. Oil on board. Courtesy of the artist

and form them into sculptural or utilitarian objects; others create work that is destined for fine art galleries and others aim their work at the humble souvenir market.

From this perspective we can see how souvenirs are a creative expression of place, made by artists and crafts people who understand the tourist destination intimately and re-present the essence of the site to enhance the tourists' fleeting and unrepeatable experience of the destination. For instance, artists such as John Smith and Henri Hunsinger produce work that engages with souvenir materials and the tourist aesthetic, and also rests comfortably in souvenir shop and fine art gallery.

While some artists and souvenir makers source raw material from the site, other artists take only inspiration from their surroundings and seek to re-present the form and spirit of the place through their chosen mediums. This group we

Figure 6 Penny Smith, *The Mountains* from the *Landscape series*. Ceramic and decal.
Courtesy of the artist

might refer to as representative souvenirs that include painting, photography,
print making, ceramics and other art forms that do not source actual media from
the site. The prints from Maria MacDermott and Penny Smith's ceramics are fine
examples of this method of engagement. While both artists work with different
media, their individual practices demonstrate an understanding of serial
production that is central to the tourist aesthetic.

In MacDermott's series of small postcard size prints, made from her original
paintings of Lake St Clair, Tasmania, the artist has repeated the landscape motifs
of the area, varying them according to changes in the weather and light. By maintaining recognisable geographic features within her paintings, MacDermott
unites the series as a cohesive group. Yet, in responding to the nuances of light
and weather, she has produced work that lends itself to the touristic demands of
integration and differentiation. Tim Burns is another painter to engage in serial
production. In his *Blackwood* series, we can see how the artist has engaged with
the first of Tasmania's minor species craft timbers to be utilised in the production
of souvenirs.

Crafted and representative souvenirs make up two of the three categories of
souvenir. A third mode of souvenirs is found in the habit of collecting samples of
places, such as sea shells, coloured rocks and plant and animal specimens, which
as Stewart (1985) informs us, influenced the development of the photographic
souvenir.

Within the boundaries of tourist sites, such as the Southwest World Heritage
Area, and the Daintree Rainforest, are found prescribed paths, signalled photo
opportunities and other curated terms of engagement. The photograph is the
most popular and socially approved method of creating souvenirs and, according to Stewart (1985), it is directly related to the pressed flower souvenir, as both
freeze time for later contemplation and interrogation. In earlier times the

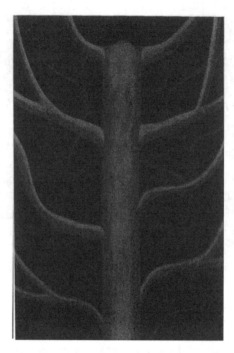

Figure 7 Tim Burns, *Blackwood* from the series. 1999. Oil on canvas. Private collection

collection of flora and fauna samples was almost an expected activity for record-ing and understanding a visited site. Now the once perceived harmless and endearing collecting and pressing of wild flowers might be greeted with the same revulsion as a wall sporting safari trophies. Today such methods of record-ing place and one's experience of it have been thoroughly substituted by the photographic image. If not executed first hand then a further substitute may be obtained in the form of the postcard, calendar and poster. In the work *Alpine stream in mist, Mt Eliza* from Peter Dombrovskis, we have an excellent example of this process. His wilderness images are collected by thousands of tourists that visit Tasmania and a collection of his images are also held in the State's Tasmanian Museum and Art Gallery. Interestingly, it was Dombrovskis' image of Rock Island Bend that brought Tasmania's Southwest wilderness area to world attention, his photography appears to have had a significant impact in the political debate regarding the damming of the Franklin River and the subsequent world heritage listing of the Southwest wilderness area.

Tourism and all that it conjures is perhaps distasteful or at least unattractive; however, ' . . . the compulsion to travel – to look, to perceive, to absorb and perhaps even to understand something that will alter one's preconceptions – is deeply ingrained in Western culture' (Lippard, 1999: 87). Like objects of fine art, this is also the role of the humble souvenir, designed and formed by the artists and craft people of the tourist destination for the purpose of enhancing the tourist's under-standing of the site. The art contained within this exhibition engages with the thematic of place and world heritage, through the imagination, expression, creativity and humour of those that understand it intimately from a prolonged engagement.

Acknowledgement

Developed with assistance from Contemporary Art Services Tasmania.

Correspondence

Any correspondence should be directed to David Hume, Plimsoll Gallery, University of Tasmania, Hobart, Australia.

References

Graburn, N.H.H. (ed.) (1976) *Ethnic and Tourist Arts: Cultural Expressions from the Fourth World.* Berkeley: University of California Press.
Kleinert, S. and Neale, M. (2000) *The Oxford Companion to Aboriginal Art and Culture.* Melbourne: Oxford University Press.
Lippard, L. (1999) *On the Beaten Track.* New York: New Press.
Stewart, S. (1985) *On Longing.* Baltimore: John Hopkins University Press.

Commentary
Elephanta Island: World Heritage, Cultural Conservation and Options for Nature Conservation

Graham Walters

Department of Health and Human Sciences, London Metropolitan University, London, UK

Elephanta Island lies within a large natural harbour 7 km east of Mumbai, India, and is the site of several cave temples devoted to the Hindu deity Siva dated 4th to 9th century AD. The number, scale and quality of the bas-reliefs and sculptures within the temples, together with their uniqueness and setting, secured inscription as a World Heritage (Cultural) Site in 1987. Otherwise, the silvan nature of the island contrasts vividly with the densely populated city nearby that is largely bereft of urban greenspace. Could conservation measures for the cave temples have incidental benefit for the natural environments of the island, providing an economical means of securing a natural conservation area for Mumbai inhabitants? Exploring this apparently simple question revealed a complex situation necessitating consideration of issues well beyond the techniques of either cultural or nature conservation.

Keywords: Elephanta, World Heritage, nature conservation, mangroves

Elephanta as a World Heritage Site

Elephanta Island attracts 900,000 visitors a year, of which 300,000 visit the cave temples (Mehta, 1998). Such intensity of frequentation raises issues that impinge on the island residents as well as on the island environments and cave temples. As these issues are closely interconnected, it is impossible to consider conservation of the cave temples, or any potential incidental conservation of natural environments stemming from cave temple management, without also considering wider issues that include four major areas of interest. These are:

(1)   The condition and maintenance of the cave temples.
(2)   The socioeconomic situation of the islanders and their requirements.
(3)   Management of the large numbers of pilgrims/tourists.
(4)   The roles and management of the natural environment.

While the Archaeological Survey of India is responsible for the cave temples, it is the Indian National Trust for Art and Cultural Heritage (INTACH) that has been charged with producing a Comprehensive Master Plan intended to provide the required integrated and coordinated strategy that addresses the requirements of all interests (Mehta, 2002). This is particularly challenging since a large number of individuals, groups and organisations have been involved in vigorous debate concerning the alternative requirements of different stakeholders. The debate has included controversy concerning alternative measures for cave temple conservation both planned and implemented, as well as the extent to which island residents are influenced by the heavy tourist flux. While the range and duration of the debate has ensured thorough consideration and helped considerably in moving forward the process of policy development (Dilawari, 1995; Mehta, 1998; Padte, 1997; Sengupta, 1996), the essential processes of appropriate policy implementation, monitoring and review have yet to be demonstrated. The major concerns to date have centred on inappropriate conservation techniques, lack of action, inadequate services and facilities for the island inhabitants, and pressures associated with tourist numbers and inappropriate behaviour of some tourists within a site of religious sanctity (Jayakar, 1997; Mehta, 1998, 2002; Sengupta, 1998). However, environmental issues that have been addressed have mostly not included the potential of the island in terms of nature conservation and its relevance to residents of Elephanta, still less its relevance to the population of Mumbai.

The Environments of Elephanta within a Regional Context

The island comprises basaltic rock rising to 169 m, contrasting with the lowlying wetlands of much of Mumbai harbour. Its forest approximates to the natural tropical moist deciduous and semi-evergreen forests (Lattoo, 1987; Santapau & Randeria, 1955) of the Western Ghats that extend on high ground from the Gujarat/Maharashtra border, 200 km north of Mumbai, 1,300 km south to the southern tip of India. The forests of the Western Ghats have been identified as one of 18 global 'biodiversity hotspots' of utmost importance due to their high values of diversity and endemicity (Myers, 1988). Lattoo's (1987) work on the flora of Elephanta is the only recent investigation of the vegetation. No species or communities of note are reported from the terrestrial systems, but their value should be regarded more in terms of their representativeness, a criterion often used when considering areas for natural conservation measures (e.g. Moss *et al.*, 1996) that has as much validity as the more commonly cited rarity, uniqueness, or size of area. The forests, however, are not unmodified, unsurprising in view of the island's history of human occupation dating back at least to the 4th century AD. The forest history is unknown but areas are likely to have been at least partially cleared more than once. Currently the forest exists in patches, used by the islanders for grazing, fuel wood and for waste disposal (Sengupta, 1998). Also, 30,000 trees of exotic, evergreen, species have been planted by the Ministry for Forests and the Environment to ensure a year-round green aspect to a forest that would naturally be mostly leafless during the dry season (when most tourists visit the island) (Lattoo, 1987; Padte, undated).

Although forests have undoubtedly been reduced in the region with the growth in population and spread of towns and the city (*Times of India*, 2002), Mumbai is unique in having the large, forested Sanjay Gandhi National Park immediately to the north. The forests of this outstanding city asset far surpass those of Elephanta in terms of size, diversity and recorded data, and the undoubted value of the Park may well have reduced perceptions of the conservation value of the Elephanta forest. In contrast, the mangroves that fringe the island have attracted more attention as they have suffered loss or degradation due to jetty construction (Chakravarty, 2002; Mehta, 1998) and the smothering of the aerial pneumatophores by layers of discarded plastics litter (Sekhar, 2002).

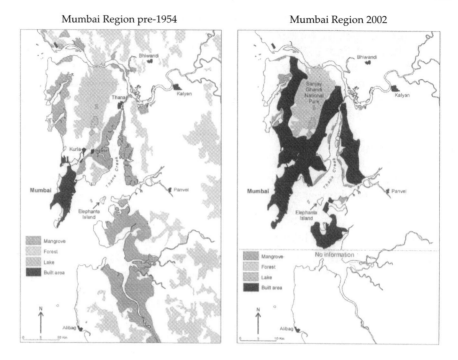

Figure 1 Elephanta Island
The figure indicates the location of Elephanta Island within Mumbai harbour, and shows the regional loss of mangrove concomitant with the expansion of Mumbai during the latter half of the 20th century. Forest cover in 2002 is indicated only for the Sanjay Gandhi National Park. The extent of the city and mangrove for 2002 is derived from satellite data (Digitalglobe) and the growth of other towns is not indicated.

Regionally, mangroves were far more extensive than today (see Figure 1). Their decline is largely due to the expansion of Mumbai from 5,300 hectares in 1954 to the present 40,400 hectares and thus there is increasing interest in their value and conservation as losses around Mumbai continue (Sekhar, 2002; Sharma, 2001a, 2001b, 2002c; Untawale, 2002). Given both these local losses, and the plight of mangroves globally (Farnsworth & Ellison, 1997), the remaining mangroves on the shores of Elephanta Island have a significance greater than their small area suggests.

Conservation of Elephanta Island's Environments

The sole recorded conservation activity for the island's forests is the planting of large numbers of exotic trees on the presumption that visitors to the island prefer to see a green and leafy forest. Planting of exotics often has agricultural or horticultural value, but in most cases is not a practice that will enhance the conservation value of natural habitats. Such horticultural modification of a semi-natural system moves the forest further from a state of naturalness, perhaps indicating an official position that viewed Elephanta's forests more as gardens rather than natural habitats, and it is not possible to predict the consequences on the existing forest or its fauna. Conservation activity associated with the cave temples includes work on the caves and temples themselves, and measures to regulate the visiting tourists. Cave temple works have been restricted to the immediate environs of the caves and they have no significance to the condition of the natural environments. Meanwhile, visitor regulation seems to have been minimal for a long period (Mehta, 1998), although it appears that visitor impact during the period 1987–1997 was restricted to waste production and disposal with some visitor pressure on woodland in the immediate vicinity of the temples. Therefore, the absence of intensive cave temple conservation measures leads to the conclusion that there can have been no incidental benefits to the island's natural environments.

However, the long period of debate concerning the island's future, including its natural environments, has stemmed from the problems relating to the plight of the cave temples. Plans for more directed, focused and effective temple conservation now fully integrate the requirements of the island residents, widely recognised as being largely non-beneficiaries of the tourist income while suffering from lack of even basic services (Sengupta, 1998), with a sustainable approach to environmental exploitation (Mehta, 2002). Plans for such environmental use include mangrove regeneration, better energy provision to reduce the use of the forests for fuel wood, water catchment protection, and the establishment of a marine bird reserve. They also include tourist management, which will involve provision of designated recreation and picnic areas to reduce diffuse pressures across the island, the regulation of visitor numbers and movement at the temples, and provision of environmental education via interpretative signs. Such measures are all part of the projected Comprehensive Master Plan (Mehta, personal communication). The widespread view is that the most effective forms of conservation most likely to result in long-term success are those with an all-embracing perspective, including full involvement of local communities (Panel on Biodiversity Research Priorities, 1992). Mehta (2002) noted that declaring the whole island as an Environmentally Sensitive Zone (a legislative designation), as has been repeatedly requested, would confer conservation protection with the support of the law to all environments, whereas at present only the cave temples enjoy such protection. The continuing disparate interests of the wide variety of stakeholders with varying political power will make this desirable outcome a formidable challenge indeed.

Correspondence

Any correspondence should be directed to Graham Walters, Department of Health and Human Science, London Metropolitan University, North Campus, 166–220 Holloway Road, London N7 8DB (g.walters@londonmet.ac.uk).

References

Chakravarty, I. (2002) Tourism development in small islands: A case study of Elephanta Island, Maharashtra, India. *Tourism Recreation Research* 26 (3), 15–23.
Dilawari, V. (1995) In the name of heritage tourism. A visit to a world cultural heritage site: The Elephanta Caves. *Indian Architect and Builder* (Anniversary Issue), 148–50.
Farnsworth, E.J. and Ellison, A.M. (1997) The global conservation status of mangroves. *Ambio* 26 (6), 328–34.

Jayakar, P. (1997) Inaugural address. Elephanta Caves seminar: Management of a World Heritage site. Indian National Trust for Art and Cultural Heritage, Greater Mumbai Chapter, Mumbai.

Lattoo, C. S. (1987) Ecological observation on the vegetation of Elephanta Island. Unpublished PhD Thesis, University of Bombay.

Mehta, T. (1998) Elephanta: INTACH initiatives toward appropriate management. *Amanat* 1 (1), 1–3.

Mehta, T. (2002) Protecting the site. In G. Michell *Elephanta* (pp. 132–5). Mumbai: India Book House.

Moss, D., Davies, C. and Roy, D. (1996) *CORINE Biotopes Sites – Database Status and Perspectives 1995*. Topic Report No. 27/1996. Copenhagen: European Environment Agency.

Myers, N. (1988) Threatened biotas: 'Hotspots' in tropical forests. *Environmentalist* 8, 187–208.

Padte, R.H. (1997) Address by Surpanch Gharapuri to Elephanta Caves seminar: Management of a World Heritage site. Indian National Trust for Art and Cultural Heritage, Greater Mumbai Chapter, Mumbai.

Padte, V.H. (undated) *Elephanta: Ancient & Modern History. Latest Guide Book*. Mumbai: Rohit.

Panel on Biodiversity Research Priorities (1992) *Conserving Biodiversity: A Research Agenda for Development Agencies*. Washington: National Academy Press.

Santapau, N. and Randeria, A.J. (1955) The botanical exploration of the Krishnagiri National Park, Borivli, near Bombay. *Journal of the Bombay Natural History Society* 53, 185–200.

Sekhar, V. (2002) BMC, residents to protect mangroves. *Times of India* (26 February).

Sengupta, C. (1998) *Elephanta Island: Heritage and Livelihood*. Mumbai: Tata Institute of Social Sciences.

Sengupta, R. (1996) Don't blame it on cement. *Outlook* (22 May), 64.

Sharma, V. (2001a) Versova's mangroves endangered by debris dumping. *Bombay Times* (16 August).

Sharma, V. (2001b) Land sharks claim mangroves in Thane Creek. *Bombay Times* (24 August).

Sharma, V. (2001c) Manori creek mangroves are victims of the axe effect. *Bombay Times* (3 September).

Times of India (2002) Vilasrao backs bid to resettle families in Chandivli (8 May).

Untawale, A. (2002) Mangrove park plan on salt pan land assailed. *Times of India* (11 June).

Afterword

Michael Hitchcock
International Institute for Culture, Tourism and Development, London
Metropolitan University, London, UK

According to the World Heritage Convention, 'Cultural Heritage' comprises a monument, group of buildings or site of historical, aesthetic, archaeological, scientific, ethnological or anthropological value. 'Natural Heritage' is defined as outstanding physical, biological, and geological features; habitats of threatened plants or animal species and areas of value on scientific or aesthetic grounds or from the point of view of conservation.

In accordance with UNESCO's mission these cultural and natural sites comprise, together with many others, a common heritage, to be cherished as unique testimonies to an enduring past. The disappearance of any of these sites would be an irreparable loss for each and every one of us, but despite UNESCO's support many of these sites are threatened.

The Convention Concerning the Protection of the World Cultural and Natural Heritage has been signed by more than 150 states, known as the 'states parties', and was adopted by the General Conference of UNESCO in 1972. UNESCO's mission is to define and conserve the world's heritage by listing sites whose outstanding values should be safeguarded for all humanity and to ensure their preservation through closer cooperation among the participating nations. Heritage legislation, like any other kind of legislation, is of course established by national law, but these laws are influenced by the many multilateral and bilateral conventions dealing with heritage, the best-known being the World Heritage Convention. The Convention may thus be regarded as a starting point for heritage legislation worldwide, especially in states with an underdeveloped heritage legal structure. It may also be seen as an attempt to spread best practice, but what should not be overlooked is that the endorsement of the Convention was ultimately a political act, hence the title of this collection of papers.

By signing the Convention, each nation promises to conserve the sites situated within its borders, some of which may be designated as World Heritage Sites. Responsibility is shared by the international community as a whole for the preservation of these sites for future generations. UNESCO's World Heritage mission is to encourage states to sign the Convention to help protect their own natural and cultural heritage. UNESCO also invites nations that have signed the Convention to nominate sites within their national territory for inclusion on the World Heritage list.

Looking back over 30 years, it has become clear that the Convention lacked an important provision from the outset, the need to conduct research on how well the Convention was fulfilling its brief in scientific terms. Given the stated scientific aims of the Convention, the absence of an attendant research programme to accompany the implementation of the Convention would appear to be a serious oversight, but one should bear in mind the spirit of the era in which it was conceived. The priority at the time when the Convention was conceived was to establish a legally recognised heritage conservation system worldwide, and research on how this was to be achieved was some-what of an afterthought. This is not to say that research on World Heritage Sites has never been undertaken because there are a number works (e.g. Shackley, 1998) that have set out to do this, but it has never been high on UNESCO's policy agenda.

Another pressing concern is that when the Convention was drawn up it was a unique legal instrument focusing on tangible heritage, but in the last decade new listings and alternative sources of authority (e.g. National Geographic) have emerged. What then remains special about UNESCO's remit and how do its achievements compare with those of others? Without systematic research these questions are difficult to answer, but some kind of comparative assessment needs to be undertaken if the World Heritage Centre is to continue making its judgements and to function efficiently. Given that the Convention has not invari-ably been popular, notably in the USA where non-national law is challenged as unconstitutional, then its workings and outcomes need to be subjected to a more rigorous and preferably independent examination. But where is this impartial scrutiny to be found? Obviously, the 'states parties' have the ultimate legal control, but they arguably have too many vested interests, not least in the impor-tant economic benefits derived from tourism to World Heritage Sites, to be regarded as independent assessors. What this collection does is to highlight the importance of research by what may be called the 'scientific community', the worldwide network of universities and research bodies, whose members submit the results of their research to peer reviewed journals.

The big question is of course funding because UNESCO lacks the resources to conduct the kind of research that the World Heritage Centre knows that it needs to conduct if it is to function efficiently and fairly. Looking at the acknowledgements on the papers in this collection, it is clear that where funding for research has been forthcoming, then one cannot point to any single source. In most cases funding has been provided by each researcher's university and, generous though those institutes of higher education have been, it is clear that this represents an *ad hoc* approach to what deserves after 30 years to be more systematically appraised. Mindful of the difficulties and costs in conducting such research and reaching out to all stakeholders, this collection also includes a paper by Lask and Herold that discusses a possible methodological solution. In particular it discusses the inauguration of an 'observation station' that could act as a forum for World Heritage research and public participation.

The importance of conducting research is underscored by the paper by van der Aa, Groote and Huigen who document a case in the Wadden Sea where inscription costs are seen as outweighing the benefits for those who live and work in cultural landscapes that are being nominated. Local opposition cannot be ignored, especially when the perception is that certain stakeholders have more to lose than to gain through being on the List. Over 30 years have elapsed since the adoption of the World Heritage Convention and it can no longer be assumed that inscription is an honour for local populations and a useful leaver for organisations concerned with tourism and conservation.

The intention here has been to move beyond a piecemeal approach to World Heritage research and to bring together papers from a range of disciplines and geographical locations. In view of the sheer diversity and geographical spread of World Heritage Sites it is not possible to provide a complete overview in terms of research. This collection, however, provides the most comprehensive perspective to date in terms of disciplinary insight and geographical reach. The nations covered in detail by this volume include The Netherlands, USA, Mexico, Fiji, Kyrgyzstan, Vietnam, Lebanon, Peru, Singapore and Indonesia, though many more countries are mentioned. The disciplinary backgrounds of the authors embrace geography, sociology, law, art history, anthropology, tourism studies, business and management, with some authors belonging to more than one subject. This volume not only highlights what these diverse sites might have in common, but also examines how the concept of World Heritage has been translated effectively into numerous different cultural and environmental settings over the last 30 years.

As indicated in Harrison's introduction, an important theme raised in the collection is the legal ambiguity in the management of World Heritage Sites since, contrary to expectation, the Convention does not imply direct intervention by UNESCO in the management of these sites. Instead, what is implied is joint sovereignty over designated sites, which then becomes for all intents and purposes subject to the policies and legislation concerned with World Heritage Sites (Bianchi & Boniface, 2002: 80). One of the contributors to this collection, James Tunney, points out the weaknesses of the legal status quo pertaining to the conceptual domains of tourism, culture and heritage. He argues in favour of a holistic approach, or at least an awareness of one, that intersects these issues with the evolution of world trade law, a domain that is becoming increasingly significant in law in general. We may live at a time of global legal plurality, but legislation on international trade may provide a map for other emergent arenas of international law. At present world trade legislation is relatively confined to narrow commercial transactions, but Tunney sees a potential challenge for the domains of tourism and heritage. The issues raised in this paper could be seen as an emerging research agenda concerned with World Heritage law.

A related theme is the way policy and management intersect, and how the World Heritage Convention is applied, especially when many different stakeholders are involved. This particularly true of the USA where Williams notes that, although there may be a high degree of compliance, numerous issues remain to be resolved if World Heritage Site designation is to remain an effective form of protection internationally. As noted by Wall and Black, of particular concern here is the centrality of the states parties to the Convention, and the tendency towards top-down planning at the expense of local people. Involvement of local people is not simply a planning matter, but is an ongoing management concern linked to such issues as the effective training of guides (see McGrath's paper) and the visitor's experience (see Shackley's paper). As is noted by Adams, there are also implicit assumptions in UNESCO about the character of sites, which contrast markedly with the actual reality, not least when there are rivalries among local actors.

Another important and related theme running through this collection might be called 'heritage for whom?' or 'contested heritage'. Of particular interest here is the relationship between tourism and World Heritage and how the benefits of development are distributed. At the bottom of these debates lie the complex links between heritage and tourism, and the ways in which attitudes to heritage vary over time and place. Unresolved questions relating to colonialism feature prominently in the papers by Harrison and Thompson, to a lesser extent in those of Evans and Winter. The legacy of colonialism exerts an ongoing influence on nationalism in the developing world where newly constructed national identities are often expressed in terms of ethnicity and are as much concerned with self-expression and self-assertion as they are with historical evidence, precedent or cultural revival. Singapore, for example, which came into being shortly before the adoption of the World Heritage Convention, has had to meld together a multi-lingual and multi-ethnic state with heritage as one of its nation building strategies. As is noted by Saunders, however, Singapore may lack its own World Heritage Site, but sees itself as a regional cultural hub and is connected via its transport links to many World Heritage Sites.

One of the commonest undertakings of a formerly colonised people is the restoration of its cultural image with the fostering inter-group cohesion group and the enhancement of the group's external status. Such endeavours invariably and understandably become embroiled in the desire to acquire World Heritage Site status. By the same token a countervailing trend can also be detected in contexts such as Fiji where the edifices of colonialism are often left in the hands of the formerly colonised who may be indifferent to their global significance. The experience of colonialism may have influenced the way certain nations, today's 'states parties', are conceived, including the status accorded certain aspects of their heritage, often leading to a focus on what might be called 'monumentalism', which reflects largely European concerns. Such values are also detectable in what attracts tourists, and this often leads to misunderstandings in interpretation and comprehension. The focus on temples, such as in Angkor in Cambodia and Borobudur in Indonesia, detracts from what are primarily cultural landscapes, in which the major structures are but a part.

A related tension that is encountered in several papers is the relative balance given to cultural or environmental conservation in any given site. The management of many sites involves both natural and cultural considerations and the effective combination of both remains a challenge. Can, for example, conservation methods designed for cave temples in India, as is asked by Walters, have incidental benefits for natural environments; and what kind of methodologies should we adopt to evaluate what appears to be a simple question, but which in reality turns out to be complex?

Another tension is the link between World Heritage and international tourism on one hand, and between World Heritage and domestic tourism on the other. Do the economic imperatives of attracting international tourists also detract from the role these World Heritage Sites play in domestic tourism, and their relationship to the communities living in and around them? Contemporary consultants working on behalf of UNESCO and the World Tourism Organisation may stress the need for community consultation when World Heritage Site status is sought, but what should UNESCO do about sites that were inscribed long before such concerns became commonplace? Ongoing help with management plans to ensure that community interests are addressed is one potential solution, but another might be to include a community dimension in the dynamic evolution of tourism and heritage law.

Approaching a similar theme from another perspective communities van der Aa, Goote and Huigen question whether or not World Heritage Site status remains the highest accolade that a site can receive. The perceived costs of inscription are increasingly seen as outweighing the benefits, especially when local populations have to share their landscapes with increasing numbers of outsiders with all the attendant concerns of overcrowding and environmental degradation. What is suggested here is that UNESCO should adopt a more sophisticated awareness of the role of local opposition to the nomination process because such resistance may not comprise direct opposition to UNESCO, but may reflect entirely different concerns. Ideally, UNESCO's operational guidelines should be more specific about what local stakeholders can influence and to what degree in the outcome of the consultation process.

To complicate matters, what is often the case with World Heritage Sites is that there may be many varieties of stakeholders with different interests and competing agendas. This is a striking feature of Maddern's account of Ellis Island, which has to accommodate a bewildering array of heritages, while simultaneously supporting the USA's drive to create a common ethos of citizenship. It does this moreover within the context of increasing mobility and spatial interconnectivity, and in order to retain credibility and legitimacy Maddern argues that World Heritage Sites must become spaces of intercultural dialogue, where ethnic animosities and inter-cultural tensions can productively be addressed. This suggests that World Heritage Sites should place less emphasis on coherent narratives where the rough edges of real inter-communal relations are smoothed over and should encourage a more dynamic and perhaps unfinished, even messier, version of historical events. A common tension within World Heritage Sites is whether their narratives should reflect national concerns, often with ethnically or ideologically situated agendas, or transnational ones that place emphasis on what these sites have in common with one another. Should Ellis Island be primarily concerned with the story of migration to the USA, or the story of migration in general and where Ellis Island fits into it?

To retain credibility and legitimacy in an age of increasing interconnectivity, should World Heritage Sites become spaces of intercultural dialogue where tensions could be productively addressed? In so far as they are concerned with the narration of the past, the aim at such sites could be to promote transnational rather than national spaces of citizenship and to incorporate ethnic and other social groups, national and international, which may claim to be stakeholders. If such claims are contested, then the World Heritage Site should be a scene of dialogue rather than conflict, where attempts to continue to include and resolve differences rather than to police or exclude those who challenge official narratives.

Correspondence

Any correspondence should be directed to Michael Hitchcock, International Institute for Culture, Tourism and Development, London Metropolitan University, 277–281 Holloway Road, London N7 8HN (m.hitchcock@ londonmet.ac.uk).

References

Bianchi, R.V. and Bonniface, P. (2002) The politics of World Heritage. *International Journal of Heritage Studies* 8 (2), 79–80.

Shackley, M. (1998) *Visitor Management: Case Studies from World Heritage Sites*. London: Butterworth-Heinemann.